A Portrait of
Brazil
in the
Twentieth Century

The Universe of the "Literatura de Cordel"

MARK J. CURRAN

Order this book online at www.trafford.com
or email orders@trafford.com

Most Trafford titles are also available at major online book retailers.

Printed in the United States of America.

ISBN: 978-1-4907-0835-5 (sc)
ISBN: 978-1-4907-0834-8 (e)

Library of Congress Control Number: 2013912866

Trafford rev. 09/12/2013

 www.trafford.com

North America & international
toll-free: 1 888 232 4444 (USA & Canada)
fax: 812 355 4082

This book is dedicated to the poets, printers and public of the "Literatura de Cordel" of the Twentieth Century.

Table of Contents

Preface

This book in its essence is an overview of Brazil in the Twentieth Century. It is a portrait of a people and their country unlike any other. The story is told by the folk-popular poets originally from Northeastern Brazil, poets who believe they are gifted with the talent of poetry by God himself and live their lives as "representatives of the masses." The estimated one hundred thousand chapbooks of verse that comprise Brazil's "string literature" [literatura de cordel], an estimate by Joseph Luyten, noted researcher of "cordel," are a repository of beliefs, social mores and a view of life unlike any other in Brazil. Aside from being the primary source of entertainment and learning for a significant number of Brazilians, they were the "newspaper in verse" of the masses of the Northeast. The poetry records and shares much of the essence of all the Brazilians and their life in the twentieth century and beyond.

Since 1966 I have traveled to the towns, the markets, and the fairs of much of Brazil to listen to the poets sing or declaim their verse before an avid public, this in addition to visits to the homes of the poets to learn more from them. I have studied at research libraries and cultural institutes, met local experts, scholars and writers, and perused great private and public collections of the "cordel." The result is my own high quality collection of "cordel" comprising over three thousand originals and dozens of Xerox copies, the basis for the portrait to be completed in this volume. The body of poetry has been my "vocation" since 1966 and this is what enables me to tell the story of Portrait.

"Cordel," as it is known, is the written record of the culture of the humble class rooted in the formative past of Brazil's Northeast. I believe that "cordel" is a major document of Brazilian culture, albeit from the common man's point of view. Through it one can truly learn of the evolution of the cultural roots of many Brazilians. In fact, "cordel" tells the story of people and places far beyond that of its roots in Brazil's North East; it tells much of all Brazil. Thus, I offer the reader this document: A Portrait of Brazil in the Twentieth Century. The Universe of the "Literatura de Cordel."

Why Brazil? Because it was an important part of my own life as professor of Portuguese and Brazilian Studies at Arizona State University from 1968 to 2011and as student, traveler and researcher in Brazil for all my adult life, but more importantly, because Brazil matters. Aside from being a major player in the past, present and future of planet earth due to its immense size, resources, and ecological and economic presence, Brazil is also one of the most interesting, most vibrant and most culturally fascinating of earth's countries. It is far more than the land of Carmen Miranda, carnival, soccer, the Amazon, and Bossa Nova as the reader shall soon see. It is in addition a country faced with the homogenizing forces of International Capitalism, Free Market Economics and the great levelers, television, the internet and all the applications of social media today. I believe that we are rooted in our past and can learn from it, and that the wisdom of the ages, of the elders and of the <u>folk</u>, that is, of the poets and public of "cordel," may in fact be of at least equal if not greater value than the wisdom of programming produced by much of mass communications today. We in the First World can learn from the folk-popular cultural roots of Brazil and the accompanying value system they entail. It is in fact the slow evolution and disappearance of the reality documented in Brazil's "<u>literatura de cordel</u>" that motivates this book. It would be sad to forget the past and present of the Brazilian reality seen in "<u>cordel</u>" and to not heed its messages.

Why "<u>cordel</u>?" Because it captures twentieth century Brazil in unique fashion; it documents a people and a nation in a colorful and accurate way. The estimated one hundred thousand chapbooks of stories in verse [<u>folhetos</u>] printed by the folk-popular poets of "<u>cordel</u>" since the end of the 19th century are the raw material for this portrait. These thousands of story-poems consist largely in the fictitious mode of narrative stories, in original and invented poetic duels called "<u>pelejas</u>," and cordelian accounts of everyday life and events. A perusal of the album headings and sub-headings of the table of contents of this book reveals the "Vast Universe of "<u>Cordel</u>," of Brazil itself.

There are as well personal reasons to do this book—to complete a career, to return what I have been privileged to receive from the poets and their public to them in this homage to their contribution to Brazil, and to complete a vision—a portrait of a people and country unlike any other. The poetry of "<u>cordel</u>" is indeed modest and of humble roots. For the reader of this book who is an observer outside the cordelian reality, the greatest value of "<u>cordel</u>" (perhaps the largest body of truly folk-popular poetry left in the Western tradition) is not only the humble quality of the poetry itself, but what it <u>says</u> of a people and nation. My aim is to capture this message in <u>Portrait</u>.

This book in the English language [1]targets as potential readers above all fellow North Americans and secondarily others with a familiar knowledge of English. There are untold people throughout the world that have an interest in Brazil, in its vast culture, in what

Brazilians think, believe and enjoy. And a good many of these people do not know the Portuguese language, thus this effort. I modestly suggest that the book could be used as one among other texts for a basic Brazilian culture or civilization course in English. The book is for those interested in Brazil, the cultural formation of a large segment of its people, what they enjoy in life, the obstacles they face in life and how they view their own country and the world. The traveler, the arm-chair tourist, the student of Brazilian Portuguese language, culture, history, politics, religion, or society will find something of interest. For sure the reader will have an insight provided no where else into many Brazilians and their view of their country.

---

[1]   A larger version of this book exists in the Portuguese language as "Retrato do Brasil em Cordel" by the Ateliê Publishing Company in São Paulo, 2011. The practicality of making this important folk-popular poetry tradition available to an English speaking public is the reason for this book.

Introduction

This book is a portrait of a people and a country <u>via</u> the "<u>cordel</u>." It is a portrait analogous to the photographic rather than the painted, that is, a series of snapshots making an album (a chapter), the sum total of ten albums being a portrait of a large portion of Brazil and its people. The snapshots will be the cordelian booklets of verse themselves. <u>What</u> they tell us is in essence the basic religious beliefs the poets and public of "<u>cordel</u>" hold, their consequential moral behavior, their heroic models for living, the problems they have traditionally faced and their solutions to them, their distractions and entertainments, their views on the major current events and political leaders of their country and of the world, the new challenges they faced at the end of the millennium, and finally, their hopes and aspirations. All the above in one sense expresses their world view, a way of life as they see it. In the end it is Brazil seen from the vast universe of "<u>cordel</u>."

As one of the most famous of the poets once said, and he was not alone, "To do a poem all I need is a title."[1] Titles will be the labels to the snapshots that make up the ten chapter-albums of <u>Portrait</u>. The titles in effect will introduce us to the booklets in verse which in turn will lead us to the Brazilians who write, listen to, read and <u>believe</u> in "<u>cordel</u>." They will show us what the participants in "<u>cordel</u>" think, what they believe, what is relevant and important to them, and how they deal with the challenges in life itself. So, once again, titles are keys to this portrait; they will indicate the most common denominators of the snapshots of <u>Portrait</u>: who, what, when, and where. It is the job of the author, and perhaps more importantly, the reader, to add the "why," each according to his own curiosity and satisfaction. As the eyes are the windows of the soul, so the titles of the story-poems [<u>folhetos</u>] are the windows to the portrait. We modestly suggest that even they alone will provide insight into the vast universe of "cordel" in this portrait of Brazil and the Brazilians.

Since the aim of <u>Portrait</u> is to tell a story—to retell what "<u>cordel</u>" (a folk-popular medium) says about Brazilians and Brazil, this book is not theoretical in its approach but rather, descriptive and above all informative. Any terminology it may use is limited to that necessary to help make clear what the poets and poetry is saying (for instance the term "cordel" itself). Portuguese terms are included in brackets after the English translation of the same. The language of Portrait is that common to an everyday description of life. Even the worn clichés we use much of the time to get us through life can be useful in the telling of the story. So, Portrait has a very specific flavor—that of the language and "wisdom of the masses" [sabiduria popular] as the folklorists call it in Brazil. This book takes a prompt from the best known of Brazilian novelists, Jorge Amado, when he admitted his cultural and artistic debt to the humble masses of his native state of Bahia during the commemoration of his fifty years as a writer in 1981 in Salvador da Bahia. If there is anything of value in Portrait, it is the creation of the cordelian poets themselves.

An academic explanation of "cordel" itself is found in the many articles and books published about it; a bibliography of selected works follows the text. A summary of the phenomenon for those already familiar with "cordel" and a primer for the newcomer follows.

The "literatura de cordel," literally translated in English as "string literature" due to the fact the booklets of verse are often sold in the marketplace draped over a wire or string or attached to the same by clothes pins, is that body of folk-popular narrative poetry originally from Northeastern Brazil. It was known originally by folklorists and scholars as "popular literature in verse" ["literatura popular em verso"]. The folk-popular tradition that "cordel" continues came from Europe, most directly from the Portugal of the 18th century, but also from France, Spain and Italy. It existed in diverse forms as well in other countries in Spanish America, its closest "cousins" most notably the songs in verse of nineteenth and twentieth century Mexico, the "corridos," and the poetic duels and songs of the gaucho poets of Argentina.

"Cordel" was written by humble poets, printed in small chapbooks on fragile paper and was sold in the fairs, marketplaces, street corners and public meeting places of Brazil's Northeast for all the twentieth century.[2] It was found originally in both the tiny towns of the backlands and interior and in the major coastal cities of Northeastern Brazil like Recife, João Pessoa, Aracajú, Maceió, Natal and Salvador da Bahia.

In the late nineteenth century massive numbers of poor migrants left Brazil's Northeast. The migration was due to severe droughts in the interior, and subsequent migrations followed throughout the twentieth century in a desperate attempt to survive poverty and outright starvation. The poets of "cordel" moved with the poor migrants. Thus one finds "cordel" in the Amazon Basin (the rubber gatherers recruited in the late nineteenth century and again during World War II were from the Northeast), the industrial Mecca of São Paulo and Rio de Janeiro in the Center-South, and even in Brasília, the new capital since 1960. Most of the labor force to build Brasília from 1955 to 1960 came from the Northeast.

The humble booklets of verse called "folhetos de cordel" have been the primary form of entertainment and news for the masses of poor northeasterners since approximately 1900. Pioneer poets like Leandro Gomes de Barros, Francisco das Chagas Batista or João Melchíades Ferreira da Silva of the teens of the century were followed by a large number of poets who entertained, informed and taught their humble readers during the heyday of cordel from the 1920s to the end of the 1950s. Production became more sporadic with the modernization of communications in Brazil via the transistor radio and television in the 1960s.

"Cordel" came into vogue for a certain middle and upper class public in much of Brazil in the 1970s and 1980s for several reasons. First was the realization on the part of the Brazilian intelligentsia that the cordelian tradition indeed was an important part of the national cultural heritage. Cordelian scholars urged that it be collected and preserved in the national archives, that it be taught in high schools and university as part of Brazilian literature and in fact that university degrees be granted for those specializing in it. Second, "cordel" became known to the art world and its collectors because of the colorful woodcuts used as cover illustrations for its booklets of verse, this primarily since the 1960s. It came to be an art form sought out by an international audience with the advantage that it did not require knowledge of Portuguese to appreciate it.[3] Equally important in those years was the increase in visibility of the improvised, oral, poetic duel of the oral improvisers of verse [cantadores] whose performance was easy to divulge on radio and TV. Many of these poets also write "cordel," and the poetic duel in printed form called a "peleja" is a mainstay topic in "cordel." Ironically, it is this oral aspect of "cordel" that remains most visible today in Brazil with the gradual decline in production of the written poems in chapbooks.[4]

Because of the widespread availability of television with its entertainment and news programs and the advent of the internet today, "cordel's" former production has fallen drastically. It is much diminished as the "newspaper of the poor" and the main source of their entertainment, a role it performed until approximately the late 1960s and sporadically since then. But it still has occasional big moments—the campaign for direct elections and the end of the military dictatorship in the mid-1980s and the ups and downs of national economics and politics since then. The impeachment of President Fernando Collor de Mello and the scandal of national political corruption in the early 1990s are only the latest of the major events chronicled by the poets. Events totally unrelated to the "normal" cycle of cordel like the great celebration of "One Hundred Years of "Cordel" at the SESC-POMPÉIA in São Paulo in 2001 headed by renowned journalist Audálilo Dantas and the First International Congress of the "Literatura de Cordel" at the José Américo Foundation in João Pessoa also provided a certain stimulus to the poets and poet-singers of "cordel."[5]

The portrait of Brazil in "cordel" is the reality portrayed in thousands of booklets of verse produced in the one hundred years—plus existence of "cordel." It is a reality colored by the framework "cordel" is built upon: the folk-popular literary tradition in Europe prior to the arrival and assimilation of "cordel" in Brazil at the end of the nineteenth century. The stories in prose and poetry from Portugal, Spain, France or even Italy which were adapted to verse by the cordelian poets in Brazil offered a vision of life and a framework that literally exploded into an encyclopedic view of life in Brazil in the twentieth century. "Cordel" is made up primarily of the following categories:

a   The stories and poems from Europe transposed to the Northeastern poetic mode with strophes of six or seven lines of verse with abcbdb or abcbddc rhyme. These stories primarily were about love and adventure, princes and princesses, medieval knights, fairy tales or religion.

b   The oral tradition of the improviser of oral verse, the "cantador," in the poetic duel, [peleja], a tradition as old as classical Greece and alive in a modern variant in nineteenth and twentieth century Brazil.

c   The assimilation of the above to Brazil by the cordelian poets, the original creation by the same Brazilian folk-popular poets throughout the twentieth century and the role of the cordelian chapbook as the "newspaper of the poor" and the poet "the spokesman of the masses" during the same time.

The dean of Brazilian folklorists Luís da Câmara Cascudo stated as early as 1939 that the world view of the original "cordel" was essentially folkloric: rewarding the good and the just, punishing the evil, a worldview derived from a medieval Catholic tradition and shared by most of the folklores of western tradition.[6] That worldview was maintained in an amazing adaptation, evolution and what amounted to a creative response to the original body of story-poems in the form of hundreds and even thousands of stories in verse composed and produced by the poets originally from Brazil's Northeast. The sum total of the same portrays in effect a very large slice of the Brazilian reality of the twentieth century.

Portrait will tell of a Brazil that is in good measure disappearing, a Brazil with a foundation of traditional beliefs, values, social mores and interpretation of the major and minor events of life in a profoundly moral way. We recall a title from one of the short stories of a favorite American writer, the immensely talented Flannery O'Connor: "All that rises must converge." In this case all that matters in "cordel" does converge. Story line, protagonists and even basic linguistic turns of phrase appear in the most unlikely and disparate story-poems.

An evil, modern plantation owner appears like a vile, medieval king. A twentieth century bandit is described like one of Charlemagne's knights. But what all have in common is a basic worldview that is essentially religious and moral and is played out in a contest between Good and Evil, with a cast of characters that includes God and the Devil and Saints and Sinners (the Brazilians themselves) on the stage of life and death, heaven and hell.

Portrait's goal is to present the vast universe of "cordel"—the cordelian portrait of Brazil—in its simplest but most brilliant and pleasing hues. Because it is the product of the poor, disenfranchised Brazilians, it is indeed the "unofficial story" of Brazil, its unofficial portrait. The scope of the portrait is awesome, difficult to handle because of its immensity, but revealing for the same reasons. To use an old axiom, one must see the whole through the sum total of its parts. The mechanics of Portrait are as follows. Each album (chapter) is identified and introduced by a cliché or saying which expresses an important facet of life and is based upon hundreds of actual chapbooks from "cordel" comprising tens of thousands of lines of verse. The cadence and rhyme of cordelian poetry do not translate well to English, but its content does. Since it is obviously impossible within the space of one book to reproduce even a fraction of the totality of "cordel," quotation in English translation of excerpts of poetry, and summaries and paraphrasing of selected story-poems, often the best known, are the basic techniques used in Portrait. Commentary on the texts by the author along with anecdotes of incidents of travel and interaction with the poets completes the picture borrowing the journalistic technique of the sidebar.

Finally, titles of each story-poem are given first in English, for the purpose of this book, once again, is to present a portrait of the Brazilians and Brazil in English to the non-Portuguese speaking public in the United States and elsewhere. However, in poems actually quoted, summarized, or paraphrased, the original Portuguese title in brackets follows the title in English for the flavor it gives to the reader who may know that language. Portrait, not without coincidence, takes the form of ten albums (chapters) in homage to the traditional western epic, for the cordelian portrait really is a folk-popular Brazilian epic.

Although not directly a topic of this book, it is important to know that this humble literature of the poor of Brazil's North East has played a far different role in Brazilian culture than the chapbooks of verse themselves or the performances of the oral singers of verse. "Cordel" and the cordelian reality have influenced erudite artists in Brazil, some of whom are major players in the big picture of Brazilian Culture. José Lins do Rego borrowed from its themes and style in his novels about the sugar cane civilization of the coastal Northeast. Brazil's best known novelist Jorge Amado who is famous for his stories of Bahia and its Afro-Brazilian heritage also used both the poetry of "cordel" and its poets as narrators in his novels. Even João Guimarães

Rosa, often termed "the James Joyce of Brazil," in his Brazilian masterpiece <u>The Devil to Pay in the Backlands</u> wrote a backlands epic which shares a sub-stratum of themes with "cordel" and both reflect the Western epic tradition. There are others: João Cabral de Melo Neto in poetry, Ariano Suassuna in the drama and Alfredo Dias Gomes in both drama and TV soap operas [<u>novelas</u>], Glauber Rocha in new-wave cinema and Elba Ramalho and others in music. It is by virtue of the "high" culture of these artists that most middle and upper class, urban Brazilians have originally known of <u>cordel</u>, albeit often in an indirect way.[7] To end this short introduction and begin the portrait, here are the slices of life of the Brazilians and Brazil that "<u>cordel</u>" portrays:

Album I.	God Above and Below: In This We Believe
Album II.	The Manifestations
Album III.	The wages of Sin—What Not to Do
Album IV.	A Model to Live By: the Heroes of "Cordel"
Album V.	Life Is a Struggle and Life Is a Saga
Album VI.	But We Have Our Distractions
Album VII.	In Politics We Hope, but Do Not Trust
Album VIII.	There Is a Big World Out There
Album IX.	Life Is Not Getting Any Easier
Album X.	This Is Not the End

---

[1] This is from an interview with the poet and publisher Rodolfo Coelho Cavalcante at his house in the Liberdade District of Salvador da Bahia, July, 1981.

[2] Keep in mind once again, that this book is written from the perspective of the "cordel" in its heyday in the twentieth century. The author of course recognizes the "new" and "different" "cordel" of the twenty-first century, but that is a matter for another book by another author.

[3] This author has witnessed the excitement of North American fans of folk art snapping up the wood block prints of J. Borges in the International Art Market of Santa Fe, New Mexico. The

large majority of such folks do not know Portuguese and most have never been to Brazil or know much about it.

4 That trend is still generalized, but there has been a real upsurge in production in recent years due to the use of the computer to type out the poem and the printer to its side to print it, thus avoiding the costly use of the printing shop, the former only means of getting a poem into print. There is an entire new generation of modern cordelian poets currently writing in Brazil.

5 It is extremely important to note that since the first version of Portrait done in the 1990s, there is a true "Renaissance" of the poetry in Brazil with literally dozens of new poets in all the states of the Northeast and some new ones in the South-Center of the nation. In a conversation with this writer in 2005 Assis Angelo, well-known northeastern culture icon in São Paulo, told me that he believes that cordel in 2005 is almost reaching the numbers of production at its height in the 1960s. Be that as it may, the number is truly impressive. To what do we owe this happy moment? This author believes, after speaking with many of the poets in attendance at the "First International Congress of Cordel" in João Pessoa in 2005 that there is more interest in Brazilian schools, from the primary to the secondary and up to the colleges, but in addition to that, the internet has awakened and created much access to cordel. But it should be noted that the booklets of verse themselves in print are also present in today's Brazil and in great quantity. Woodcut artist, poet and publisher Marcelo Soares believes that this is due to the use of the computer not only to write the cordelian story, but to the printer at its side to print copies of the poems, thus avoiding the exorbitant cost of the printing shop, a factor which really hurt the poets and publishers at the end of the twentieth century.

6 Luís da Câmara Cascudo, Vaqueiros e Cantadores, Porto Alegre: Editora Globo, 1939, p. 16.

7 Mark J. Curran, A Literatura de Cordel, Recife: Universidade Federal de Pernambuco, chapter 4, 1973.

Album I

God Above and Below: In This We Believe

Introduction:

B razil is known as the largest Roman Catholic country in the world with more than ninety per cent of its population professing some link, formal or informal, to this religion.[1] But beyond this, scholars always speak of the "religiosity" of the Brazilian people. The experts speak in the same breath of the concept of religious syncretism, the mixing of diverse aspects of different religions, as a major characteristic of religion in Brazil.[2] This is of course most notably seen in the mixture of Roman Catholicism and Afro-Brazilian religions, the result of a long history of slavery, imposition of the white man's faith on the Blacks and their long odyssey of outwardly obeying the slave owners but inwardly keeping at least some measure of their own faith traditions. The result is a continuum of African religion in Brazil today, from that closest to African roots, the "candomblé" and "xangô" of the Northeast, to the most amorphous, the "umbanda" known primarily in Rio de Janeiro.

Thrown into the syncretic mix are the communication with spirits via the séance and the belief in reincarnation of the Spiritism of Allan Kardec from nineteenth century France and vestiges of Indian animist practices seen in a hodgepodge of Catholic, African and native beliefs. The fundamentalism of Protestant sects dating from the 1880s, the strong present-day movements of Pentecostalism ("Church of the Universal Kingdom of God") and today's powerful Mormon evangelization complete the large part of the picture. If one takes all this in, he is beginning the process of understanding religion as it is in Brazil.

But the "deep roots" or underpinnings of Brazilian religion are in the Roman Catholic faith brought by the Portuguese colonizers and imposed on those not born into it. This is the reality that has existed for almost five hundred years and has left an indelible mark on the people and the country, and this is the primary religious reality of Brazil in the Twentieth Century as seen in Brazil's "literatura de cordel."

It should be no surprise that one of the major topics of "cordel" is religion, (some say the most important) and thus a seminal part of Portrait.[3] The flavor of religion in old "cordel," however, is neither syncretic nor ecumenical. It is Roman Catholicism first of all, but Brazilian Roman Catholicism and finally, Catholicism of the colonial Northeast. It is "Old Church" religion with some surprising aberrations of the same. When Holy Mother Church is absent or in a weakened state, as is the case in the backlands where there was a shortage of priests spread over a geographic immensity, little or no formal education in religious matters for the humble, illiterate masses, and religion came in short intense doses of the annual Missions, strange things could and did happen. [4]

Local religious leaders, sanctioned or not by Rome, and mostly not, came out of the woodwork and led a desperate, impoverished but courageous flock in a search for unorthodox solutions to the important questions in life. Thus a major topic in the study of Northeastern Brazil is "Regional Mysticism" or as known by the elite and non-participants, "Religious Fanaticism."

But orthodox or not, the poets and their public are asking the same religious questions as their educated fellow Brazilians. Is there a God? Who is he? Where is he? In what form do we see him? Is there life after death? If so, how do we get there? In what does our salvation consist? Where is our salvation? Is the kingdom of God on this earth? If so, what form does it take and who can lead us to it? Are there a real hell and a devil and what is his role? Are Jesus, Mary and the saints our guides? What about local saints? What about local cult leaders like Antônio Conselheiro, Father Cícero, and Friar Damian? What about the Protestant sects [nova-ceitas]? And the Spiritualists? And should not our local and national leaders follow the same guidelines of what we believe? What happens if they do not? And ultimately, how does it all end?

The kaleidoscope of Brazilian religion becomes clear in "cordel," but most clear in its traditional Catholic and popular Catholic variants. The key word here is "variants," because there are many surprises, most of them in the realm of what is called "popular or folk Catholicism." If asked, the poets will say for the most part they were originally Catholic, but just as the entire country's religious spectrum has evolved, so have they. Most still are at heart Roman Catholic, but with a local flavor. A minority today will espouse Protestantism, others Kardec Spiritualism or even Afro-Brazilian "umbanda." Many see no problem taking the best from all four. But all say they must write what their public believes and expects, and that until very recent times is traditional northeastern backlands Catholicism.

So the religious foundation of Catholicism as found in the Northeast will provide the point of departure for a religious and moral vision that will guide the poets throughout the twentieth century, particularly as the "secularization" and "modernization" of Brazil in recent times will test old beliefs and application of the same to new, thorny moral issues. Because of the immensity of the question and the fact that religion is the most important topic in all "cordel," the matter is taken up in two albums, Beliefs (Album I) and Manifestations (Album II). Album I will investigate God and the saints, Satan and the sinners, and the apocalyptic view of the end. It will show us the basic beliefs, that is, the traditional beliefs with some superstition thrown in. Out of them comes the primary vision of the entire portrait, the religious and moral vision which guides poets and public in their interpretation of and reaction to events, persons and values yet today in a rapidly changing Brazil. In this the first album of a portrait of a people and a way of life, we see:

1   Jesus, Mary, the Apostles and Saints
2   Satan, Above and Below, Hell and Hellfire
3   Signs of the End of the World and the Apocalyptic Vision

1 Jesus, Mary, the Apostles and Saints

The Story-Poems of Jesus

In the first of these story-poems [folhetos], one sees the traditional Catholicism of the Northeast as divulged in the readings and sermons at mass based upon actual scriptural accounts from the Bible, especially those read and heard during Holy Week. One learns of the basic faith of the Northeasterner in Jesus Christ, Son of God, and Savior of Mankind, in poems based on scripture itself when the poets cite one or another of the evangelists, poems with titles like the Birth, Life and Death of Jesus. These poems in effect often substitute for a reading of the gospels for the rural believers. The teachings of Jesus during his ministry are paraphrased in verse and in language common to the cordelian public, and special emphasis is given to his passion and death. Variations have titles like The Sufferings of Jesus, The Passion of Christ, the Imprisonment of Christ, or Jesus Christ in the Garden, including one particularly lachrymose and melodramatic in tone: Who Would Not Have Cried When Jesus Suffered. In almost all the stories the tone is serious, the style formal, the subject of great respect and not to be fooled around with! Up to this point, other than being in verse and in the Portuguese language, the stories could be the same recounted from the pulpit of any Catholic Church in any Catholic country and express the same beliefs and values.

A second type of story about Jesus is quite a different matter. Poems abound which tell of the miracles of Christ, but not in a retelling of familiar gospel episodes themselves, but from popular and oral tradition in the form of "miracles" or "examples." Taken at times from episodes in the New Testament, they are far more often based on legend and combine Biblical fact and fiction by virtue of a true creative bent by the poets. The popular bards often insert a great sense of humor and irony into these delightfully entertaining stories about Jesus and St. Peter and their travels. But it is precisely this brand of religiosity—serious, but subject to humor and irony—that is truly Brazilian in character.

The scenario in these poems is almost always nearly the same: Jesus and St. Peter are on the road and stop to beg lodging for the night. Peter is Peter, impetuous and not always very smart. Jesus allows him a lot of leeway and the result is generally trouble, but trouble always remedied in the end with Jesus' saving the day and with a resulting moral teaching. Generally Jesus and Peter are taken in by a poor man and his wife (the givers of hospitality always begin poor), giving beyond their means in goodness and charity. Peter, seeing the goodness granted, begs Jesus to reward the poor man and woman. Jesus, a bit more skeptical than in the New Testament Gospels, obviously knows how the story is going to end—wealth brings arrogance and evil actions, and the virtues of the poor disappear. To humor Peter but to also prove his point, he grants the reward: the poor hosts become rich, arrogant and unforgiving and must be taught a lesson before repenting and returning to their original humility and goodness.

What makes the Jesus and Peter stories so fun are all the variations, often expressed with humor and irony, and the fact they are set generally in a scenario with all the accoutrements of the Northeast: Jesus and St. Peter sleep in hammocks, the poor man becomes a rich owner of a sugarcane plantation and mistreats his slaves. He is put to the test by Jesus in a variant where Jesus miraculously separates rice from its hulls by fire and the greedy owner tries to do the same and burns up all his crops, buildings and wealth (thus justice is done, punishment given). A variation is found in the story of the arrogant blacksmith who burns up his mother in his forge after seeing Jesus "miraculously" make an old woman young again (because she had true faith in him) by the same process, a poem also rich in humor, strange as that may be. So the real "Master of Masters" is Jesus and it does not bode well for the blacksmith to try to be greater than he. Arrogance and ambition lead to evil ways; faith and humility lead to the righteous path and salvation.[5]

Such poems as The Man with the Rice and the Power of Jesus and the Story of Jesus, Master of Masters or Jesus and the Evil Blacksmith are wonderful stories which demonstrate the essence of the poet's role: to entertain first of all, but to inform and teach as well. And the story lines with their events and characters while readily entertaining the cordelian public, more importantly teach the values of the traditional faith. This is exemplified by a variant of the story when Jesus grants three wishes to the generous poor man, an obvious take-off of the oriental exemplary stories and fairy tales, and greed eventually forces him to sell his soul to the devil. He dies unrepentant, is wanted neither in heaven by St. Peter (due to his sins) nor in hell by Satan (for his cleverness in outsmarting the devil himself) and is left to wander the earth wallowing in his own evil ways.

An important corollary to the life of Jesus but with a totally different tone that tells us much of the Brazilians and their "religiosity" is the poem dealing with Jesus as patron saint and miracle worker at a pilgrimage site in Brazil's Northeast. Here the non-Brazilian reader is introduced to an often bizarre Brazilian reality, the realm of popular Catholicism verging on superstition, but a central fact in Brazilian traditional life. Suffice to mention two different cases in point: the important shrine of Good Jesus of The Rock [Bom Jesus da Lapa] and Good Jesus of the Good End [Bom Jesus do Bomfim], the first in the backlands of the state of Bahia along the São Francisco River, the second the major pilgrimage church in Brazil's first capital and most famous colonial city, Salvador da Bahia.

Both variants are based on concepts originally Catholic and orthodox, but in an evolved form that is anything but that. Jesus Christ, Son of God, Redeemer of Mankind—these are concepts which thus far are certainly orthodox in nature. But at both religious shrines, Jesus Christ has been converted into a miraculous, but different Jesus involving one of the most important customs and beliefs of Brazilian popular Catholicism: the religious promise called "ex-voto" in Portuguese.

When one wants something from his god, he must ask for it. The traditional Catholic way is through personal prayer, a major aspect of orthodox teachings of the church. But in Brazil and many other Latin Catholic countries, the custom is taken to another level. If one's request is granted—the cancer goes into remission, the job is found, the girlfriend comes back—proof of one's gratefulness and at minimum an expression of good faith is to "pay the promise," or do something showing you acknowledge the help of the saint and believe in his/her powers. It may take the form of placing a photograph of the person healed in front of the image of the saint (or in this case, Good Jesus) in the local church. But in northeast Brazil there are special places where the saints are very present in miraculous ways, places which often are distant and difficult to get to. Where orthodoxy diminishes is at those sites deemed miraculous but which are immersed in half religious custom, half folk superstition, and, to put it bluntly, bordering on the strange. These places are not rare and form the basis for some of the most interesting, colorful and important of customs and beliefs in the cordelian Brazilian Portrait.

Good Jesus of the Rock [Bom Jesus da Lapa], is a shrine in a town on the banks of the São Francisco river which is said to be the "River of National Unity," joining northern and southern Brazil. The river runs north from the interior of the state of Minas Gerais, curves east after its long trajectory across the dry backlands of Minas Gerais and Bahia, borders the state of Sergipe and empties into the sea at Penedo, Alagoas. "Lapa" means rock and that describes the scene well: from the flattest of plains on either side of the river, out of nowhere rises a huge rock filled with many caves, some large enough to house an entire chapel or church. This is the home of Good Jesus who is considered particularly miraculous and draws poor pilgrims from all parts of Brazil, but mainly the Northeast.

SIDEBAR. This author reached the site in 1967 via a wood burning sternwheeler of the old São Francisco Navigation Company, now defunct but in its time one of the marvels of Brazil. Riverboats imported from the Rhine in Germany, the Mississippi in the United States and some made locally, transported commercial traffic along the river until the 1970s. It was one of the most "folkloric" trips in Brazil, not unlike the Mississippi of Mark Twain one hundred years earlier. In April, 1967, I bought a ticket for about $20 U.S., double bunk and three meals a day, on a sternwheeler for a fourteen day trip to Joaseiro da Bahia with the purpose of contacting poets and buying "folhetos" along the way. I met a cast of characters unlike any other in my travels in Brazil: courageous river pilots trained in the same school of navigation as sea-going captains, ruddy crew members, passengers, including a little old lady who would "walk" on her knees from the dock to the shrine of Good Jesus of the Rock to pay a religious promise, humble backlands girls ironing at night with antique irons filled with hot coals, a Paraná riverboat captain from the Paraguay border checking out the "other" river, a swaggering, scary, beer-drinking, pistol-toting ranch owner who threatened to swim across the river with me on his back (after drinking many "Brahmas," the German inspired Brazilian beer) and last, but not least, the local miner who reminded me of a crusty character from Bogart's The Treasure of the Sierra Madre, who in an incredible scene out of a Hollywood movie offered to take me to his amethyst, tourmaline, aquamarine and topaz mine a few miles from a river port. While spending a leisurely seven days aboard, rooming with a retired riverboat pilot who filled my ears with fact and fiction and lore of the river, I read Jorge Amado's classic novel of the area, Red Harvest ["Seara Vermelha"]. The adventure should have ended in Joaseiro, but I got off several days early to rendezvous with a friend in Salvador da Bahia and ended up experiencing yet another adventure. But that's another story.

Lapa is in a part of Brazil where life can take on strange twists: it is in the same backlands as the War of Canudos of 1896-1897 (a conflict of religious fanaticism to be considered soon in Portrait) and the scenario of Brazil's best novel The Devil to Pay in the Backlands ["Grande Sertão: Veredas"], an epic of good and evil, God and the devil, courageous bandits and love in the backlands. In effect, the shrine became the reason for an annual pilgrimage by the people and poets of the Northeast, the latter visiting it each year during feast days to tell and sell the story of Good Jesus. The highlight of the Lapa is the "miracle room" filled with Plaster of Paris body parts (fingers, hands, arms, legs, even heads) of cured believers as well as models of sternwheelers "saved" from disaster by Good Jesus. There is a stone tower outside the entrance to the cave wherein lies the church of Good Jesus which could come directly from a nineteenth century romantic painting depicting a scary Germanic fairy tale, a tower from any of many small castles of Europe. At the entrance to the shrine old religious harpies [beatas] dressed in black met the pilgrims, many who come on their knees for kilometers. During our visit in 1967 beggars abounded. All manner of shops with souvenirs of Good Jesus surrounded the plaza in front of the tower and shrine, and one of the most colorful of markets or fairs in Brazil was not far away. END OF SIDEBAR.

To begin, one must see the Story of the Monk Francis of Solitude, Founder of Lapa ["História do Monge Francisco da Solidão, Fundador de Lapa"] by the poet Minelvino

Francisco Silva from the city of Itabuna in the cocoa region of southern Bahia.[6] Dubbed the "Apostle Troubadour" for his many excellent "folhetos" about religion, a staunch Catholic and defender of Rome but immersed in the popular religion of Bahia, he was a staple for years at the annual festival of Good Jesus in Lapa. Basing his poem on a religious pamphlet sponsored by a monsignor of an undesignated parish, he tells of the original inhabitants of Lapa, the Coroados Indians, and the arrival at the site of Portuguese soldiers of fortune and hunters of gold and slaves [bandeirantes] in seventeenth century Brazil, men responsible indirectly for opening up much of the country to colonization. Seventy-seven years later marks the arrival of the Portuguese Francisco Mendonça Mar in the capital of Bahia in Salvador in 1679 at the age of twenty-two. After unsuccessful jobs in the city, one resulting in being thrown in jail, he had a vision which told him "Search for your Calvary in the cave." The vision led him on a difficult journey [travessia] across the interior of Bahia with a major encounter with a wild mountain lion or jaguar-like cat [onça]. Following the model of St. Francis, he pulled a thorn from the paw of the cat which in turn became tame and followed him and defended him against enemies on the journey which ended at the Rock of Lapa and its caves [grutas]. Guided by an image of Jesus and a devotion to the Virgin Mary, Francisco settled in Lapa as a monk in a life of prayer. News of his good works arrived in Salvador to the Archbishop who ordained him a priest in 1702. The fame of his good works and the miracles of the image of Christ he brought with him were the beginnings of the fame and pilgrimages to Lapa.

The second shrine of Good Jesus is far different in character, but the story it tells of Brazilians and their faith is no less impressive. It tells of the beautiful church in the district of Bomfim in Salvador da Bahia where the patron saint, Jesus Christ himself, is revered in yet another of the amazing phenomena of Brazilian religiosity: the syncretism of Catholic worship inside the church and African "candomblé" worship outside, Jesus and his Afro-Brazilian counterpart, Oxum Oxalufá. One of the most colorful sights in Brazil is the Thursday of the Novena to Good Jesus, a feast day when dozens of dignified, beautiful and happy African-Brazilian ladies dressed in all their finery come and busily wash the steps of the church in homage to Good Jesus and offer baskets of fruit or flowers to Good Jesus and Oxalufá, the greatest of the African gods [orixás].

Perhaps the best poem portraying the mixture of it all is by the poet-reporter José Costa Leite who knew his public and what they most liked. The poet visits the great popular festival of Bomfim in Bahia and tells of his pilgrimage in Story of the Devotion of the Lord Good Jesus of Bomfim ["História da Devoção do Senhor Bom Jesus do Bomfim"].[7] He recounts the beginning of the shrine with its image of Good Jesus brought to Salvador by the Portuguese sailor and hero Teodósio de Faria in 1754. The chapel, now a basilica recognized by Rome for miraculous powers, may be the locale of Brazil's most famous festival of Catholicism, popular Catholicism and Afro-Brazilian syncretism. The poet compares it in importance to the shrine of Father Cícero in Juazeiro (the most important in the cordelian portrait, to be seen) and to St. Francis in Canindê, Ceará State. He tells of the pilgrims who travel from all over the country to "pay a promise." He describes the novena as a festival where you pray and then play at the nearby "Carnival at the Shore" [Carnaval da Ribeira] on the last day of the Novena. But most important is the special attention the poet gives to the washing of the steps of the Basilica by "Bahianas," the ladies in the Afro-Brazilian cult of "candomblé." These ladies in all their finery complete a six-kilometer procession from the great church of Conceição da Praia in the city proper to the Itapagipe Peninsula and the Basilica of Bomfim to wash the steps of the basilica and then enter and place baskets of fruit and flowers in honor of Good Jesus (and perhaps more importantly, Oxulafá, the greatest of the African gods or saints who is identified with Jesus.) He describes the "miracle room" (all the shrines have one, some creepier than others—the height of popular Catholicism in Bahia!).

Mary Our Mother

On a much smaller but no less important scale the figure of the Blessed Virgin Mary plays a role in Portrait. The official Mary, canonized saint of the Roman Catholic Church, Mother of Jesus Christ, and patron saint of parishes throughout the world is present in the cordelian portrait as is the Mary of Brazilian popular Catholicism, the Mary of legend and "miracles," of the medieval and modern Marian cult.

The "traditional" Mary, mother of Jesus and suffering mother at his passion and death, is portrayed in poems like The Seven Swords of Pain of Holy Virgin Mary ["As Sete Espadas de Dores da Santa Virgem Maria"].[8] The poet recounts Simon's prophecy of the seven wounds of Christ and the subsequent seven sorrows of Our Lady: first, the prophecy of Simon, second, the flight into Egypt (an early narrative model for the important difficult journey motif [travessia] throughout the cordelian portrait), third, the disappearance of Jesus and finding him preaching in the temple, fourth, Jesus taken prisoner, fifth, Jesus scourged and spit upon in the streets, sixth, Jesus on the road to Calvary, and seventh, the death of Jesus in Mary's arms.

Also following the pattern of Jesus stories, there are cordelian poems which abound in the portrait which treat the feast days dedicated to the Virgin Mary, particularly as a local patron saint, perhaps the best case being the "The Festival of Nazareth" [Círio de Nazaré].[9] The Basilica of Nazareth is dedicated to the Virgin Mary, patron saint of Belém do Pará, an important city and state in northern Brazil near the mouth of the Amazon. As with Lapa or Bomfim in Bahia, one learns of the festival itself, a great popular religious spectacle in Brazil, and then the miracles and "examples" rising from it.

A good portrait of the Nazareth festival is The Festival of Nazareth [O Círio de Nazaré] by a visiting pilgrim poet who incidentally attends to offer his poem as a souvenir to the masses of people. For fifteen days beginning the second Sunday of October, the people pray, repent and celebrate the feast of their patron saint known locally as the Virgin of Nazareth. Like Bomfim, people from all over Brazil and even outside of Brazil attend with much fervor and carrying on. The image of the Virgin is carried in procession from the Cathedral to the Basilica of Nazaré, the street strewn with flowers before her. The procession is however headed by the fireworks float "to make the people happy" and the "miracle" float on which the bystanders literally throw models of heads, arms, legs and such, thus "paying the promise" for healings by the Virgin. The Brazilian Navy even takes part with an official float. Thus the popular festival, begun in 1616, takes its course with shoeless pilgrims following the float of the Virgin with an air of respect.

But on the other hand, days of celebration, eating, drinking and debauchery follow the procession. Local dishes are a must like "regional duck" [pato no tucupi]. There is an amusement park for the kids and regional drinks including a drink made from a local palm [o açaí]. Tourists abound, national media figures come to be seen as well as to see, and even a variant on the improvisers of oral verse of "cordel" is present: the "coconut singers" [violeiros de côco]. The poet says that only the great festival dedicated to St. Francis in Canindé, Ceará, can compare. One begins to see how important local religion is in this carnival atmosphere.

Dozens of other stories about the Virgin exist, from melodramatic, teary homages to prayers and more Examples. But Portrait closes this section with perhaps the best known of the poems involving Mary: The Punishment of the Arrogant Soul ["Castigo da Soberba"],[10] a poem reported early in the twentieth century in oral form and then in written variants, but made famous in one of the best known of Brazilian plays The Rogues' Trial ["Auto da Compadecida"] by Ariano Suassuna in the 1950s. The play first gained local fame in Recife, Pernambuco, then on the national stage in São Paulo and Rio, in Brazilian cinema in the early 1970s, and a TV mini-series in 2000. It is based primarily on the stories of "cordel" which are adapted to sophisticated Brazilian drama.[11]

Portrait places this poem along with Money ["O Dinheiro"],[12] (the role of money and the satire of clerical abuse of the same), by the pioneer cordelian poet Leandro Gomes de Barros in the teens of the twentieth century and the same poet's Debate of the Protestant Minister with the Vulture[13] (to be seen later) as the best poems on religion in the cordelian portrait. There is good reason to believe that all three were written and printed in "cordel" by the great Leandro Gomes de Barros, or if not, at least transposed to verse by him from the oral variants existing in late nineteenth century northeastern Brazil.

The Punishment of the Arrogant Soul could be included anywhere in this album because so many basic concepts and beliefs converge in it. It is the story of final judgment for an arrogant soul in purgatory, but a judgment strangely familiar to a Brazilian's idea of a court of law on earth. The accuser and prosecutor is Satan, the judge Jesus himself, but it is Mary the lawyer for the defense in her role as intercessor, a basic tenet in traditional, popular Catholic beliefs, that is most important. The portrait is extremely entertaining due to the language and humor which evoke the reader's appreciation of the trial. But underlying the entire story is the role of Mary as mother of Jesus who is God and also man and the very human corollary of the good, obedient child who can refuse no favor or request from his loving mother. Thus, the sinner is given a second chance, even though Jesus was going to condemn him "by the book," and the devil can only console himself with an aphorism: "Women stick their noses in everything." In summation, it is this basic belief and practice, faith in Our Lady as Mother of God and intercessor through prayer of the faithful, that comprises the true basis of Catholicism in so many countries of the world and in particular the northeastern backlands of Brazil. There can be no better example of "<u>cordel</u>" as religious portrait of a people and nation.

The Apostles and the Saints

Closing this initial look at the portrait of Brazil and its people by way of its religion, Portrait must make mention of all the story-poems dealing with the apostles and the saints. They are a curious amalgam of stories closely linked to the gospels and/or the far-fetched exempla we have already seen in reference to the person of Jesus and the Blessed Virgin Mary. Oral tradition across the centuries in Europe left the popular literary tradition replete with such stories, and they were passed on to Brazil and adapted or recreated in "cordel." All are meant to entertain, but each also informs and teaches.

The poets also write humorous poems [gracejos] meant to entertain but bring a message as well. Such is the story of How Saint Peter Entered into Heaven[14] ["Como São Pedro Entrou no Céu"] when the poet-reporter José Soares recounts the fight between St. Simian who originally had the keys to the pearly gates and the upstart Peter for control of the same. With support from the apostles arriving at the gates of heaven at the same time as Peter and with Jesus' help, Peter arrives at his final destiny. But Jesus had to placate St. Simian via a clever management decision: he named him bookkeeper of heaven, keeper of records of all the souls entering the gates.

Like the Greek gods of old, the saints tend to take on all too human characteristics in the cordelian accounts, so the same St. Simian is forever portrayed in Life and Death of St. Simian[15] [Vida e Morte de São Simião] as the hardheaded, persistent and clever saint that only the great leveler, the Grim Reaper himself, can get to take his place in heaven, this in spite of humorous attempts by St. Peter, St. Michael the Archangel and Jesus himself to extricate the saint from his earthly existence.

St. Anthony, protector of young maidens, saintly "matchmaker" for weddings, and patron saint for those who lose things, is also omnipresent in the literature. Using a similar framework as the humorous exempla of Jesus and St. Peter on the road in poems already seen, in one famous poem St. Anthony disguises himself as a simple country friar who explains to a devotee the how and why of the death of the latter's horse, his son, and his wife in apparent contradiction to the faithfulness of the man to the saint who acted ironically to save the devotee's life and soul itself. This was the plot of Story of a Man Who Had a Dispute with St. Anthony,[16] an old story also claimed by João Martins de Atayde.

There is a plethora of saints' stories in the portrait, many in traditional form as from the Lives of the Saints, others in the realm of fantasy: How Judas Iscariot Died, Story of the Martyr Saint Etelvina the Cearense Saint, Homage to St. Lucia, Life and Miracles of St. George, a funny modern day reaction to the astronauts on the moon The Revolt of St.

<u>George with the Invaders on the Moon (the Brazilian image of "the man on the moon" is that of St. George slaying the dragon)</u>, <u>Battles and Victory of St. Cyprian against Adrian the Magician</u>, <u>Life and Death of St. Raimundo Nonato of the Mulundus</u> and countless others. They complete this part of the cordelian portrait, telling the stories of lives of the saints but above all praising the virtues of Christians who emulate the same.

2 Satan Above and Below, Hell and Hellfire

If the Catholic of Brazil's old Northeast (and his descendants today in Rio de Janeiro, São Paulo, Brasília or the Northeast itself) is to do good, obey Jesus and attain heavenly salvation, that means <u>not</u> doing evil, following the "dark side" of Satan himself and ending up in the fires of hell. And just as Jesus, Mary and saints of the gospels are recreated across the centuries in local legend, so it is with Satan. But the devil plays an unorthodox and surprising role in the religiosity of the <u>cordelian</u> public, the topic of this section of <u>Portrait</u>. He plays in the shadow of Jesus, but also of Mary, the apostles and saints. God and the devil: this is the dichotomy which permeates both elite and folk-popular culture in Brazil. It is the reality of Glauber Rocha's <u>God and the Devil in the Land of the Sun</u> ["Deus e o Diabo na Terra do Sol"], one of the most avant-garde films ever made in Brazil, a product of the "New Cinema" [<u>Cinema Novo</u>] of the 1950s and 1960s. God and the devil is the sub-stratum reality of <u>The Devil to Pay in the Backlands</u> ["Grande Sertão Veredas"], the masterpiece by João Guimarães Rosa in 1956, arguably Brazil's best novel.[17] The notion is central to Brazilian folk-popular culture as well. But behind all this and most important is that it is a reality of Roman Catholicism both orthodox and popular and of Christianity today.

The Biblical Satan, be he Lucifer, Beelzebub or other nomenclature, is interspersed throughout the story-poems, but it is the "popular" Satan who has a ubiquitous presence in the life of the northeasterners. This is the devil of folk legend and popular Catholic tradition growing and evolving through the centuries. In some ways this devil, although always potentially frightening in a bloodcurdling way, like Jesus, Mary, St. Peter, St. Anthony and others in the cordelian stories, becomes almost human, acting like people the reader knows but with a little something "special" about his demeanor. The devil is absolutely necessary in the portrait just as he is in the real life of the poets and public of "<u>cordel</u>," and he is seen in these variants:

Jesus and the Devil: Complaints of the State of the World
St. Peter, the Apostles, the Saints and the Devil: the Folk Imagination
Satan and the Fairy Tale Tradition: <u>The Marriage of Lucifer</u>
The Devil, Hell and Who Is In It (Northeastern Bandits, Communists and Evil Politicians)
The Moral <u>Exempla</u>: Satan and the Lessons to Live By
A Modern Phenomenon: Satan and the Biggest Pop Star of Recent Times: Roberto Carlos

Jesus and the Devil: Complaints of the State of the World

The belief behind these "folhetos" is that the world created by God, saved by Jesus and inspired by the Holy Spirit has gone to hell in a hand basket. Satan, designated by God himself as master of hell, is thoroughly stressed out and a bit overwhelmed by his own good fortune—humanity's corruption. He thus must go to heaven, convince St. Peter to let him in the gate and have a personal appointment with Jesus to let him know what has happened to his creation. Satan is legalistic, having already gone head to head with the top lawyer in heaven, the Blessed Virgin Mary, so he wants it all in writing, a contract signed by God (Jesus) giving him the right to haul all the corrupt sinners he can round up off to hell. Jesus is a bit casual, and reacts to the onslaught of corruption with "I would not worry about it too much if I were you" ["o que há de mais no mundo?]"

Titles abound like One of Satan's Complaints to Christ, The Second Complaint of Satan to Christ, The Second Complaint of Satan to Christ over the Corruption in the World or Jesus' Explanation and Satan's Outburst. They all follow the pattern just described, but the crux of the matter is found in a classic poem by Vicente Vitorino de Melo from the interior of the state of Pernambuco, The Second Complaint of Satan to Christ [Segunda Queixa de Satanás a Cristo]. [18] Vicente wrote his "first complaint" in 1940 and is back with this one in 1967 because no one repented the first time around, or just as likely, it promised good sales. Satan, like any common person, has to battle St. Peter to get into heaven because he has this "reputation." Pride [orgulho] caused his downfall, the big sin of being too big for his britches, thinking he was as good as God. After standing in line with everyone else wanting to get into heaven, he finally gets his chance to let it all out: the litany of evils in the world, all in an almost formulaic language present in most of these stories. The good ole' world is about to end, corruption is rampant, immoral and vulgar sexual behavior is everywhere, and religion has disappeared. No one pays any attention to the Catholic priests, and even more, the worst carrying on is in the atrium and even inside the church itself! And the May celebrations for Mary! And of course there is carnival, three days of gambling, dancing and sex. And, well! The novenas in the countryside! If you want action, go to a saint's day and novena in a small town! When the praying ends, the partying begins! The poet deliciously describes anything that smacks of a good time and modern days. Jesus answers: "If they repent, I will pardon them all." The Virgin Mary pops in on the conversation and the devil of course loses his composure: women are always sticking their noses where they do not belong! He and Jesus were just having a man-to-man talk and she butts in. The devil makes snide remarks about heaven being run by the bureaucrats, and Jesus who cannot refuse his mother, shows the devil the door. He vows even greater evil for the world, but the poet ends praising Jesus—Father, messiah and merciful judge [compadecido] of humanity's sufferings. The devil is the fall guy.

These poems, done to remind the public of the state of the world, were best sellers because one could have his cake and eat it too, that is, profess his religion and its message and at the same time experience a little vicarious pleasure from the plethora of sinful activities the devil describes. The poems express the mindset of many people in Brazil from the beginnings of "cordel" in the early 1900s to the 1960s: the old roots and rules and stability are disappearing and now are mainly nostalgic memories. The world is now an upside down world and people are wild and crazy. But in the end one hears Jesus and returns to the fold or suffers the consequences. The poet and the public are having fun, but the message is not forgotten.

St. Peter, the Apostles, the Saints and the Devil, the Folk Imagination

Out of the Biblical descriptions and the evolution of popular belief and tradition over the centuries come the story-poems which entertain, teach and inform basing their lessons on the battle of good and evil between the saints and the devil. One of the best is a story by the Pernambuco poet José Costa Leite, known for combining religion and humor: <u>Satan Working on St. Peter's Farm</u> ["Satanás Trabalhando na Roça de São Pedro"].[19] This poem known as a humorous story [<u>gracejo</u>] depicts St. Peter and Satan as close neighbors, each working a farm across the river from the other. St. Peter has much less land but double the crop; Satan is hard working, but not so smart and far less successful. The latter proposes a partnership and St. Peter agrees: Satan will do the work; St. Peter will do the overseeing. They plant in succession manioc, corn, tobacco, sugar cane, potatoes and squash, staples of agriculture in the North East. The devil sweats and toils, the crops are wonderful, and St. Peter then tricks the devil out of his share of the harvest. Manioc comes first and St. Peter gives the devil the choice to take what is above ground or below. Thinking it better to take all the greenery he sees, Satan takes the worthless part of the plant above ground, and St. Peter ends up with the tuber itself, the good part. Next comes the corn, but not to be taken in again, the devil "learns" from past experience and takes what is below the ground and gives St. Peter all he can see above ground. Foiled again! The humble northeasterner in town for the local fair or market, probably a sharecropper or small farmer, upon hearing the declamation of the poem howls with laughter seeing the slow devil deceived time after time by the clever, roughish Peter. Converging with other story types and themes, Peter thus becomes a traditional northeastern rogue [<u>pícaro</u> or <u>quengo</u>], one who must live by his wits to survive!

Satan and the Fairy Tale Tradition: <u>The Marriage of Lucifer</u>

One of the oldest and best of the stories of the devil in "<u>cordel</u>" is a classic with the title <u>TheMarriage of Lucifer</u> ["O Casamento de Luzbel"].[20] It is quite clear that this is a case of story line, protagonists and format converging in this folk-popular literary tradition. The central issue, the old religion with its battle between good and evil, in this case personified in the devil's machinations against an innocent maiden and her life-long defense by the Blessed Virgin Mary through a guardian angel, is combined with the tradition of the long, narrative poem in the fiction mode of "<u>cordel</u>" [<u>romance</u>, <u>história</u>], to be seen in a future album. The result is a story in three 32-page volumes of six-line strophes [<u>sextilhas</u>] which takes the reader on an entertaining trip through earth, purgatory and hell, mixing religion with the marvelous and fantastic elements of the fairy tale.

One of the old cordelian classics attributed to João Martins de Atayde in the heyday of the poetry from the 1920s to the 1950s and sold to a major publisher in Juazeiro do Norte, Ceará State, in the late 1950s, this classic has survived to this day. It reveals concepts of faith, moral standards, and best of all the creative bent of the poet combining in fiction faith, beliefs and the world of fantasy.

The Devil, Hell and Who Is in It (Northeastern bandits, Communists and Evil Politicians)[21]

All that matters in "cordel" converges. One of the most interesting and colorful of the snapshots of Portrait is the story of the real life bandits of the Northeast. From the legendary bandits of the eighteenth and nineteenth centuries like Cabeleira or Lucas da Feira to the very real bandits of the heyday of "cordel" in the twentieth century, Antônio Silvino of Paraíba and the infamous Lampião and Maria Bonita, the figure of the bandit [cangaceiro] from Brazil's Northeast is a chapter in itself in the history of the country. [22]

Reference to the bandits in regard to history and society will be seen in a later album, but here one sees a link to popular beliefs, superstition and religion: the bandits were believed to have mysterious powers such as an ability to ward off bullets which derived from incantations and prayers they learned. It was common knowledge that Lampião had a special fondness for the powers of "The Miracle Worker of the Backlands," Father Cícero, and more than once went to Juazeiro do Norte to see him. But relating to this album, if a bandit was able to escape the law in an almost miraculous fashion, it was believed that he had a pact with the devil himself. On the other hand, the bandits, especially Lampião, were considered the epitome of evil and mean enough to challenge the powers of Satan himself. Thus an entire sub-theme of fiction and fantasy was created in the cordelian stories of the arrival of Lampião or Antônio Silvino in hell. In these latter stories the poets let their imagination flow free, generally in a humorous vein.

The best known of these stories is The Arrival of Lampião in Hell ["A Chegada de Lampeão no Inferno"][23] by José Pacheco, a poem imitated, plagiarized and stolen by other poet-publishers over the years. In the story Lampião arrives in hell, burns its market and crops (just like the local bullies did in real life in the tiny towns of the backlands, an episode all too well known to the public of "cordel"). The doorman of hell is a young black boy (like the young blacks on the sugar cane plantations), and most of the devils are black as well (a racial prejudice common to the times in the interior of the Northeast). And this hell is just like small town government in the northeastern backlands: there is a bureaucracy with the same hoops to jump through before Lampião can get to the "central office" to talk to Satan. The poet's humor rests on irony because Satan fears the bandit will steal what he has worked so hard for so long to save (like a good citizen). He calls out the troops, all the devils of hell and all coincidentally black; Lampião thinks he must be in Abyssinia! The poet lists the names of the devils (like in epic poetry), some from northeastern tradition, some comic names, and Lampião defeats them all. But since heaven did not want him nor did the devil, he is now back in the northeast backlands [o sertão] and if you do not believe it, you can write to the devil himself in hell!

The concept of Lampião going to hell and "raising hell" in hell caught on and was imitated by many other poets. So naturally stories began to evolve with the bandit in hell courting the daughter of the devil, dealing with a devilish mother-in-law (the mother-in-law [sogra] is one of the most maligned characters in northeastern folk beliefs or, for that matter, most folklores). The poet, Apolônio Alves dos Santos, one of the mainstays of the Northeastern Fair in Rio de Janeiro during the 1970s and 1980s, repeats part of the story line from the Pacheco classic,[24] leading up to Lampião's battle with the devils, but departs to tell of the arrival of the devil's daughter. She wrestles Lampião to the ground; both feel a "great sensation" and make love on the spot. But once again the poets write to get a laugh: the devil's code of honor is ironically the same as that of the traditional northeasterners. Since Satan's daughter has been "dishonored," the culprit must either marry her or die. Lampião accepts with the condition he can govern hell. The devil accepts but wants it all "legal," that is, in writing, so that they can be his inheritors! The poet ends by noting that this was Lampião's second lover, granting that Maria Bonita was the first in real life.

A final snapshot is The Battle between Antônio Silvino and Lampião in Hell, ["A Briga de Antônio Silvino com Lampião no Inferno"].[25] The poet warns that this is a "modern" plot. What could be more interesting than a meeting of the "Terror of the Backlands" (Lampião) and the "Justice Maker of the Backlands" (Antônio Silvino). There is no record of any encounter or battle in real life, (Silvino preceded Lampião by almost one generation), but in cordelian terms, it would be a battle rivaling Achilles and Hector. In this fantasy, Lampião has been elected mayor of hell, so it now has lights and paved streets (a correlation to politics and economic development in tiny towns in the interior of the Northeast). He is set to marry Satan's daughter but in an Afro-Brazilian "xangô" ceremony (a clue to what the poets and public think of the Afro-Brazilian rites in Pernambuco). Antônio Silvino arrives, challenges Lampião for the post of mayor, and a traditional battle ensues: trading of gunfire, then a duel to the death in hand to hand combat using the cold steel of long knives. Lampião gets the worst of it, culminating when Antonio Silvino bites his nose (a very un-heroic bit of humor). The devils arrive to reinforce Lampião, but the Archangel Michael appears and whisks Antônio Silvino off to heaven and his just reward. What makes all these poems so good is the way the poets take real life values, beliefs and situations and apply them to the scenario of hell, thus bringing real life and their views on it even to fiction.

And of course the poets could apply the same principles, the same scenario, and the same humor to another very real evil: the communists and other evil politicians and international leaders. So one sees <u>The Arrival of Stalin in Hell</u>, <u>The Arrival of Mussolini in Hell</u> and especially <u>The Arrival of Hitler in Hell</u>.[26] Communism is almost always associated with the devil by virtue of its traditional and inherent atheism and materialist (as opposed to spiritual) view of the world. The old Marxist axiom, true or not, "Religion is the opiate of the people" had huge consequences in the traditionally Catholic Northeast. Poems like <u>Discussion of a Priest with a Communist</u>, <u>The Dragon of the End of the Era</u> (where Communism is equated to the Beast of the Apocalypse and the devil), <u>Message of Our Lady of Fatima and the Horrors of Communism</u> (with the message that Communism is diabolical and those who believe in it will end in hell), and the subversive plans of International Communism are always seen as works of Lucifer. So it is no surprise Stalin ended in the hell of "<u>cordel</u>."

But the Corporatism of Mussolini and the utter Fascism of Hitler did not escape either, and the poets wrote hilarious poems panning a buffoonish Mussolini and a sexually starved Hitler who would chase the daughter of Satan (or his mother) in hell. Real life events of the despotic leaders enter a different album of <u>Portrait</u>, but one learns much of the character and attitude of the Northeasterner in these humorous stories set in the fictional hell of "<u>cordel</u>."

Satan and the Moral Example [Exemplo]—Lessons to Live By

Once again there is a parallel: just as Jesus, Mary, Joseph and the saints serve traditionally as models and produce miracles accordingly, so the devil follows oral—folk tradition and popular religion in stories of example, but stories warning the reading public to avoid evil and the fires of hell. In these poems the devil is always a step or two behind Jesus, the saints or even the human protagonists; he is a bit slow of mind and most often ends fooled and foiled.

A Modern Phenomenon: Satan and Roberto Carlos

Religious beliefs, poetic fiction and real life can often merge, as in an event that made lots of money for the poets in the late 1960s, a happy accident when life, folklore and religion became one. The Beatles had arrived on the international stage with a popularity that would not only change the popular music of much of the western world, but also the social customs and morality of the times. Rock and Roll with its blues, country and gospel roots, with Bill Haley and the Comets, Carl Perkins, Little Richard, Chuck Berry and especially Elvis Presley, had prepared the way for the Beatles' success. But their long hair and secular message sent a tidal wave of change through the USA and also Brazil. A talented, good-looking young man from the state of Espírito Santo, enamored of the new music and styles, adapted foreign rhythms, music and customs to the youth of Brazil. Roberto Carlos and friend Erasmo Carlos single handedly began a new music the "iê, iê, iê" (from the "yeah, yeah, yeah" of Beatle lyrics) or in loose terms, Brazilian rock. With long hair down to the shoulders, tight pants and a come what may attitude, Roberto Carlos sent the teeny boppers to swooning like never before in Brazil.

SIDEBAR This author was a firsthand witness to the new scenario. Much as Elvis had won the hearts of teenagers in America in the mid-1950s with the historic appearance on the "Ed Sullivan Show" and the Beatles later with a similar appearance, Roberto Carlos became "King of Brazil." Teens en masse adopted the long hair, the tight trousers, the plethora of new slang Roberto used in his songs and mainly the peculiar Brazilian rhythms adapting British and American Rock to Brazil (including the twist [twiste]). I always believed this was U.S. vengeance to "Gringos can't samba." The herky-jerky movement of Brazilian teens in the late 1960s dancing to Beatles' and Roberto Carlos' music was a sight to see. It was a time when this author could take the stage in Campina Grande, in the Paraíba interior, or even a nightclub on Recife's famous Boa Viagem beach, play ersatz rock and roll and be a hit. Enough said. One should add that the "iê, iê, iê" evolved into an incredibly talented, very sophisticated and original Brazilian rock that would dominate much of Brazilian music to the 1990s. END SIDEBAR

Chance would have it that one of Roberto Carlos' first and biggest hits was "I Want Everyone to Go to Hell" ["Quero Que Todo Mundo Vá Para o Inferno"]. Things could not have worked out better for the poets of "cordel!" Dozens of poems were written and sold like hotcakes on the streets in late 1966 and 1967: The Life and Success of the singer Roberto Carlos, The Letter from Satan to Roberto Carlos, The Letter Satan Sent to the Singer Roberto Carlos, The Answer by Roberto Carlos to Satan's Letter and other spin offs like The

Encounter of Satan and Roberto Carlos, The Arrival of Roberto Carlos' Caravan in Hell, Sin and Confession of Roberto Carlos and finally The Woman Who Bit Her Pillow Thinking It Was Roberto Carlos.

The stage was already set: cordelian customers' orthodox belief in Jesus, Mary, the apostles and saints and the role of the devil and the existence of cordelian stories meant to entertain, with the devil matching wits with humans. But this was a new twist (no pun intended). In the song Roberto Carlos is really angry with all those who cannot understand or appreciate the new music, and he simply sends them all to hell. This engenders the plethora of story-poems in which the devil complains (one recalls the motif of the complaint, the devil complaining to Jesus about the state of the world) via letter to the singer that hell is full up [lotado], and he the devil does have limited resources, so stop singing the song!

Roberto of course must answer, so a second series of letters and responses engenders more poems and money in the pockets of the poets. One must recognize that it is the happy merging of several totally unrelated phenomena that caused a situation which would result in the sale of thousands of cordelian poems on the subject: the craze for rock and roll and Roberto Carlos, the tradition of cordelian publication, the devil in Brazilian popular life, and the unrelated meeting of the three.

3 Signs of the End of the World and the Apocalyptic Vision

Given that Jesus Christ saved mankind through his suffering and death on the cross and that he will come again to judge us all, what remains to be known is when and under what circumstances? The answers lie in the pronouncements of the scriptures and modern day prophets; those answers are a major snapshot in <u>Portrait</u>. The traditional northeastern Catholic who often wonders if he has already suffered the pains of purgatory on earth has a serious interest in what he calls the "signs" of the end of the era or the signs of the coming, or simply, the end of the world. Grounded in New Testament sayings of Jesus and particularly in the Book of Revelation, the poets could depend upon steady sales of a story-poem with this topic. And material was abundant: the popular religious leaders in the backlands, some legitimate voices of the faith preaching from apocalyptic literature, others, by far the most famous, and the leaders of cults based on the notions of Sebastianism, messianic belief, and personal repentance and penance in the face of the Last Judgment. In fact one could hardly consider himself a poet of "<u>cordel</u>" without at least one good title on the topic. But the particular way each story is told varies greatly, and the poets' knowledge of sacred scripture and ability to turn a poetic phrase produced poems always a little different from one another.

But even beyond this is the preoccupation of the believer: when is the second coming, how will I know and what can I do? These are the great concerns of these stories. The popularity and sales of such poems indicate there was fascination with the topic. But just as in the stories of the devil and his complaints to Jesus about corruption in the world, these stories as well spend a lot of time listing the many, many pleasures (sins) of the world for, one suspects, the vicarious enjoyment of the public. Therefore, they suggest a variation on an old supermarket newsstand axiom: if you cannot do it; you can at least read about it.

The practice of updating poems of prophecy by changing the dates and years as they pass, but keeping the same text and prophecies may be an indication for the cynically minded of the sincerity or lack thereof of the poets. But one must recall that the poet had to sell the poem to continue as poet, so the public must have believed in and enjoyed the stories.

One of the oldest, traditional poems of the hundreds that exist on this topic is <u>The End of the World</u> ["O Fim do Mundo"] from the João Martins de Atayde press in Recife. [27] The poet traces the tradition of Judeo-Christian prophecy from God's words to the prophet Isaiah and tells his public that there are always new prophecies of corruption in the world, from real wise men, so pay attention! The visions of Moses, Aaron and Elijah are coming true today! The poet says he has been a hard worker with little pleasure in life, so he suffers no nostalgia [saudades] for the "good ole' days" and will be glad when the end comes. He traces how God created the world, but as evil and corruption grew, God became disgusted with his creation and decided to end it all with the Flood. Well, says he poet, bad times are here again, the cataclysm is near.

So how will it end? At 5:00 (the poet does not designate a.m. or p.m. or day) the sky will turn red, leaves will drop, rivers will dry up, oceans will become violent and the world will be turned into a "funereal drama." Five angels will come (usually it is four) and burn the four corners of the earth with winds and rains of fire, and humanity will be scalded. The dead will be awakened in their tombs and will proceed to the final judgment. St. George will come down from the moon (he is in effect the "man in the moon" in Brazilian popular belief, riding on his steed with sword and armor), sword in hand and weigh the sins of mankind (usually it is St. Michael the Archangel who will come with his scale of justice and do this). Angels will announce the end with the sound of heavenly trumpets; Death himself will come to reap his share of the harvest. St. Peter and all the saints (the poet lists twenty or so) will come to receive the just; Lucifer will collect the damned. The poet delights in listing the sins that will take those unlucky ones to the ten gates of hell and its thirty compartments. Dante or Quevedo have nothing on the poet's description; doctors and lawyers still take up a lot of the space in hell, so little has changed. But hell is full, so the devil's complaints to Roberto Carlos were true.

Manoel Tomaz de Assis took advantage of the sighting of a comet which he does not designate by name to write one of the best apocalyptic poems, The Planet Is a Sign of the World to Be Punished ["O Planeta E' um Aviso do Mundo Ser Castigado"].[28] His thesis and the basic belief of such literature is that the comet is a warning, and God always sends a warning when he wants to punish mankind for its transgressions. In this case there is going to be a real donnybrook ["pega-pega"]. The battle will mark a true "epic journey of great difficulty and trials" [travessias]. The causes are clear: the cinema and nudity on the beach where the girls bathe in a one-piece suit [maiô] with no skirt over it. "The devil is loose on the streets" (a major northeastern saying). The war with Communism is another sign and Satan is behind it all! The poet reminds his readers, "When a saint is in the car, the devil is in the rumble seat," and the proof is that there is more samba than praying during the novenas! There is another sign: a radio in every house blaring out "indecorous" music, seducing the youth and implanting a moral rottenness via its "disastrous words."

What is one to conclude? More recent comet stories are statements from poets in major metropolitan areas and in the age of national television networks, men on the moon, cell phones and the internet. But even then, the same poets still do not renounce the end of the world, the final judgment and the basic existence of sin in the world. But the vast majority of the "end of the world" poems do come from and represent an earlier era in the North East. And the beliefs and values they represent, of God and the devil, Good and Evil, rewarding of the just and punishment of the evil, a second coming of the great judge, and of a final judgment, permeate traditional "<u>cordel</u>" and the snapshots of the manifestations of religion presented in the next album of <u>Portrait.</u>

---

[1]   Joseph Page, <u>The Brazilians</u>, Reading: MA, Addison-Wesley, 1995.

[2]   For such information, consult Luís da Câmara Cascudo, <u>Dicionário do Folclore Brasileiro</u>, Vol. 1, 2, Rio de Janeiro: MEC, 1962; Charles Wagley, <u>An Introduction to Brazil</u>, Revised edition, New York: Columbia University Press, 1970; and, Page, <u>The Brazilians.</u>

[3]   Manuel Diégues Júnior in his "Thematic Cycles of Popular Literature in Verse," <u>Literatura Popular em Versos, Estudos, I</u>, Rio de Janeiro: MEC-Casa de Rui Barbosa, 1973, said that the theme of religion would comprise, possibly, twenty per cent of the entire volume of "cordel," and is for certain the oldest theme in "cordel." We might add the following: if one were to add the "cycles" of Father Cícero Romão Batista, Father Damian, and the moral "exempla" stories related to religion, for certain it would be among the largest of all "cordel."

[4]   Waldemar Valente, <u>Misticismo e Região</u>, Recife: MEC, 1963.

[5]   The paraphrased story was by Manoel D'Almeida Filho, <u>Story of Jesus, Master of Masters</u>, Aracaju, n.d.

[6]   Minelvino Francisco Silva, <u>Story of the Monk Francis of Solitude, Founder of Lapa</u>, Itabuna, Bahia, n.d.

[7]   José Costa Leite, <u>Story of the Devotion of Our Lord of the Good Jesus of the Good End</u>, Condado, PE, n.d.

[8]   José Costa Leite, The Seven Swords of Pain of Holy Virgin Mary, Condado, PE, n.d.

[9]   Cunha Neto, The Festival of Nazaré, Belém do Pará, n.d.

[10] This seminal text for "cordel" is found in:Leonardo Mota, Violeiros do Norte, Fortaleza: University Press of Ceará, n.d., pp. 201-213.

[11] See Ariano Suassuna, Auto da Compadecida, 4th ed., Rio de Janeiro: Agir Edta., 1964.

[12] Leandro Gomes de Barros, O Dinheiro, in: Leonardo Mota, Violeiros do Norte, pp. 213-215.

[13] Leandro Gomes de Barros, Debate de um Ministro Nova Seita com um Urubu in Gustavo Barroso, Ao Som da Viola, Rio de Janeiro: Departamento de Impresnsa Nacional, 1949, pp. 429-435.

[14] José Soares da Silva, Dila Editor, Como São Pedro Entrou no Céu, Caruaru: n.d.

[15] Manoel José dos Santos, Vida e Morte de São Simião, Condado: s.d.

[16] João Martins de Atayde, Editor Proprietário José Bernardo da Silva, História de um Homem que Teve uma Questão com Santo Antônio, Juazeiro do Norte: 1954. The author perhaps may be José Galdino da Silva Duda, this according to Átila de Almeida Filho, Dicionário . . . , p. 214.

[17] We did a study on the theme which won the Orígenes Lessa Prize in 1985: "'Grando Sertão Veredas' na Literatura de Cordel', in Brazil/ Brasil, n. 14, year 8, 1995, pp. 9-50.

[18] Vicente Vitorino de Melo, Segunda Queixa de Satanás a Jesus Cristo sobre a Corrução no Mundo, n.p., 1967.

[19] José Costa Filho, O Satanás Trabalhando na Roça de São Pedro, Condado: n.d.

[20] Luís Costa Pinheiro, Editor Proprietário José Bernardo da Silva, 3 volumes, O Casamento de Luzbel, Juazeiro do Norte: printing of 1957.

[21]   The cordelian villains were not limited to Brazilians: famous villains of international wars like Kaiser Wilhelm, Mussolini, Hitler, Juan Perón and even Saddam Hussein (and most recently George W. Bush) were also sent to hell by the cordelian bards. Portrait will see this matter in Album VIII, "There's a big world out there."

[22]   There is a large quantity of books and studies about banditry in "cordel," but the sources that have been most useful to us over the years include the classic books by Gustavo Barroso, Ao Som da Viola; by Luís da Câmara Cascudo, Violeiros e Cantadores and Flor dos Romances Trágicos; and a more recent book by Ronald Daus, O Ciclo Épico dos Cangaceiros na Poesia Popular do Nordeste, Rio de Janeiro: Fundação Casa de Rui Barbosa, 1982.

[23]   José Pacheco, A Chegada de Lampião no Inferno, Juazeiro do Norte: no publisher indicated, 1949.

[24]   Apolônio Alves dos Santos, Lampião no Inferno, n.p., n.d.

[25]   José Costa Leite, A Briga de Antônio Silvino com Lampião no Inferno, Condado: n.d.

[26]   All these titles are by the popular cordelian poet of Salvador da Bahia, Cuíca de Santo Amaro in the 1940s and 1950s. See our book Cuíca de Santo Amaro Poeta-Repórter da Bahia, Salvador: Fundação Casa de Jorge Amado, 1990.

[27]   João Martins de Atayde, O Fim do Mundo, Recife, 1948.

[28]   Manoel Tomaz de Assis, O Planeta É um Aviso do Mundo Ser Castigado, n.p., n. d.

Album II

The Manifestations

1 Sebastianism, Messianic "Movements" and Popular Catholicism

As was said in the introduction to Album I of Portrait, the gamut of Brazilian religiosity seen in "cordel" runs from the most traditional of Roman Catholicism to the local variants of popular Catholicism to Protestant, Kardec Spiritist and Afro-Brazilian options. After the traditional Catholic component seen in Album I, the largest share, by far, of "cordel" is dedicated to the poem-stories treating Father Cícero Romão Batista, the "Miracle Worker of the Backlands," and a close second, the poems of the evangelizing, fire and brimstone Capuchin preacher of missions, Friar Damian, believed by many to be the successor of Father Cícero. But to understand either case, one must see an extremely important event and pioneer story in "cordel," The War of Canudos ["A Guerra de Canudos"] and its leader "Good Jesus Antônio Conselheiro." In order to understand what happened at Canudos, one needs first to know about Portuguese Sebastianism.

Sebastianism is a phenomenon dating from a real event in 1578 from Portuguese history. It is a folk-popular belief that was passed down to a sector of the Brazilian population, principally the uneducated, impoverished masses of the Northeast interior. Valdemar Valente, a scholar who deals with Northeastern "mysticism," writes of the history of Sebastianism and attributes both belief and preaching of the same to no less than the famous Jesuit missionary Father Antônio Vieira in the earliest days of Portuguese colonization. The belief is that King Sebastian, the teenage ruler of Portugal in the late sixteenth century who was extreme bordering on fanatical in his own religious beliefs, dreams and quest, took a small army of Portuguese soldiers to North Africa, today's Morocco, to make war against the infidels, the hated Moslems. In his mind he was simply taking the war for the Reconquest of Portugal from the Moslems, a war that basically ended at the end of the 12th century, to its final and logical conclusion. In what turned out to be a foolish utopist enterprise, the small army

31

was soundly defeated and all were killed including the king. But his body was never found, and slowly, surely and amazingly, the belief grew that one day young King Sebastian would return in all his glory to take tiny Portugal to new heights of grandeur. Thus, the concept of a secular "messianic" figure, a savior of sorts, was created. [1]

This belief, modified in the strangest ways, took root in backlands Brazil. In effect, the poor masses, disenfranchised, helpless and miserable, not only looked to the Second Coming of Christ in the spiritual realm, but the arrival of another type of savior to rescue them from earthly pain and suffering. The two "messiahs" became intertwined in the minds of many.

Real incidents of self-proclaimed saviors, or those proclaimed by others, created major events in Northeast Brazil that in a small way changed the course of the nation. One such event, not recorded in "cordel" because it took place before this folk-popular register of history came into its own, was the amazing event at "Pretty Rock" [Pedra Bonita] in the backlands of Pernambuco. A charismatic, self-proclaimed "messiah" led a fanatical following of local residents to disaster. Led by the belief that King Sebastian or another savior would return to save them, the members of the cult threw adults, children and dogs to their death off the top of the "Pretty Rock." Their blood would "cleanse, purify and prepare the way" like the blood of Jesus the Lamb, for some kind of final solution.[2]

A second event, this time recorded by folk poets including a soldier-poet who would be one of the pioneers of "cordel," was the War of Canudos.[3] In 1896-1897 a self-proclaimed popular leader, "Good Jesus Antônio Conselheiro," led the rabble of back landers, largely poor farmers but fierce gunmen as well, to battle local police, state militia and national armies in a war to the death where the rebels fought against the might of the New Republic! The story was among the first of the great journalistic, popular registers of "cordel." But it became, according to some, the "greatest work of Brazilian literature" and a national epic when Euclides da Cunha, a reporter during the Canudos campaign, reworked his reports and notes into the book Rebellion in the Backlands ["Os Sertões"].

But the longest lasting and greatest popular cult, second only to the stories of Jesus, Mary, the apostles and saints themselves in "cordel," is that dedicated to the person of Father Cícero Romão Batista, the "Miracle Worker of the Backlands" and subject of the largest religious pilgrimages in northeastern Brazil.[4] Portrait is incomplete without him. The young, dedicated and good priest, Father Cícero, became known as a wonderful clergyman, counselor, giver of charity and leader in Juazeiro do Norte, Ceará, located in a tiny region, an oasis in itself, in the center of the arid backlands of the North East.

A single event changed everything: in 1879 while celebrating mass before a small group of the faithful in Juazeiro, the sacred host was believed to have turned to blood in the mouth of a communicant, the "holy woman" [beata] Maria Araújo. Word spread, and the poor and desperate of the backlands and soon the entire Northeast would come to Juazeiro to ask for the help of Jesus, Mary and the saints through the intercession of Father Cícero. A true popular cult arose based on a combination of his legitimate good works and the masses' belief in innumerable miracles attributed to him. So Father Cícero became a messiah of sorts, a savior for the lowest of the low, an option for those who had no options, and finally, a religious-political leader who would become the spiritual leader of a popular revolution against the establishment and established government of his state of Ceará in 1914. The man became legend and a phenomenon in Brazil. After his death, the legend also became Sebastianist in character when pilgrims and poets wrote of his promises to "come again" to lead them to salvation. As a result, he became, along with Jesus Christ and the politician Getúlio Vargas, one of the greatest heroes of "cordel."

Years later the phenomenon continued with another priest of extreme veneration, bordering on a being a cult figure. Friar Damian [Frei Damião] was a Capuchin monk and missionary blessed with a preaching career in the backlands far longer than most human lives. After the death of Father Cícero it was Friar Damian who became the former's spiritual successor in the eyes of the poor masses of the Northeast. A cult of sorts grew up around him as well, and he became another symbol of popular Catholicism in Brazil.

To see the manifestations of popular Catholicism in the Brazil of today's "cordel" one needs to see this triumvirate and it is best to proceed chronologically in their development.

Good Jesus Antônio Conselheiro and the War of Canudos

In 1896 and 1897 a self-proclaimed counselor, leader and messianic figure known as "Good Jesus Antônio Conselheiro" led a rabble of poor peasants and ruffian gunslingers in what amounted to an amazing military campaign against first of all local police, then state militia and finally the cream of the Brazilian Army. In the end he was killed as were most of his followers, but the story became a national epic in Euclides da Cunha's masterpiece Rebellion in the backlands[5] and an important chapter in the cordelian Portrait.

The Brazilian historian José Calasans in his The Folkloric Cycle of Good Jesus Conselheiro helps to introduce us to the poems about the man and the event, the first snapshots in this album of Portrait. He summarizes the popular voices and their notions:

- that Jesus Christ sent "Holy Anthony" to free his followers from punishment
- that the Good Counselor abstained from women and kept the rule of chastity in order to be pure to fulfill his "divine mission"
- that Antônio Maciel, the name the counselor had in his native Ceará before migrating to Canudos, murdered his own wife and mother
- that he performed "miracles" in the construction of his churches by being able to isolate "evil" rocks from "good" ones in constructing the churches
- that his mission was "divine"
- that he preached the return of Sebastian, not as the young King of Portugal but rather as the opposing force to the New Republic and restorer of the monarchy
- that the forces of the police and army detachments fighting against him were really the Anti-Christ
- that he directed the military campaign with supernatural powers
- that his defeat of the first three military expeditions sent against him was truly a miracle
- that he would turn the river near Canudos, the Vassa Barris, into blood and the rocks of Canudos into bread for his people
- and most importantly, that after his death in the campaign, he would return in glory to lead his followers once again in the campaign against the evil Republic.[6]

The poems of "cordel" on Antônio Conselheiro are few in number primarily because this folk-popular poetry was in its infancy at the time of the war in 1896-1897. They are however extremely important because they are the foundation for the concepts of mysticism and Sebastianism that will be so important in the later stories of Father Cícero and Friar Damian.

The first complete poem in "<u>cordel</u>" itself (there are short poems and excerpts extant from oral snippets collected by Euclides da Cunha prior to the cordelian version) is by a participant in the campaign, a soldier turned poet, João Melchíades Ferreira da Silva.[7] He wrote the poem years after the campaign when he was now retired from service at Canudos and the Acre War and a cordelian poet-chronicler for a printer in João Pessoa, the capital of Paraíba. In eighty strophes of six lines each he summarizes the first three expeditions and details the fourth and final in which he served as a combatant. Aside from details of the battle itself, he cites statistics as to the armaments, the number of soldiers and the names of other combatants. But his vision is clear and direct: the Army was battling a "bandit chief," who "rose against the Republic" and eluded his followers. He sees the rabble and followers of Antônio Conselheiro as no better than Antônio Silvino and Lampião, the famous bandits of the Northeast (to be seen shortly). The poem in fact was written at the height of bandit troubles, and the Counselor is described in exactly the same terms: the most perverse of men, of evil instinct. Deserters, horse thieves, criminals and sorcerers—these are the men who filled the "army" of Conselheiro. The poet details the campaign until the sound of the victory trumpet on October 5, 1897. He sees Canudos as a patriotic victory of the Brazilian Republic over bandits, of Good over Evil.

Some believe Antonio Conselheiro received inspiration from and learned the art of preaching sermons from no less than Father Cícero Romão Batista, thus leading us to the next snapshot.

Father Cícero

With an understanding of the undercurrents in northeastern popular religion percolating down through history and seen in such events as "Pretty Rock" and Canudos, one can appreciate an even larger and longer lasting popular religious cult in the Northeast: the case of Father Cícero Romão Batista in Juazeiro do Norte, Ceará. His story is first and foremost in the cordelian portrait; literally hundreds of story-poems in "cordel" treat the phenomenon. Many of the story-poems were written during his long life, but just as many have been written since his death (reality becomes myth and Father Cícero becomes a messianic figure along the Sebastianist line).[8] Many of the poems tell first of all of his life and deeds. A second type of story-poem relates his "teachings," with titles referring to sermons, messages, counsel or prophecies. The latter are reported from eye-witnesses to the sermons, but just as often may be "created" versions of the same passed down from mouth to mouth by the religious pilgrims. A final type, and perhaps the largest by number are the dozens of stories based on hearsay, legend and now myth, the stories of "miracles," visions, dreams, encounters and the like during the life and since the death of this incredible man.

SIDEBAR This writer in 1966 did his own pilgrimage, first of all to collect the story-poems so important to "cordel," but secondly, to see if I could capture the essence of the importance of Father Cícero. The trip was by local bus from Recife, Pernambuco, on the Atlantic Coast, to Juazeiro, Ceará, and became a twenty hour trip through the three climatic zones of Pernambuco state and across the state border into the oasis of the Cariri where Juazeiro is located. The bus was similar to a tiny school bus in the United States with uncomfortable, straight back, hard seats and packed for the most part with very poor northeasterners making their way to homes in the interior. Stifling heat during the day and bumpy roads caused babies and even some adults to throw up, the mess initially wiped up with newspapers and later ignored by a hassled driver. The paved road turned out to last for a total of only two hours, from Recife to Caruaru, "the Princess of the Agreste," a euphemism for the main city in the pastoral zone of Pernambuco. Immediately after Caruaru the pavement ended and we were in for eighteen bone crunching, hot hours until an after-midnight arrival in Juazeiro. The trip took us through the damp, green, gorgeous sugar cane zone along the Pernambuco coast, the green hilly pastoral area near Caruaru, and finally for my first look at the land of the true northeastern epic tales from "cordel"—the bone dry, cactus and bramble filled backlands of the interior [sertão]. The latter zone, the dry backlands, was the land of northeastern cowboys [vaqueiros] dressed from head to toe in heavy leather "armor," thus dubbed the "knights of the backlands," of bandits and religious "fanatics." We passed by the area where the infamous bandit Lampião was born, near the Serra Talhada. The stop for the big Brazilian noon meal [almoço] was at what they call a sort of ranch [arraial], a stop in the middle of nowhere with a "restaurant," a rough setting of tables under a thatched roof. Unprepared to go it alone with snacks, I joined in with the locals in the repast of rice, beans, chicken, and jerky [charque], the specialty of the backlands. We all ate from community bowls and I spent most of the time wondering if this was how I was to meet my end. (Unfortunately I have one of the most delicate stomachs in the West, a fact known to my students.) But since the miraculous Father Cícero was the point of the entire journey, my still incipient faith sustained me.

Arriving well after midnight to a part of Juazeiro which was nearly pitch black due to very limited street lighting, we tried to hail the doorman of the local hotel (you clap your hands loudly and say, "Hey, you there in the house!" ["ó de casa!"]. The quaint backlands custom did work; a night watchman came but said there indeed was no room at the inn. But to my good fortune, I came to experience the true religious pilgrim's experience, that is, a fifty cent hammock in a "pilgrim's lodging," [rancho de romeiro], a room with an earthen floor furnished solely with two hooks from which a hammock was hung. Sleeping in my clothes and covering my head and arms with a jacket against surprisingly cool night air and the many mosquitoes, I fitfully passed that night. In retrospect, things should not have been any other way. In pilgrim's parlance, it was a small price to pay (and with little suffering) for the benefits [graça] gained.

Days followed when I believe I saw almost all that I needed to in order to form an intelligent first impression of Juazeiro and the good father: the main church [matriz] of Our Lady of Sorrows (the church Father Cícero created from the old original ranch chapel), his final residence now turned into a museum, the cemetery, chapel and grave of Father Cícero, the incredible "miracle house" where the faithful leave proof of their promises (which made a lasting impression on me), and finally the "Garden" [Horto] which housed the dreams of Father Cícero, a huge church complex outside the town.

What really stayed with me were some isolated images burned in my mind and heart relating to the "cult" of Father Cícero. I recall the high pitched voices of the faithful, mainly women and "holy women" [beatas] in a vespers ceremony at the main church, the crowds at the cemetery, chapel and tomb of the priest, and the dirty, ragged, poor old "holy women" who practically accosted me as I entered the "House of Miracles." They seemed akin to harpies as they screeched offers to tell the story of "My Godfather," ["Meu Padrinho"] for a few coins. And I was privileged to see and hear the blind player who for a coin or two sang songs and poems about Father Cícero while accompanying himself on the Arabic viola [rabeca]. Then there was the absolute modesty of the house where Father Cícero lived and died, his bed the poets talk about kissing in respect, the vestments in a glass case, and old daguerreotypes of Cícero's parents. Finally, there was the immensity of the compound dedicated to the works of the priest, the "Garden" [Horto]. END OF SIDE BAR.

Since there are literally hundreds of story-poems about Father Cícero, one is challenged to boil it all down to its essence. An imperfect overview can be accomplished in one poem. The poet Severino Paulino da Silva in Birth, Life, Death, Education, Sign and Destiny of Father Cícero Romão ["Nascimento, Vida, Morte, Educação, Signo e Sorte do Padre Cícero Romão"][9] begins his narration in verse with the directive that his story is for Catholics only. He tells of Father Cícero's birth on March 24, 1844, in the town of Crato, Ceará, to Joaquim Romão Batista and Joaquina Vicente, the latter a member of the society of "the Mother of the Incarnate Word." Father Cícero's godfather was a powerful local landholder and political chief [coronel] of the area. The poet minces no words, saying "Blessed be the womb/ of the hand that conceived him" and that the sun shone on all Ceará that day (as it does most of the time, especially during the periodic droughts). Baptism, first communion, Latin lessons and high school under the tutelage of a Priest, Father Inácio Rolim, followed.

With the death of his own father, Cícero felt the need to support his mother and two sisters, so he entered the seminary in 1865 in Fortaleza, the state capital. The poet goes on to tell that Father Cícero was ordained in 1870 at the age of 26, and the ordination was shortly followed by a trip to Rome and an audience with the Pope. After an initial appointment in another small town in the Cariri region, Cícero was named priest at the chapel of the "Juazeiro Ranch" ["Fazenda Juazeiro"]. According to the poet, he invited "heretics and bandit chiefs" and all others to catechism classes to study the "light of Holy Catholicism." His teaching and counsel brought him fame as did his charitable work during the most famous drought in the Northeast, the famous "drought of two sevens," 1877.

It all changed in 1879 when during a mass a local "holy woman" [beata], akin to the traditional "church mouse," called Mocinha or Maria de Araújo, received holy communion from Father Cícero, and the host reportedly turned to blood in her mouth. Word spread like wildfire of the "miracle," and an investigation was held by the local bishop who during the interim prohibited Father Cícero from celebrating the sacraments. The poet reports a famous sermon at this time when Father Cícero tells the faithful to be patient, asks God to bless them and continues to preach his message of faith, repentance and the sacraments in the formal church, with special reverence to Our Lady of Sorrows, the patroness of the church of Juazeiro.

The poet then changes direction to describe miracles attributed to Father Cicero—the repentance of a "fallen" woman, the finding and rescue of an old woman lost in the countryside, and several Lazarus-like episodes of bringing people back from the dead (a man knifed by a ruffian, a girl burned to death). The poet concludes one should believe these miracles and says he has no time to waste convincing "heretics" to the contrary! One miracle even involved a doubting Protestant, the administrator of a sugar cane mill in Pernambuco who ridiculed Father Cícero's powers and dared to fall from the top of the mill if the powers were real. He fell, but was not killed and later was miraculously healed when he admitted the powers of the priest!

The result of the miracles was a steady flow of religious pilgrims, most in dire need of healing and financial help, who flocked to tiny Juazeiro to hear the priest's sermons given each night to the pilgrims [romeiros] after the saying of the rosary. The growth of the cult was such that Juazeiro grew from a desert ranch to a tiny town, then a larger town, and finally a city, all due to the fame of the priest. It was during these years that Father Cícero first became mayor and then with the help of his political henchman, Floro Bartolomeu, Federal Congressman and Vice-President of the State of Ceará, this after a bloody local war.

The same poet Paulino then moves on to Father Cícero's death, when "Christ's image shed tears on the cross and the earth trembled!" He shares a prayer Father Cícero gave the faithful before his death and the contents of his last sermon: Care for the sick, pray the Rosary, keep the holy days, fast when the Virgin says to, and do not be deceived by the evil one. The end of the world is coming; drought, hunger and war will come. The evil Protestants will bring other religions and the Beast will wander the earth! But the faithful will be saved.

In fact, on July 24, 1934, Father Cícero did die. His body was prepared for viewing from the open window of his house, and thousands gathered to pay respect. The poet ends describing those who will buy his story—the good and the faithful. He says it will not interest the Protestants or the atheists. And for sure it will not interest those who buy the cordelian "corruption" stories just to get their kicks from the sins described therein! This story is meant to be a souvenir for the good Catholics who go to Juazeiro to remember the good father.

The lengthy story-poem just described is similar to dozens of others, all recognizing the powers of the tiny priest from Juazeiro and in effect the many miracles attributed to him. The myth was being created. And the cult grew. Another poet writes that Juazeiro was nothing when Father Cícero arrived. He gave the sacraments to the poor at no charge. When he became mayor of Juazeiro by popular vote in an election, the opposition spread the word that he was a bandit [cangaceiro]. The news spread that that was why the bishop suspended him from his duties. But he never abandoned the poor, nor they he, providing medicine in time of plague, sustenance in time of drought and most of all hope. Pilgrimages and pilgrims survived days of travel to Juazeiro, miraculously saved from fierce wild animals on the road. Father Cícero's famous bull, also considered magical, was allowed to wander the streets of Juazeiro, a symbol of his powers! And now he is canonized (the "Brazilian Catholic Church" requested the confirmation of its own "canonization" of the Saint of Juazeiro by Pope John Paul II during one of his recent trips to Brazil.)

Friar Damian, Successor to Father Cícero

In one sense it was simple: Father Cícero died in 1934, but a Capuchin Friar had arrived in the city of Recife in Brazil's Northeast to preach the "Holy Mission" in 1931. He inherited both the role and the fame of Father Cícero as preacher of the holy faith and prophet of the end of the world, and as such he took a message of repentance and salvation to the poor of the Northeast. At a very late moment in his life, while in his 90s, he was still preaching the missions and was nationally visible when then presidential candidate Fernando Collor de Mello arranged to attend one of his masses (an indirect endorsement as a good, traditional northeastern Catholic?) in the 1989 campaign. Friar Damian did not quite reach the mythical stature of Father Cícero, although some would debate even this, but he undoubtedly fulfills a function and role as a holy and miraculous priest that indeed substitutes in the minds of the poor outlanders for those of Father Cícero.

The poets generally write of Friar Damian in the first person as witnesses and participants at one of his famous missions. Rodolfo Coelho Cavalcante from Salvador da Bahia, a poet who brings his own strong non-Catholic religious convictions to his stories but admits he must write to please his public, wrote <u>Friar Damian the Missionary of the Northeast</u> [Frei Damião—o Missionário do Nordeste"].[10] He makes a point of saying that the poets of "<u>cordel</u>" write the truth; if there is exaggeration, it is in the minds of the readers who gossip about what they read. He opens by saying that when Father Cícero died, God sent another "major figure" to preach the word. But carriers of the word are always persecuted, so Father Damian is no exception. Detractors call him a sorcerer, say he has a pact with the devil and preaches only stupidities. But the poet says no; he is the most truthful of all!

The poet says he was selling his story-poems in a nearby town, heard the Friar was going to preach, and made a point of going to see him. Whatever happened, it would make a good story with good sales! Rodolfo describes the mechanics of the mission: Friar Damian arrives in town and immediately a pilgrimage is started, usually with a procession. Then the priest climbs up to a platform or dais with a speaker system, gives a quick greeting to the crowd and begins the sermon which the poet paraphrases: The end of the world is at hand, do not make fun of the Eternal! The modern customs and ways are nothing but blasphemy! The Old Testament prophesied the coming of Christ, the Light, but the devil followed and corrupted the world. The worst is materialism—sins of immodest dress and the like. The new generation is corrupt and sinful. And that is <u>why</u> "The Great Consuming" is here. Men on the moon and "genetic machines" are examples of science against the spiritual laws of God! Sodom and Gomorrah are nothing in comparison to the world of today!

The Friar goes on to say that he never has cured anyone; it is Jesus who cures those with faith in him and who pray to him. The Friar takes a handkerchief to wipe his "dewy" face, finishes the sermon, and stumbling a bit, climbs down from the platform. The poet concludes Friar Damian is no less than Paul of Tarsus in preaching, equal to John the Baptist in the fervor of his prayer, as humble as St. Francis of Assisi and has made the people of the backlands happy! People in sin repent after hearing him.

Arigó (the famous Brazilian spiritualist hero and personal hero of the poet) was arrested after all; Galileo was condemned; Socrates was forced to drink hemlock, and they killed Jesus! Humanity just does not accept the truth because of its worldliness. Friar Damian continues the battle!

Such is the message of the mission. Over the years, almost sixty-five at this writing, Friar Damian's fame spread, miracles were attributed to him at the times of his preaching, and the people themselves contributed to the making of the myth. So just like Father Cícero, a plethora of poem-stories, some of them the most outlandish possible, have been told and written in "cordel." They treat his miracles and his message via sermons, visions, dreams and the like.

A theological seminary study in Recife tells of no less than eighty such "miracles" about Friar Damian recounted by eighty-five informants from throughout the Northeast.[11] It was by virtue of his sermons, his teachings, his counsels and these "miracles" that Friar Damian indeed became the "new" and probably not the last of the "Saints of the Backlands" (Opinião magazine). He is the most recent and perhaps the last of the messianic figures of the northeast interior, an important snapshot of the Portrait of the Northeast.[12]

2 Protestants, Catholics and Sugar Cane Rum

The majority of the traditional cordelian public, that is, the buyers and readers from the beginnings of the twentieth century up to the late 1960s, were "old church" Catholics. Their "religiosity" was formed by decades of traditional teachings from the Catholic Catechism, the mass, the sacraments and the annual Missions. The newly arrived Protestants [crentes] shared some beliefs with the Catholics, among them the apocalyptic vision of the end of the world and the final judgment. But other matters kept them separate. A bit of history is necessary.

There generally speaking have been two large waves of Protestant missionaries in Brazil. The first came in the 1880s with traditional sects like Baptists, Assembly of God, etc. sending brave missionaries into what often was hostile territory, including the Northeast. The second wave of recent years profited from the experience of the former and brought a very different perspective and philosophy.[13] In the portrait of religion in "cordel" it is the "old" Protestants, those who pioneered in spreading the word and increasing their flock at the very time "cordel" was coming into its own, that is most relevant. The Protestantism of today is largely a phenomenon which has taken place since the disappearance of most of "cordel" and with a different cultural outlook than their forbearers. Most of the pioneer scholarly writers on "cordel," Gustavo Barroso, Leonardo Mota, Rodrigues de Carvalho, Luís da Câmara Cascudo and others, talk of the atmosphere of suspicion, distrust and downright hatred among the local Northeasterners in regard to the foreigners who came to spread a new message—a message with very different beliefs and practices which contradicted and clashed with the old ways of the Catholic believers. The first Protestants were seen at best as strange and with strange beliefs, most of which were in opposition to traditional Catholicism. At worst they were seen as direct enemies of all that traditional Catholics believed in, haters of Rome and the Pope, deviating from the true faith, and as even the work of the devil.[14] This atmosphere was reflected in early "cordel" in fiercely satiric poems against them, like Leandro Gomes de Barros' The Devil in the New Sect or The Devil Confessing a Protestant or João Martins de Atayde's Religion against Protestantism.

But local customs also played a role in other poems called "debates," "discussions" and "encounters" in which traditional Catholics and Protestant believers [crentes] or [nova-seitas] discussed specific practices of faith or customs like drinking the local preferred drink, sugar cane rum [cachaça]. And, finally, the poems dealing with prophecies of backlands religious leaders Father Cícero or Friar Damian would always rail against the Protestants as the "art of the devil," enemies of the True Faith!

Representative titles are <u>The Protestant Who Was Thrown Out of Heaven</u>, <u>Advice to Catholics against the Protestants</u>, <u>The Discussion of a Catholic with a Protestant</u>, <u>The Discussion of a Religious Pilgrim with a Protestant Preacher</u>, <u>Discussion of a Priest with a Protestant</u>, <u>Discussion of Guido Guerra with a Jehovah's Witness</u> and countless stories about sugar cane rum like <u>Discussion of a Protestant with a Sugar Cane Rum [cachaça]" Drinker</u>.

What one sees most often in these stories is old time backlands Catholicism fencing with the radically new ideas of the first protestant missionaries. The accounts are often dead serious, but frequently the poets joke and basically indict the "nova-ceitas" with jests (just as they did with Satan in the stories already seen).

The most famous and eloquent of these stories was attributed to the master cordelian poet Leandro Gomes de Barros in the first years of the 20th century: <u>Debate of a New Sect Minister with a Vulture</u> ["Debate d'um Ministro Nova-Seita com um Urubu"].[15] The poem has little new in the way of theological or liturgical issues, and the Protestant loses as usual, but the extremely clever language and ironic humor of the poet sets this story apart from all others. The Defender of the Faith is a sarcastic northeastern vulture [<u>urubu</u>] known in the North East as the garbage-man of the backlands. This eater of carrion, as the poet says, may be "just a vulture," but he is a faithful vulture, defending the True Faith to the last.

An old Protestant lady dies and Master Vulture comes upon her, expressing his good fortune to his vulture colleagues. But after a Protestant minister arrives and admits that "the devil has won a mother-in-law" with this one, but still wants to claim her, the vulture and his buddies still think it is not a waste of time to "gnaw on this one until something better comes along." When the Pastor renews his claim to the remains, Master Vulture says, "Go ahead and take the old she-devil who is just stinking up the place." Naturally offended, the Pastor launches into a traditional debate, admitting the vulture has no soul, but could still be a believer, so he invites him to join the sect where he could be baptized.

The vulture's response is an attack on the Protestants who are of the ilk that not even their skin can be made into a meal. Vulture and protestant pastor discuss where the Protestant's soul will go when he dies, and the vulture defends the "Old Religion" which has "more poetry:" fasting during Lent, fireworks on St. John's day, Midnight Mass at Christmas and the annual Missions. The standard complaints continue with the vulture on the offensive: Why do the Protestants not like the crucifix with Christ on it or the Blessed Virgin ("Didn't Jesus have a mother?"). Even vultures can see the truth in that! The Protestant defends himself, his knowledge of the Bible, and his salvation by faith. The buzzard answers, "Easier for the sun to turn into ice and the devil to walk with the cross!" He is irked by the protestant hymns; even a "common samba" is better than that and even a vulture can pray better. The Protestant's defense that he knows the Bible from beginning to end makes little impression on the old Catholic vulture who answers, "Weren't you excommunicated?"

The vulture tires of the discussion, becomes disgusted with the whole thing and tells the pastor to go ahead and take the old bag of a lady. The Protestants are all a bunch of devils trying to terrorize him. Both Master Vulture and the Protestant pastor end up insulting each other, the vulture giving the traditional sign to ward off hexes, "Protestant, I give you the figa!" (thumb and first finger crossed in the form of a cross to ward off the devil). Master Vulture modestly concludes, "I, just a brute pagan (and vulture), believe and follow the Ten Commandments, and you, baptized, deny them; you run like a devil if anybody mentions the sacraments." A witness, a bystander who happens to be a Catholic saint, applauds and cheers on the vulture who "debates well" and says "Die, you vile Protestant." The devil says, "Amen."

The sugar cane rum stories are really a variation on these poems, but with an interesting twist. The drink of the common people, the local firewater distilled from sugar cane [cachaça], symbolizes fun and good times for the Catholics. The great master of "cordel" Leandro Gomes de Barros was known for hilarious story-poems on the subject. The Protestant will sharply criticize the drink but with heavy emphasis placed on the drunkard. In The Discussion of the Protestant with a Sugar Cane Rum[cachaça] Drunk ["Discussaão de um Crente com um Cachaceiro"][16] the poet creates a happy drunk who justifies his vice all by faith: I have religion so I drink St. John's wine; the priest at mass says eat this bread and drink this wine, and when I drink Big Mountain rum, I think of the hill of Calvary! Obviously meant to be funny and to entertain, below the surface such stories really treat a serious issue and one of the major divisions in custom between the old and new ways.

The poet was aware of the turn of phrase and unorthodox defense of traditional Catholicism in the cordelian classic The Gambling Soldier [O Soldado Jogador] when a deck of cards in church becomes an unorthodox Catholic "Missal" to follow the mass.[17] So once again, the colors of the Portrait become more vivid in these stories of belief and faith.

3 Brazilian Spiritualism

<u>SIDEBAR</u> As a student doing research for my dissertation in Brazil in 1966-1967 I was extremely curious about learning about and experiencing this important aspect of Brazilian reality, particularly African spiritualism. As a student of Brazilian Literature, one could not ignore the works of the Bahian novelist Jorge Amado. Steeped in the syncretism of Catholic and African religions in Bahia, Amado made it an important part of his novels, and in fact the value of Afro-Brazilian culture in Brazil became his main thesis (see especially the novel <u>The Miracle Shop</u> ["Tenda dos Milagres"]). I attended as well during November and December of 1966 in Amado's Bahia many, many nights of "<u>capoeira</u>," the Afro-Brazilian dance-self-defense.

In an earlier phase of research in Recife and the Northeast Interior in 1966 and while living in Olinda, the first capital of Pernambuco just outside of Recife, I had made initial visits to the Afro-Brazilian "<u>xangô</u>" rites in Recife and had looked forward to seeing the "purest" of such rites in Brazil, the "<u>candomblé</u>" in Bahia. No doubt my enthusiasm and in fact love for this aspect of Brazilian culture would lead me to many more visits to Salvador and what I call my "Bahian" trilogy: books on Jorge Amado, Rodolfo Coelho Cavalcante and Cuíca de Santo Amaro, the latter two major cordelian poets in Salvador from 1940 to 1986.[18] It was only years later when I was "educated" in "umbanda" by a very unsuspected source, Sebastião Nunes Batista, a friend and colleague of "<u>cordel</u>" research at the Rui Barbosa Foundation in Rio de Janeiro. Sebastião was a son of the famous Francisco das Chagas Batista, one of the major pioneer poets of early "<u>cordel</u>" in Paraíba. He was also a believer and practitioner of "<u>umbanda</u>," convinced of its Golden Rule and principal of Reincarnation. <u>END SIDEBAR</u>

Though the poet João do Cristo Rei may have railed against a Kardec Spiritualist and called him a "Protestant" in a snapshot of Father Cícero and his cult in Juazeiro do Norte, this aspect of Brazilian religion is present in the cordelian portrait, but admittedly in a minor way. Few stories actually treat the subject, and there is an undercurrent of distaste in the generic sense when all such dealings with mediums, magic, etc. are thought of as mumbo-jumbo and the work of the devil.

"Traditional" accounts of religion by students and scholars of "<u>cordel</u>" have often classified Spiritualism in Brazil with an inherent bias. The "spiritual" aspect of Catholicism, that is, the existence and presence of the soul beyond material life on earth or the wispy appearance of angels and apparitions of Mary are generally accepted. But the "high spiritualism" of the séance, the communication with spirits of the deceased via specially gifted "mediums," and of course the rebirth or reincarnation of the same soul are anathema in traditional Catholic dogma and are often seen as works of the devil (Father Cícero and Friar Damian did not deviate from such teaching in this matter). Even more farfetched for the Catholic is the basic tenet of Afro-Brazilian religion that the gods or "saints" can literally come down and take possession of the believer during the ritual songs and dances of "candomblé," "xangô" or even "umbanda". And the "low spiritualism" of animistic nature, primarily from Indian and African origins, is simply dismissed.

So as culturally important as these religious beliefs are in their totality for Brazil, their image in "cordel" and hence for the cordelian public is by and large a negative one. The poets, writing for a traditionally Catholic and often superstitiously Catholic public, will generally make fun of the cults, just as they did with the Protestants who were turned into vultures, monkeys, dogs and the like for blaspheming against Father Cícero or Friar Damian. One needs to keep in mind however that the Protestants in general were seen as far more of a threat to the old ways than practitioners of Brazilian spiritualism.

Samples of spiritualist poems are ABCs of Spiritualism, ABCs of the Mediums, The Death of Arigó the Famous Medium of Minas Gerais or The True History of Chico Xavier, many of these poems were written by the well-known Rodolfo Coelho Cavalcante, a practicing Kardec Spiritualist most of his adult life. Undoubtedly there are more, but these suffice for the snapshots of Portrait.

Some representative titles about African cults are ABC of Umbanda, The Hex Turned Against the Hexor, The Hex of the Black Woman Backfired, Macumba in Bahia, Mysteries of Macumba, Why We Combat Umbanda, Saint George and the Dragon or Iemanjá Queen of the Sea and Her Admirers. A good many of these stories are from poets in Salvador da Bahia, the first colonial capital of Brazil and a city with perhaps the largest black population (some of whom are customers of the poets) and consequently the largest number of places of worship [terreiros] of the African cults. More than anything else one sees the references to the practitioner of black magic [catimbozeiro, xangueiro] and the like in the cordelian stories used in a generic context to mean those who use magic, black magic, hexes or the like to get what they want. Such activity is obviously condemned by the traditional, old church as pagan, evil and the work of the devil. But all these stories shed light on Portrait. Attitudes, beliefs, and humor of the poets and their public are revealed, sometimes in surprising ways.

Kardec Spiritualism

One poem says it all: Rodolfo Coelho Cavalcante's <u>ABCs of Spiritualism</u> ["ABC do Espiritismo"], a story the poet wrote in 1968 with a photo-cliché of Leon Hippolite Denizart Rivail, or Allan Kardec, on the cover. The poet does his best to explain the phenomenon: he tells how Kardec was inspired to reinterpret Holy Scriptures and create Spiritualist Doctrine, basing his new law on the scripture "Man is born and reborn, and then is born again" (citing the case of Elias from the Old Testament).

Of course it follows that there can be no heaven or hell for that makes a tyrant of God, and instead the souls or spirits of the deceased "enjoy the pleasures of 'Elevated Planes'." The sinner of a past life can be rescued from that life and begin to live another. The Spiritualists also rest their case on the Biblical phrase "In the house of my Father there are many dwelling places, and it is right I should go before you." So the heavenly "mansions" are reserved according to the Spiritualist interpretation of the word of Jesus for the "spirits of light." And at the same time there are other "exterior regions" where those who were guilty of sin in past lives can be for a while.

The "Do unto others" precept of Spiritualism is based on the saying: "He who lives by the sword, dies by the sword," ["<u>Quem com o ferro ferir/ Mesmo ferro há de sentir</u>"]. So it is not God who punishes, for that is impossible, but the person himself according to how he lives. As you sew so shall you reap and "No eternal punishment!" ["<u>Nada de castigo eterno!</u>"]. The poet says, "That's just an invention!" According to the poet (and Allan Kardec) Jesus simply showed that "hell is the sad situation or state in which the spirit is in tribulation," so once again, there is no heaven or hell. So on earth or in space all troubled spirits live in their own "hell" because they feel at fault. But, to the contrary, there are other spirits who are "illuminated." And the greatest illumination of all is Spiritualism itself, for "those who feel their way in the darkness of the errors of ideology, of false philosophies." How else can you explain a child born crippled, poor or blind and another a genius like Mozart? How can you explain the rebel Martin Luther or the stupidity of Nero?

The poet believes it necessary to remind us of the case of King Saul who prohibited his people from "consulting the dead" yet consulted a medium himself! And did the medium not confirm what was to happen to him? According to the poet, what Saul did was control the practice of "mediunism" and controlled "consultations" of "low spiritualism." He was just trying to control the commercialism and fanaticism of his time.

The poet continues his explanation: Spiritualism correctly understood is Religion and Science! A father cannot pay for what his son did; a son cannot pay for what his father did.

Each person pays for his own bad actions, and the person suffering in this world sinned today or yesterday!

But there is evil about: selling the gift of communication with spirits ["mediunidade"], using cartomancy or lighting candles can all be witchcraft but never Spiritualism! Xangô, Dois-dois, Omulú are all "saints" of "candomblé" and have nothing to do with Spiritualism! The latter is the "Light" of the teachings of Jesus!

The poet closes saying that "Without being fanatical/ I am a believer in Spriritualism." He quotes sayings from Kardec at the foot of each page. Portrait emphasizes this story-poem first of all because it does summarize the belief system of those who are pure Kardecists in Brazil and because the poet Rodolfo wrote many poems in "cordel" with this slant. Yet the poet at the same time admitted that he constantly had to be aware of his public, mainly "old" Catholics, and write for them. So one has to be very careful in reading his poems to see the "real" message.

SIDEBAR Most Brazilians will have an acquaintance or a relative who practices Spiritualism, and a major belief is that there are certain individuals born with the gift or power of healing. Spiritualists essentially believe this gift is the same power that Jesus had, but of course in a lesser way. But a true practitioner can heal in Jesus' name. We met such a person in Campina Grande, Paraíba, Mr. Jaime Coelho sr. who was famous in the entire region. Pharmaceutical salesmen would leave their samples and unsold medicines with him, donating them to the "cause." Mr. Coelho explained his gift to me in great detail: he could quickly determine after talking with a patient if a sickness was mental, physical or spiritual. If physical, he would "prescribe" a medicine from his huge stock. An entire room of the house, as large as some pharmacies, was filled with shelves of the medicines. If the case was judged to be mental, he would refer to a doctor. But if it were spiritual, and often this was the case, he would pray with and over the client, often producing good results. The proof was the long line outside the compound at the back of his large lot and extending down the street, waiting for "consults." He believed that he had in a small way the same healing power of Jesus. All consults were free; he made his living with gas stations in town. END SIDEBAR

It is not known how many readers of "cordel" ever espoused Kardec Spiritualism. Even though the cordelian portrait has only a few snapshots of such beliefs, and even though the great majority of poets and public were "old" Catholics, Portrait is greatly enriched by them for the beliefs are commonplace in Brazil. The same is true for African Spiritualism and its many manifestations.

Macumba, Umbanda and Candomblé

Once again, "cordel" in general does not present Afro-Brazilian spiritualism in a good light; the "black magician practitioner" [catimbozeiro, xangozeiro] and the like are seen as practitioners of superstitions and even as members of evil cults. One needs to remember that the large majority of cordelian poets and public are cradle Catholics and in many cases a superstitious lot themselves! But one sees several points of view in the stories.

"Macumba" is ordinarily a generic word in Brazil. It refers, like Kleenex, to any one of the spiritualist oriented African religions and almost always in a pejorative sense, as in "That dirty 'macumbeiro,' be careful of him!" One can imagine Master Vulture of cordelian fame crossing himself when seeing a "macumbeiro," just like he did to the Protestant preacher. But to complete this album, Rodolfo Coelho Cavalcante, who probably was more immersed and surrounded by such stuff than any other poet of "cordel," wrote Macumba in Bahia ["A Macumba na Bahia"][19] in a totally different sense.

Rodolfo has a right to talk for he is the great searcher for truth in "cordel" and has looked into most of the religious options available in Brazil. Carlos Cunha, fan and expert of the "cordel" in Salvador da Bahia, called Rodolfo the great "evangelizer" of the medium, really a very accurate analysis.

Rodolfo begins by affirming the affinity of all the doctrines of "Occultism," be they Theosophy, Esoterism or Spiritualism with its "mediunism." There is the doctrine of "umbanda" with its dogmas of "points, songs and prism" [pontos, cantares e prisma], as well as "Quimbanda," the form of "macumba" that reigns in most of the principal temples [terreiros] according to the poet. (This author has always understood "Quimbanda" by virtue of academic readings as the cult related to the use of black magic for purposes of evil).

But it turns out the entire poem is really a call to tourism in Salvador da Bahia. The poet actually presents a very pleasant, colorful account of "macumba" as "Bahian folklore" which cannot be missed. The poem quite possibly could be a "paid" poem contracted to be written by the Bahian Tourist Commission. Be that as it may, it is a great snapshot of an important part of Brazilian culture. Portrait paraphrases and summarizes its contents.

The poet says there are more than one hundred temples of "quimbanda" and "umbanda" in greater Salvador, each with its "terreiro" or place of worship. "Umbanda" exists for charity, but "Quimbanda," "in truth, plays a different role" (perhaps corroborating our own understanding that it is the cult associated most with black magic.) The poet continues, saying that professors come from all over to research "candomblé" (meaning in this context all the African cults in Bahia): the essence of "concrete psychism," where the "mediunidade" is the mechanism for the "manifestation." It matters not, be it the doctrine of Ghandi, Kardec, Calvin, Martin Luther, Rostaing, even Constantine himself, or the African religions—they all have one mission, "Inter-communication with the Celestial Divine."

But then the poet says that "Macumba" is a "heavy" religion, but it also is folklore. Afro-Brazilian religion has its code: the female cult leader [mãe de santo] works with her god spirit or saint [encantado] to perfection. In the old days there were crooks who took advantage of the members of the religions and blasphemed the principals of "Umbanda" and twisted the ideas of "Quimbanda" into something evil from what was really splendid.

Rodolfo lists many of the major African cult saints and their Christian equivalents: Oxalá—Our Lord of Bonfim, Oxosse—St. George, Iansan—Our Lady of the Sailors, Omulu—St. Lazarus protector of lepers, Exú—any demon, and Ogun—St. Anthony. They are all gods of the cult and come down to work, some cleansing, some indoctrinating; they are beings from another world with a profound power, even to punish!

They come down during the ritual, all in procession, dancing in the rhythm of the drums. And the faithful of the cult, the "horses" [cavalos] are "mounted" or possessed by the saints, dancing beautifully, all different in style, greeting the recently arrived saints in song and dance.

The poet tells the reader when and where one can visit the "terreiros." And he warns to not make fun of them, for with "manioc flour mixed with cooking oil" ["farofa de azeite"] anything can happen (a hex)! If called upon properly, the leaders of the cult, the father or mother of the saint, can help the sick, the financially strapped, and alcoholics.

Even though the cults are primitive religion, they are, the folk poet must admit, folklore and culture of Old Africa which are a part of the literature of the entire nation! (Rodolfo suspects that they perhaps even came from Islam or the Vedas of old.) He reasons that the Bible itself is full of references to the occult sciences, so combating "Candomblé" is certainly wrong. After all, "Our Catholic Church" has its miraculous saints which manifest themselves mysteriously from time to time, in the poet's words, "transcendental beings from a 'Celestial Orbit'." So the "mediumism" [mediunismo] of the spiritualist cults has both a good and bad side, working respectively for good and evil.

As a troubadour and poet Rodolfo feels he has done his job. In fact, he is very fuzzy and at times tends to confuse and merge all the African rites as well as Kardecism. Such is the message his public receives in the printed story-poem. It is a snapshot which enriches this portrait of Brazil and the Brazilian "Cordel."

4 A Return to Orthodoxy: the Pope and the Holy, Roman, Catholic and Apostolic Church

The final snapshot of the great theme of religion is a return to cordelian roots in the belief, hope and loyalty to the Popes of Rome, a recent but perhaps viable alternative to Bom Jesus Anthony Conselheiro, Father Cícero and Friar Damian.

The authority of the Pope and of the Church in Rome lies at the roots of traditional Northeastern Catholicism. "Peter, you are rock and upon this rock I build my church." But Liberation Theology and its adherents in Brazil have butted heads with "Peter" more than once in recent decades. Catholicism in many parts of the Northeast today has taken on a dramatically different tone than everything so far described, yet nothing described is irrelevant. With the Second Vatican Council in Rome in the early 1960s and the resulting "fresh breeze" allowed to flow through the open doors of St. Peter's, and more importantly, with the coming into its own of the Progressive Church via Liberation Theology in no small part aided by the Brazilian bishops and theologians, and finally, with Rome's reaction to Liberation Theology and the Christian Base Communities, the portrait of Northeastern Catholics and their church is today radically (no pun intended) different. At the center of the issue lies the authority of Rome and the Pope, the teaching ministry of the church and the mission of the church on earth. The Kingdom of God may be in heaven in eternal life, but should and could it not also be in the hearts of men here and now, and amongst the poor of Brazil as well?

The popes have always received the greatest respect and obedience, and a traditional event in the cordelian portrait is the death and succession of the man chosen for the Chair of Peter. Witness poems like <u>The Death of Pope John XXIII</u>,[20] the rotund, cheery main force behind the opening or "<u>aggornamiento</u>" in 1963-1964. Later, the brief sojourn of Pope Paul VI and his sudden death in 1978 were related in stories like <u>The Death of His Holiness Paul VI in Rome</u>.[21] But no man or event ever affected Brazil like the person and reign of Pope John Paul II, the "Pilgrim Pope" known most for his mission of evangelization, of taking the Gospel once again to all nations. He would be known as "John of God" or "<u>João de Deus</u>" in Brazil. He would be the first pope who would set foot in Brazil in 1980, the first pope who would speak directly and preferentially to the poor. He would speak to the workers (coming from the great workers' state of Poland itself), but also would call for a return to the discipline and allegiance to Rome, but now in the modern age.

One of the major moments of modern "<u>cordel</u>" was the diluvium of poems written and sold on the streets on the occasion of John Paul II's first visit to Brazil in 1980 and followed by the near tragedy resulting from the attempt upon his life just one year later in Rome. Over one hundred different accounts were published by poets who wrote in faith but also saw a propitious economic moment and knew that their public would welcome the pope with open arms and buy the stories about him in part as an expression of their traditional faith.

The plethora of poems which reported the pontiff's visit to Brazil in 1980 is comprised of stories from practically all the major poets of "cordel" remaining at that time. Almost all the major cities and states of the Northeast are represented as well as many elsewhere. Most of the poems deal with the pope's daily itinerary and the events happening in each city. This was easy for the modern cordelian poet: each step of the journey was reported on live national television. Many of the stories are simply a transposition to verse of the journalistic moment. But from them the reader can gain a perspective that reassures that the roots of Catholicism are alive and well in Brazil.

The great majority of poems of the visit, and there were dozens printed all over the Northeast and in Rio, São Paulo and Brasília, express the tremendous outpouring of love, religious sentiment, good will and hope for the future that the Pontiff's visit produced in Brazil. This pope would visit a prison in Brasília, would impulsively and spontaneously give his gold ring to the poor of a slum in Rio as a symbol of hope, and would thus touch the hearts of all Brazilians in "the most sublime and unforgettable spectacle I have ever seen" (Apolônio Alves dos Santos in his Visit of the Holy Father to Brazil and His Talk with President João Figueiredo on June 30, 1980).

Another poet, Azulão of Rio de Janeiro, a staunch believer in workers' rights and the workers party, would emphasize John Paul's respect for the workers of his own Poland and the world and the needs of the peasants.[22] A pope that hates "snobbishness, power and richness" and who is on the side of the humble and disenfranchised is clearly idolized by the poet and his public. Once again, a pope who insists on visiting the proletarian sections of town and kisses the soil of the country he visits as a symbol of God's gift of the land to mankind is in turn "a gift from God to us, a man like Jesus."

Just one short year later an astounding event rocked the world and was again reported in "cordel," the attempted murder of Pope John Paul II in the plaza of St. Peter's during a weekly audience.[23] A young Moslem extremist from Turkey shot the pope several times, most seriously in the intestines. After immediate surgery at the best hospital in Rome the pope slowly recovered from this traumatic, earthshaking event. The same poets who wrote of John Paul's trip to Brazil covered the crime, for that was how it was journalistically treated—a horrible, disgusting and perverse crime! The language used by the poets to describe the assassin is that of an "inhuman Turk," a perverse criminal with an inhuman heart, the same language used to describe the worst of villains in the cordelian cycle of adventures. The poet Apolônio Alves dos Santos of Rio de Janeiro concludes that Brazil is indeed filled with evil, despotism, kidnappings, bombings, muggings and terrorism. In these times all Brazilians pray for their leader, the Pope.

As might be expected, Abraão Batista in Juazeiro do Norte, Ceará, knowing well his pilgrim public who come to visit the shrine of Father Cícero, sees it all as a sign of the End.[24] He says the future is now, the Beast of the Apocalypse is running loose, and if God does not intervene, the devil will take all. He claims that he has learned to write of prophecy, and St. Malaquias had predicted the event saying that the pope is associated with the sign of the half moon, coincidentally the symbol of Turkey!

Whatever the tack and the message of the individual poet, it is respect, if not always belief, that above all is seen in these poems. The Brazilian who is eclectic in his religious beliefs, feels down to his bones a respect and a love for this man who represents what is good and hopeful in the world. He is the representative of Jesus Christ himself, the "rock" of St. Peter, and a tie to the beginnings, this in spite of the kaleidoscope of beliefs and customs seen in these two seminal chapters of a people and their country. As the poet Rodolfo Coelho Cavalcante said of the pope in his poetic cordelian biography, "Ours is an apostolic nation born under the banner of the Catholic religion,"[25] and so it is in Portrait.[26]

---

[1]   Waldemar Valente, Misticismo e Região, Recife: MEC, 1963; see also Luís da Câmara Cascudo, Dicionário do Folclore Brasileiro, 2nd. Ed. Rio de Janeiro: MEC, 1963, pp. 686-689.

[2]   In Brazilian fiction it is worthwhile to read: José Lins do Rego, Pedra Bonita, Rio de Janeiro: José Olympio Edta., 1961.

[3]   The chronicle was reported by Professor José Calasans in Canudos na Literatura de Cordel, São Paulo: Ática Edta., 1984. A previous version by the same author carried the title O Ciclo Folclórico de Bom Jesus Conselheiro, Salvador: Tipografia Beneditina Ltda., 1950.

[4]   A good source for the story is by M.B. Lourenço Filho, <u>Juazeiro do Padre Cícero</u>, 3rd ed., São Paulo: Edições Melhoramentos, n.d. See also Edmar Morel, <u>Padre Cícero o Santo de Juazeiro</u>, 2nd. ed. Rio de Janeiro: Civilização Brasileira, n.d.

[5]   Euclides da Cunha, <u>Os Sertões</u>, preface by Manuel Cavalcanti Proença, Rio de Janeiro: Edições de Ouro, 1966.

[6]   See Calasans, <u>Canudos na Literatura de Cordel</u>.

[7]   João Melchíades Ferreira da Silva, <u>A Guerra de Canudos</u>, n.p., n.d., in Calasans, <u>Canudos . . . .</u>

[8]   The best recent book on the phenomenon of Father Cícero is by the writer Candace Slater, <u>Trail of Miracles</u>, Berkeley: University of California Press, 1984.

[9]   Severino Paulino da Silva, <u>Nascimento, Vida, Morte, Educação, Signo e Sorte de Padre Cícero Romão Batista</u>, Juazeiro do Norte: n.d.

[10]   Rodolfo Coelho Cavalcante, <u>Frei Damião o Missionário do Nordeste</u>, Salvador: n.d.

[11]   From the magazine <u>Opinião</u>, article with no author indicated, n.p., n.d.

[12]   Since the first draft of <u>Portrait</u>, Friar Damian died, but the poets remained faithful to his figure, and new titles appeared, marking his end and his memory. Among them <u>Father Damian, the last saint of the backlands 1898-1997</u>, <u>The arrival of Friar Damian in heaven</u>, and <u>Friar Damian the saint of the Northeast</u>.

[13]   Joseph Page, <u>The Brazilians</u>, pp. 373-375.

[14]   See the following sources once again: <u>Ao Som da Viola</u>, <u>Violeiros e Cantadores</u>, <u>Vaqueiros e Cantadores</u>, and one additionally: Rodrigues de Carvalho, <u>Cancioneiro do Norte</u>, 3rd. ed., Rio de Janeiro: Instituto Nacional do Livro, 1967.

[15]   Leandro Gomes de Barros, <u>Debate de um Ministro Nova-Seita com um Urubu</u> in: <u>Ao Som da Viola</u>. The complete text is repeated in: Mark J. Curran, <u>Antología Bilingüe da la Literatura de Cordel</u>, Madrid: Editorial Orígenes, 1991.

[16] Leandro wrote, among others, O Adeus da Aguardente, A Criação da Aguardente, A Defesa da Aguardente, Discussão do Vinho com a Aguardente, e, O Filho da Aguardente. It was known that the poet enjoyed a bit of a drink while he improvised verse (Curran, A Literatura de Cordel, chapter 2).

[17] Leandro Gomes de Barros, História do Soldado Jogador, Editor Proprietário José Bernardo da Silva, Juazeiro do Norte: n. d. This classic story, coming from European tradition, suffered many plagiarized versions and outright theft by other poets, with titles like O Soldado Francês or O Jogador na Igreja. A famous singer of old country music in the United States, Tex Ritter, had a top hit with his version of the story, titled "Deck of Cards" in English. Reknowned Alagoan folklorist, Theo Brandão, told us in a conversation in the 1970s that he had a manuscript of more than 500 pages on the story, tracing it from its European roots to the many versions in Brazil.

[18] See by this author: Jorge Amado na Literatura de Cordel, Salvador: Fundação Casa de Rui Barbosa-Fundação Cultural do Estado da Bahia, 1981; A Presença de Rodolfo Coelho Cavalcante na Moderna Literatura de Cordel, Rio de Janeiro: Nova Fronteira-Fundação Casa de Rui Barbosa, 1987; and Cuíca de Santo Amaro Poeta-Repórter da Bahia, Salvador: Fundação Casa de Jorge Amado, 1990.

[19] Rodolfo Coelho Cavalcante, A Macumba na Bahia, Salvador, 1978.

[20] José Soares, A Morte do Papa João XXIII, Recife, 1963.

[21] José de Souza Sobrinho, O Falecimento de sua Santidade Paulo VI em Roma, n.p., 1978.

[22] José João dos Santos, "Azulão," Visita de João Paulo II ao Brasil, Engenheiro Pedreira, 1980.

[23] Flávio Fernandes Moreira, O Atentado contra o Papa, Rio de Janeiro, 1981.

[24] Abraão Batista, A Tentativa de Assassinato do Papa João de Deus, Juazeiro do Norte, 1981.

[25] Rodolfo Coelho Cavalcante, A Vida do Santo Papa João Paulo II, Salvador, 1980.

[26] As might be expected, with the death of John Paul II in 2005, a great number of new titles came upon the cordelian scene, recounting and praising his life and works.

Album III

What Not To Do—The Wages of Sin

Introduction

Another major aspect of a people and their country must be the adherence to or lack thereof of a moral standard for the way they live their lives; thus morality is an important part of <u>Portrait</u>. It is obvious that Album I "In This We Believe" dealt with the existence of God in the form of the Catholic Trinity as well as beliefs as to the Blessed Virgin Mary, the apostles and saints, and the existence of the devil, all in the form of orthodox Catholicism. Album II dealt with variations of the same in manifestations of religion seen in Brazil's folk-popular Catholicism and in a lesser way, Protestant, African and Spiritualist religions. It is also obvious that each religion in and of itself involves not only <u>what</u> is believed, but a consequential <u>way</u> to live out what is believed. Thus the whole realm and question of morality, what is good and should be done and what is bad and should be avoided, is a corollary to religious belief. It is the "way" of religion.

<u>Portrait</u> has the underpinnings of morality, an essential vision of good and evil, seen in almost all the story-poems.[1] But in a more specific way, the poets and public of "<u>cordel</u>" and many other Brazilians share to a greater or lesser extent the beliefs and the way expressed in this folk-popular literature. For reasons of practicality, in order to capture the "vast universe of "<u>cordel</u>" in English, the issues of this chapter which of course are based on "In This We Believe" are rather an emphasis and description of what we should do, what we should avoid and the consequences of both for us. At issue is the description, both serious and in jest, of the moral state of the world, and it boils down to sin, the "wages of sin" and conversely, the rewards of avoiding sin. So this album of necessity overlaps the "belief" questions in Albums I and II.

Moral issues and their portrayal in "<u>cordel</u>" are a combination of the "real" and the "fantastic," characters and events that come from normal day to day living, that is, what is,

57

and characters and events that are dreamed, imagined and could be. As one writer put it, the fantastic in "cordel" is revealed in a narrative which is the sum of heterogeneous elements that come from fantastic legends and Biblical deeds mixed with new realities, some arbitrarily created by the poets.[2] In the "primitive culture" the same author attributed to the poets and public of "cordel," the real is confused with the unreal, history cedes itself to myth and to a land of spirits, suffering souls, saints and miracles, a place where man lives with God and the devil. The mixture will be seen in this album in the hundreds of "folhetos" which are didactic in nature and end with a moral lesson, poems called "examples" [exemplos]. The poets of "cordel" have been writing for over one hundred years about morality and it is basic to the way they lead their lives.

1 Sin and the Moral State of the World

Introduction

A very large part of <u>Portrait</u> are the hundreds of "<u>folhetos</u>" which become snapshots of every conceivable moral transgression known to the poets and their public. These stories usually only indirectly mention sacred scripture or specific teachings of religion and then only with a short reminder that sin will be punished. Emphasis is on the doing and the results, but what one sees is the moral microcosm of the poet and his readers, what they conceive as wrong and of course consequently, what is good. By and large this is the result of the old-time religion with emphasis on hell and damnation, fire and brimstone, but with some surprises.

It also is obvious from a perusal of the illustrations on the covers of these stories (a sample being beautiful young ladies in skimpy beach attire) and the lists of hedonistic practices described inside the covers, that there is more going on here than an expression of moral indignation. It is the Northeastern equivalent of the U.S. supermarket tabloids: if you cannot do it, you might as well read about it. So aside from the moral lesson he purports to provide, the poet entertains his public as well.

One must begin with the poems on "general corruption:" <u>The People of Corruption, Corruption Parading Itself in the Devil's Parade, Perdition in the World, The Horrors of Moral Decay</u>, or <u>The March of Moral Decay</u>. These link immorality to sin.

Above all it is <u>woman</u> who is most linked to living rightly or wrongly (is this because almost all cordelian poets are men and their public in the marketplace as well is traditionally male?). How does one then explain the female role model of the Blessed Virgin Mary or Mary Magdalene? Is woman to be wife and model mother or a shameless prostitute? It turns out women themselves are both the cause and effect of the lack of morality in the world and are a big part of <u>Portrait.</u> Among dozens of titles in point are: <u>A Treacherous Woman, The Pleasures of Youth and the Treachery of Women, The Value of Honesty, The Desired Woman or the Woman Without an Owner</u>, <u>He Who Has a Woman Has Trouble</u> or <u>Wife and Companion-a Poem Dedicated to Those that Suffer.</u>

But if it is the nature of woman to be temptress, of little fidelity to husband and home, she is best known in the oldest profession! The early, traditional cordelian stories condemn her: <u>The Goddess of the Cabaret (the Proud Prostitute)</u>, or <u>Near the Cabaret</u>. But recent stories reflecting changes in society present another perspective: stories like <u>ABCs of the</u>

<u>Prostitute, The Life of the Prostitute,</u> or <u>Encounter with a Prostitute</u>. In the poems on prostitution, if the woman is the root of all evil, it is also because of man's help to get her there. Even in the most condemnatory of all stories, the poets must admit that it is man, although tempted by the seductress most times, who steals the honor of the young virgin, who besmirches the young maiden's honor with promises and lies of marriage, who forces sex on the young maid in the rich man's mansion and who bribes the poor, abandoned farm girl with food and temporary shelter in exchange for her favors. And in a semi-feudal society like the old Northeast, once virtue is lost, the unlucky maiden whose suitor is without honor ends up on the streets plying the trade of the prostitute.

However, cheating on your husband or wife brings a levity absent in the preceding stories to the many stories of cuckoldry like <u>The Era of Horns</u> or <u>The Cuckolds' Union</u> or its backlash in <u>It's Not a Crime or a Sin for a Husband to Cheat on His Wife</u>. Such stories emphasize the rampant cheating as sport and as "style," and certainly are a moral commentary on the times.

But adults are not the only sinners. Teenage hormones play a role in the stories involving courtship (the old term), dating (the new term), "making out" and the "new morality." "Juicy" titles meant to attract prospective readers are frequent: <u>Modern Dating</u>, <u>The Result of Young Girls Who Make Out</u>, <u>Between Making Out and Dancing</u>, <u>He Who Likes to Make Out Only Wants to Live in Goiana</u>, <u>Making Out in the Dark</u>, <u>Reserved Making Out</u>, or <u>Making Out in the Movies</u>.

A corollary are the many poems dealing with the same subject during the annual carnival, the epitome of immoral times! Such stories often are another version of an age-old folk theme "<u>Oh tempo, oh mores</u>!" when the poets lament the loss of the good ole' days with all the goodness therein and the present days of moral corruption and hedonism. They range from comments on new styles of clothing—<u>The Mini-Skirt that Keeps Hiking Up</u> or <u>The Scandalous Fashions of Today</u>—to the accounts of scandal on the beaches—<u>The Trip to the Beach</u> or <u>The Marvels that Can Be Seen on Copacabana Beach</u>. But most entertaining are the accounts of teenage hippies, longhairs and rock and roll from the 1960s (the poet Rodolfo Coelho Cavalcante made a living writing these stories during the "moral cleansing" of the military regime).

Needless to say, the hundreds of such "<u>folhetos</u>" in the marketplace and fairs since the beginnings of "<u>cordel</u>" are no accident or fluke; immorality sells!

General Corruption

In these stories the poet almost always begs pardon from his public for daring to take up the theme of moral degradation, but at the same time feels <u>obligated</u> to do so (should the reader be surprised?). He generally will do a laundry list of evils in the world as did the poet Severino Simião in <u>The People in Corruption</u>:[3] there is no honesty or virtue anymore; no one even trusts another to pay debts on time. Even the most sacred of the sacred, the wake prior to the family funeral, will be bereft of mourners if there is no sugar cane rum and food! And the customary religious processions may have the "holy women" [<u>beatas</u>] in front, but the kids are in the rear flirting and even making out! Young ladies go to dances and even drink, they ride bicycles for two rubbing against their boyfriends, they even play soccer [<u>futbol</u>], a "religion" of its own in Brazil, and they sit on the laps of their boyfriends who drive in fast cars. Shop owners employ pretty girls by the dozens so the not so smart hillbilly in town will buy more! And carnival is the worst with the annual crop of new babies nine months later.

"Arrest 'em all," says the poet! If this were not bad enough, the world is full of "queers" [<u>veados</u>] prancing about in lipstick and rouge, hitting on other boys. Corruption is generalized like the plague. For one hundred virgins there are one hundred thousand prostitutes (a UNESCO study some time back dwelled on the incredibly high occurrence of prostitution in Brazil). Why? Because these sinners do not believe in God; money is their god and they live in sin! And it did not used to be that way!

Poets worried in 1910 about women not wearing corsets or petticoats and beginning to use makeup! Poets today can border on the vulgar and pornographic in describing the lack of moral control in the world. Erotildes Miranda dos Santos of Feira da Santana, Bahia, made a living in the 1960s utilizing nude or nearly nude photos on the covers of his poems and howled of the depravity and ruination [<u>devassidão</u>] and [<u>desmantelo</u>] of mankind. He was good at describing in a suggestive manner all the glimpses of thighs, breasts and even private parts themselves to an avid male public in the markets, the latter all listening in rapt attention! Cuíca de Santo Amaro, the "Hell's Mouth" of Bahian "<u>cordel</u>" from the 1940s to 1964 loved to describe the women of his day in tight dresses, this plus all the scandal in Salvador at the time. Antônio Lucena de Mossoró in very recent times went further by using extreme vulgarity in language, amounting to verbal abuse by today's standards, in describing homosexuals and the plague of AIDS in his versions of moral decay in Brazil, laughing all the while.

Woman, the Modern Eve

It is no surprise that the large majority of poems look at women with a slightly different view. But with humor! In <u>Whoever Has a Woman Has Work</u>[4] the poet says women are two-faced and trouble! In <u>The Pleasures of Youth and the Treachery of Women</u> ["Os Prazeres da Juventude e a Traição da Mulher"][5] the poet José Costa Leite tells us God made woman without a lick of common sense. When he gave her to Adam, that was when Adam's problems began. Women are ungrateful and unfaithful and even the devil wants nothing to do with them. But the problem is that even though they are all untruthful [falsas], they are also good looking and pleasurable [boas e gostosas]! "Pleasure to the eye but hell to the soul!" says the poet. It is rare to find a good woman, and the worst of all are the prostitutes. They convince a poor customer to set them up in a little house, and once set up as a "kept woman," ["amancebia"] then the poor innocent man discovers his new girlfriend has been "had" by everybody in town. So the poor victim ends up playing the fool! The poet concludes by saying there are only two good women in the world: the Mother of Christ and his own wife! He adds that there does not exist a woman without a fault!

Sometimes the stories match reality. The poet Cuíca de Santo Amaro in Salvador da Bahia from 1940 to 1964 wrote an endless string of stories telling of immoral women and the scandal they created in Bahia. (They were half the story; the immoral men were the rest.)

In <u>The Woman Who Committed Adultery Against her Husband</u> ["A Mulher que Adulterou o Esposo"][6] the poet rails against the infidelity of women, the cause of all evil! But he especially points out upper class women who can have affairs, and the local reporters get paid to not put it in the paper. But he, the "Moral Guardian of Bahia," did not get his share of the bribe in this instance, so here is the story of the unfaithful woman, a civil servant, caught in the apartment of . . . a professor! Cuíca promises to reveal the names in next week's story! The poet actually might write up a new version of the same story, but with specific names mentioned, and present the entire printing of perhaps one thousand copies to the guilty parties. He would then offer to sell the entire printing to them for a nice convenient price should they so desire. If not, the poems would be sold like hotcakes on the streets of Bahia in the next few days! Sometimes Cuíca had a few takers. Sometimes he was beaten up or ended up in jail. But the locals were always waiting for his latest.

The epitome of the stories of infidelity was the series of "folhetos" Cuíca wrote in the mid-1940s on a real event, <u>The Crime of Brotas</u>.[7] After warning her recalcitrant husband to stop fooling around with other women, a wife took action one night when he collapsed in bed, exhausted from that night's adventure. Cutting off his "head," she also cut off his dignity and manhood. In a second story, also based on a real event in Bahia, The Vengeance of the Man from Brotas ["A Vingança do Homem de Brotas"],[8] the husband-victim took vengeance for the affront by knifing his wife in a dark alley. But the poet, spurred on by great sales, topped the former stories with a leap into pure fiction: The Marriage of the Man from Brotas ["O Casamento do Homem de Brotas"].[9] In this story the man decides to marry again, but has to order a new "head" from the place that makes them the best—the United States. But, alas, it is so big that the airplane carrying it to Bahia crashes and he must live to lament his loss!

From the Cabaret to the House of Prostitution

The leap from woman's infidelity to prostitution is very small. From the old stories like <u>The Goddess of the Cabaret the Proud Prostitute</u> or <u>Near the Cabaret</u> to more recent "sociological" accounts of <u>Encounter with a Prostitute</u>, <u>Life of a Prostitute</u> or <u>ABCs of the Prostitute</u>, women who "fall" are depicted in a much more serious light.

<u>Near the Cabaret</u> ["Perto do Cabaré"][10] presents the images common to old "<u>cordel</u>." The poet Antônio Apolinário da Cruz recalls the good ole' days and the changes of today. In the old days the cabaret was on the edge of town; now it is in the middle of town. If you want to see what is happening in town, just watch the doors of the cabaret! Man was born to love God, to be a light in his presence, but the man with the whore at the cabaret has forgotten God and is like a wandering, lost dog, howling and abandoned.

The women in the cabaret sell their flesh to man who is a sinner; such women are worth nothing! They end with a maggot infested mouth, infesting their own children and grandchildren! Their leprous hands can blind, take away speech, even kill. They are indeed astute like the serpent, and the man who takes pleasure in them is like the vultures after the flood and Noah's ark, feasting on the dead!

The man who leaves his wife for a whore is a sinner. He breaks a sacramental vow of marriage and has the same obligation as his wife to be faithful. It is comparable to the priest's vow of chastity to God, but to each other. The man who goes with the prostitute in the cabaret has no love of God, and his jail sentence will be in hell for eternity. And if he goes to the cabaret, he becomes addicted! He has the vice of cabaret women forever. Such men are fools!

But recent stories are different. José João da Silva writing in the 1950s in Recife tells the story of a poor victim of a rich man. She is taken advantage of and loses all, living the miseries of a prostitute. But she happily reencounters a lost love of her youth who saves her and takes her into his comfortable home to live happily ever after.

Rodolfo Coelho Cavalcante, the great modern moralist of "<u>cordel</u>," veteran of personal campaigns against licentious verse in the marketplace of Salvador da Bahia in the 1940s, former Bible thumper and enthusiastic Spiritualist believer, is the defender of the contemporary prostitute. He harangues Brazilian society with its huge index of prostitution and preaches and begs the government and the new feminists to do something about it. His stories are important modern snapshots contrasting with the "old" "<u>cordel</u>."

In <u>ABCs of the Prostitute</u> ["ABC da Meretriz"][11] the poet begins in lyrical fashion (for "<u>cordel</u>," essentially a narrative poetry): the life of a prostitute is a sea of misfortune, an ocean of tears on whose bitter waves she rides in a ship of misfortune, arriving at the port of death, her sad end the tomb! But there is hope for the prostitute: God has pity on her and her soul can be saved if she repents and changes her life! She has a great model in Mary Magdalene who repented, wiping her tears shed at the feet of Jesus with her own hair! The poet reminds that there is no flesh in paradise; sexual pleasure is only in this present corrupt life.

He sees the prostitute as a "being thrown away by society." The man who purchases her favors is a criminal as well, and both live in error. Desired when young and in her prime, now drunk and begging in the streets, she is the victim of society which took away her purity and now condemns her. Her model, rather, should be the Blessed Virgin Mary who gave birth to "an angel."

Rodolfo addresses the prostitutes directly and pleas with them to leave the life of sin! Man has no right to drag you, once a pure virgin, into sin! After all, your body belongs to God. God created Eden, but the first woman was lost to sin through her disobedience to God for prohibited desire! God gave her innocence, but then also punished her. But he still offers her his grace, "rays of light," and if she accepts it she can leave "the life." The poet ends in a personal prayer to Holy Mary, asking her to take his "ABC" to the prostitute to implore her to leave this "road to hunger." He thinks aloud, "Maybe this poem can save her," and laments, "My God, when will my country be free of the plague of prostitution?" By now we see that Rodolfo really was a cordelian "preacher" and "evangelist."

Horns[12]

The poets say that if the easiest way to be unfaithful is a trip to the local house of prostitution, today it is becoming just as easy to have an affair with someone's wife! Brazil is in the middle of a plague of cuckoldry. It is, like the greater Rio poet Azulão says, The Age of Horns ["A Era do Chifre"]. In a poem that is meant to be a humorous look at the current state of affairs, the poet starts out in a serious vein: today is an age of cynicism and evil, and people are confused, their free will resulting in an era of scandalous abuse.

But then he begins the jokes. In the old days only bulls and Billy Goats had horns. Today it is high fashion and everyone either has them or wants them. Like clothing, they come in all sizes and colors. It used to be the married man who "wore" the horns, but not anymore! Even young engaged women put horns on their fiancées and this before the wedding! Women who work in the city and take the commuter train, arrive home late saying the train was late or they had to work late.

A necessary aside: Azulão is referring to a situation he knows well in the great metropolis of Greater Rio. A resident in a far off proletarian section of Engenheiro Pedreiro, he and his fellow citizens must take the run down "Central Train" [Trem da Central] of recent cinematic fame into the city to work. But this is no luxury passage from Connecticut or upstate New York into the "city," but a broken down, hot, miserable ride for the poor. Azulão describes the ride in a famous poem we shall see later. It is the poor slum dweller living outside of Rio who must take the long ride to the city to work as a maid, a doorman or the like in the rich sections of Rio.

Continuing the poem's narration: it was the boss's fault! The married man leaves his warm bed early in the morning for work and "Big Dick" jumps into his place. Girls may dance cheek to cheek, but they are looking over his shoulder at the next victim! Cuckoldry is rampant from the farm to the city, so if you want to avoid it, do not get married or do not even live together. And with divorce on the horizon (a national law permitting divorce passed in 1977) the plague of cuckoldry can only grow!

One recalls Album I, sees these snapshots, and wonders what is going on here? Where is the serious-about-religion northeasterner? He is one and the same as the poet and public of these stories, writing and reading the serious or funny comments on the moral state of the world today.

Courtship or Dating, Sparking or Making Out

BEGIN SIDEBAR. The most common signs of these immoral times are the goings on of the youth. Boys will be boys, girls will be girls and hormones will be hormones, especially in the tropics! One example suffices. In a country which had just begun mass production of automobiles in the 1950s during the regime of Juscelino Kubitschek, the country that became famous for the VW Beetle [o Fusca] and the "Big Beetle" [O Fuscão], a country that invented ingenious lotteries so that people of very modest means could pay a modest fee each month, the total being enough for the down payment on a VW Bug, this certainly was a country where making out in the back seat would take on a special flavor. In the Rio de Janeiro of 1967, in that hot summer of January through March, VW bugs would line the street which served as a parking lot along famous Ipanema Beach, the windows fogged up with an outside temperature of 90 degrees (is this what the "Girl From Ipanema" did at night?). Such were the signs of the times of "modern" Brazil. END SIDEBAR.

The poets knew they could not lose on this issue: not just the back seat necking and such, but the whole scenario of social mores and "courtship" in the 60s. After all, were the poets not just fulfilling their role as "reporter of the masses" and "watchdog of public morality?" So dozens of stories were written, the more salacious, the better the sales. But the snapshots captured a memorable time in the history of the country: Brazil was coming into the modern age. The land which had always been the "land of the future" seemed to have arrived and there was no better proof than "the New Morality."

As with other types of stories, some of the accounts are dead serious, others pure spoof for fun, and of course a few somewhere in between. The older the stories, the more "innocent" the new morality may seem to the present day reader. A sample from each will complete the snapshots.

In the "old" style in a poem dated from 1957 in Juazeiro do Norte, that hotbed of religious conservatism, the poet in Modern Courtship ["O Namoro Moderno"][13] laments the changes in customs. In the old days courting was practically done in secret, the modest maiden being courted inside the house and in the presence of her parents. Today, it is done on a whim, anytime, anyplace. In the old days the girls did not even know the term "courtship" ["namorar"], and there was no talking back to their parents' decisions for a proper husband. The girls were involved working on the plantation, and "weaving cloth from cotton" was their life (the poet presents them as in a state of near nirvana!). Today, anything goes—the boy and girl are found kissing in the marketplace. The next thing will be Communism! Men will now actually pay to get into a dance because they hear there are so many available young girls there. The poet has even seen girls singing and playing the guitar and even young female schoolteachers do the same! And, these girls are "street smart" ["prevenidas"] and not so naive today! Yes, Brazil is generally corrupt today with courting even going on at the Novenas!

Cuíca de Santo Amaro is almost as lurid in describing the "miseries" that go on in the cinemas in Salvador.[14] He complains couples are making a whorehouse out of the cinema! Movies are the ante-room to perdition, a book where maidens learn to be prostitutes, a school with no professor that teaches virgins to lose their "virtuous demeanor" ["pudor"] and wives to lose their virtue [valor]! The poet hastens to add that he does not write these stories for thrills or to glorify immorality, but because others tell him about such doings and it is his responsibility as a reporter of all things going on in Bahia to bring them and truth to the attention of the reader! This is in spite of his own first person narration of what he has seen while at the movies. The poet in real life was indeed crazy about the cinema and spent hours catching the latest features, so he had time to look around.

But perhaps the best snapshot of teenage love life is by that excellent poet in greater Rio, Azulão, in Courtship Today ["Os Namorados de Hoje"].[15] It is one of those "folhetos" that is a sociological gold mine and truly a look into Brazilians and Brazil in the late 1960s. In a way it summarizes all said so far about modern morality (and sin) in this chapter.

The poet says he picked up pen and paper to tell in verse of the unbridled loose times, to tell the truth about the beatniks and the "bossa nova" of youth courting today in Brazil. First of all are the clothes with the roles reversed, women dressing like men, men like women, and all this in an atmosphere of dancing, kissing and bodies glued together—that is what the people want!

Women cut their hair short, men wear curls; both go down the street in pants so tight you cannot tell which is which. Girls ride bicycles with pants so tight you see the rear end shaking [rebolando]; young men turn into perverts and old men slobber at the sight of any young girl.

The worst of all takes place on the commuter trains from the poor suburbs to the city. But that is just the beginning; from there it ends up in a dark movie theater. So the tearful girl with the swollen stomach writes a letter to the advice columnist who says young ladies should learn not to play with matches if they don't expect fire! So be careful of going out for a walk with the lover boy and especially of the swim at the beach. That's not a tumor growing in all the girls' bellies! The doctor says that whatever is going around can be caught only in a dark spot where there is messing around, especially at the dance halls, during carnival or at the base of a dark wall! (The reader has noted the language of this chapter, an attempt to match the exact tone of these poems written in Portuguese slang.)

But the humor turns black at this point: the "style" today is for the "serpent" who makes the mistake to "force out the tumor," and if it is born alive to kill it, roll it up in a cloth and throw it into the garbage.

Waxing philosophic, Azulão says Lucifer planted all types of evil in the world after being thrown off the celestial throne, and the results are gambling, dancing and carnival! In the heat of the drumbeat of the carnival school bands and the drinking from Shrove Tuesday to Ash Wednesday, hundreds of young girls enter "the battalions of the lost."

Courtship today is downright nauseating and disgusting: the girl takes the boyfriend home to her parents' house, the father shakes his hand, wishes them the best and splits the scene! The two have sex on the divan, and the mother watches the whole thing from the kitchen. When it gets dark, the same guy takes her to the movies, and once the film has started, he spends the rest of the night hunting for "fleas" in her blouse. And after the movie, he buys her popcorn and while she eats, he hunts for "old maids."

The results are the same: pregnancy to the ones that dance "Rock and Twist" in the "unbridled bossa nova" of courtship as it is today. Kisses and partying end up in curses of damnation.

Girls today just want luxury: a blond man, a cool car like a "Cadillac, Aero Willys, Volkswagen or a Buick," freedom, a swim at the beach, carnivals and . . . picnics! They want to read scandalous magazines like <u>Grand Hotel</u> ["Grande Hotel"] or <u>Illusion</u> ["Ilusão"], and they all want to be stars of radio or TV exchanging their honor for bohemia and damnation. The poor girls in the slums [<u>favelas</u>] all want to be American, dying their hair blond, trying to be cool and telling their boyfriends, "I'm from Copacabana." They only want to wear tight pants and speak English and are not particular who picks them up. Full of "jive" ["<u>gíria</u>"], they "move it" down the avenue. And the poor guy who falls for them and spends all his money on partying and drugs will drown in a sea of deceit.

And they do not stop at boyfriends; they will take a nice furnished apartment and easy living from a married man! Many the married man out on the town and buying them drinks at the corner bar is taking bread from his own family's table to "provide luxury to a wicked woman."

So whoever buys this poem should take the poet's advice: women, shame on you, have a little pride! Men, show a little integrity! Not wanting to offend, the poet ends saying that his intent was just to describe some of the craziness of the new courting. The poem sold like hotcakes!

More Fun on the Beach

But along with dating and "making out," the poets loved to write accounts like <u>The Marvels You Can See on Copacabana Beach</u> ["As Maravilhas que Se Pode Ver na Praia de de Copacabana"]¹⁶ to impress the hillbillies in town for market day in the interior of the Northeast or even the northeastern market in Rio de Janeiro. As the poet Manoel Apoliniário says in this "<u>folheto</u>" written "for all those who know how to read," we know that Brazilians really know how to party in Rio de Janeiro, and the main place is on the beach at Copacabana. They go to take a dip and end up drinking and in the middle of all kinds of "funny business" [<u>safadeza</u>]. Rio is the capital of Brazilian orgy!

This poem is another funny poem [<u>gracejo</u>], and although it uses the refrain of "the swim at Copacabana," it really is an excuse to talk about kissing, hugging, making out and worse anywhere today in Brazil. It begins by getting the buyer's attention with a description of the one-piece swimsuit [<u>maiô</u>] (the poet is writing in a time prior to the bikini and the "dental floss," thong or string bikini [<u>fio dental</u>]).

The poet lists all the shapes and colors of women on the beach, including the "<u>Balzaqueanas</u>," those women of easy virtue! He says he gets so embarrassed just thinking about it he can scarcely describe it; somehow he overcomes this in the next six pages. The girls arrive at the beach, throw off their clothes (always a modest skirt in the old days) and the drinking, "messing around" [<u>malandragem</u>] and immorality begin! The result is pregnant girls! And the women who put horns on their husbands at Copacabana! Today when the poet sees the couples glued together on the park benches in the tiny plazas of the Northeast, he can only think of where it all started, on the beach at Copacabana. When that girl casually lifts a leg on the beach and you see "the cavern with the black panther," it is just all too much! The "moral guardian" sadly (or happily) reports this to his loyal customers. The cover of the poem is in the woodcut style with two smiling, very happy, well-endowed young ladies in "<u>maiô</u>" and "<u>biquini</u>" with a look that suggests that "girls just want to have fun."

The Things They Wear

But it was not just the "maiô" and the "biquini." When the 1960s arrived with all they entailed, some important changes in styles of clothing accompanied the new era. One was the "revolution" of the mini-skirt. Azulão in Rio de Janeiro wrote The Skirt that Hiked Up ["A Saia que Suspendeu"][17] and told his readers there is no need to go to the beach for your thrills—just check out the mini-skirts on the city streets. They are like rockets; they only keep going up. And it is not just the young girls who wear them. One confuses housewives who want to be movie stars imitating Brigitte Bardot or Gina Lollobrigida (international sirens who made trips to Rio's carnival as "star of the year" in the 60s) with the prostitutes. The poet jokes that even the government cannot control the new styles, try as it may. Even the all-powerful state agency for food standards and controls, SUNAB, can't tell the women how long the skirts should be. Women are in control.

So the whole thing is a sign of the immorality of the times, the world turned upside down, women wanting to be men, men dressing like women, guitars instead of "berimbaus" (the Afro-Brazilian percussion instrument used in the beautiful dance-self-defense art [capoeira] in Bahia). This is not civilization! It is immorality and all are on the road to perdition. It's a matter of conscience!

No one can match the indignation of Rodolfo Coelho Cavalcante when he gets on a roll, and the new styles were one of his best. In The Scandalous Styles of Today ["As Modas Escandalosas de Hoje em Dia"][18] the poet insists he does not like to write about moral degradation, but is obligated to do so. The youth of today! At seven years they are reading depraved comic books; at twelve the boys have long hair like girls, and at eighteen they insist on being emancipated. They are worse than the sexual deviants [tarados] all over Brazil these days.

The country is a moral cesspool; everyone seems to want to go to hell. The boys in their tight pants look like young girls, and the low cut blouses and dresses a respectable gentlemen sees on the streets and buses are too much! Men are actually too shy or embarrassed to look at the brazen hussies and even turn away! (The poet Rodolfo actually kicked a young lady out of one of his classes when he taught primary school for a few years in Piaui because she wanted him to kiss her. He said she could never be a "disciple" of his with that attitude.) Ah, the old days were different: widows wore perpetual black as a sign of mourning; children would not dare to smoke. Today they all smoke Hollywood (a popular Brazilian cigarette in the 1960s). The world is slowly turning into an abyss!

The poet is just getting warmed up. He really could get started on a related hot topic from the 1960s: the arrival of Rock 'n Roll and all that surrounded it.

Hippies, Longhairs and Rock 'n Roll

A good part of the cultural shock for the "old guard" [velha guarda] generation as it was known in the Brazil of the 1960s, was dealing with the new living with abandon by the teenagers of Brazil. Several circumstances converged to create a fertile situation for change. First and most important of all was the arrival of foreign rock and roll and all that came with it. The Beatles had arrived on the coattails of Elvis Presley and American Rock. It would be the four mop haired kids from Liverpool who would set Brazil on end. The Beatles' music, the tight trousers they wore, but most of all the ever lengthening hair would cause a minor revolution in Brazil with the era of the "long hairs" [cabeludos]. Erasmo Carlos and especially Roberto Carlos would adapt the new music and beat to a Brazilian rock and roll, the "yeah-yeah-yeah" [iê iê iê] era. But as might be expected, the new music brought new attitudes of independence and even rebellion. Roberto Carlos spoke a new slang and a new Portuguese; he was "very cool" [bacana] or [legal], the catchwords of Brazilian slang at the time. He invented and put new vocabulary into his music. But undercurrents of sexual liberation and drugs followed. It was inevitable.

Concurrent to this, and some say the real cause of change, was "the fresh breeze" Vatican Council II brought to the Catholic, Christian world. Radical change arrived with the mass in the vernacular, the priest facing the fervent at mass, but most of all in putting stress on the "new" theology of "God is Love" which was welcomed by all wanting to have fun, instead of the "sin, sin, sin" and "the fires of hell" of old Catholicism. The changes thus wrought in day to day living by this the guardian of all belief and morality cannot be overstated in the Brazil of the 1960s.

But there was more; it was the age of significant scientific development and change. The transistor radio became available and affordable to masses of Brazilians who had only vaguely dreamed of the seductions of the outside world (capitalism and its advertising for starters). Satellites in space were the foundation for a new communications network which brought television and then color television to the far corners of Brazil almost overnight. The "materialism" of the United States in particular came in a wave of new programming (and advertisements) to which the Brazilians soon added their own products in a wave of incredible national creativity (the TV Globo era). And not coincidentally, the pill and easier birth control had arrived.

But concurrent to all this was a "larger power:" a military dictatorship whose hard line leaders combined their fear and hatred of international Communism and its threat to Brazil and the hemisphere with an almost folkloric desire to return to "the good old days of religion and morality." It was an era forever satirized by Stanislau Ponte Preta's <u>Festival of Stupidity that Devastates the Nation</u> [FEBEAPA][19] an indictment of the gaffes made by the early military leaders of the revolution. Public displays of affection were discouraged or even outlawed—holding hands, embracing or kissing in a public plaza were considered contrary to common decency and the high moral level of the nation, particularly in conservative states like Minas Gerais. So in an unusual moment in time folk-popular poet joined military general in condemning the "new" morality and all its manifestations, thus creating an important and extremely colorful snapshot for <u>Portrait</u>.

One poem can summarize it all. In September of 1966 in a time of full-blown "Beatlemania" and Roberto Carlos' star rising in Brazilian popular music, Rodolfo Coelho Cavalcante wrote <u>The Results of Long Hairs Today</u> ["Os Resultados dos Cabeludos de Hoje em Dia"].[20] He says it all started in Liverpool when the Beatles decided to bring a new style to the planet; they started a war with their long hair. It is a declared war on all the moral precepts and customs of today, anarchy personified! Saying they were more popular than Jesus Christ, the Beatles could not have hit a bigger nerve or created a better opportunity for the poets of "<u>cordel</u>."

The poet identifies "longhairs" with thieves, playboys and effeminates. The government should arrest them all, shave their heads and give them a dose of discipline. In an interview by this author with the poet in 1981 Rodolfo softened his stance: "My attitude is not Puritanical. I'm not against longhairs per se; just look at Jesus or Balzac, they wore long hair. No, it's when they are immoral, show no respect, smoke grass. I'm against it."[21]

But in the poem he says it cannot continue; Brazil is going to degenerate into another Sodom or even a corrupt Rome. If one of the poet's four sons comes home with long hair, he will give him a whipping! He asks to be pardoned by his readers, but says he just cannot stand it and is revolted at this "foreign custom." The next thing will be nudism and then atheism! That's the real problem: it really is Communism infiltrating the youth of Brazil, starting revolutions, throwing bombs, killing government officials (the real political unrest of the late 1960s to be addressed in another Album).

The poet says a country without order certainly cannot have progress ("Order and Progress" is the Positivist motto on Brazil's flag), so he asks the current president, General Costa e Silva, to do something about all this. It is a shame upon Brazil! The poet later said the plethora of such "<u>folhetos</u>" was really a personal campaign of his in the 1960s "to combat what was not decent." He linked patriotism to order, order to respect and the current styles and morality to a lack of respect and a challenge to the old ways. All converged in the cauldron of political turmoil of Brazil in the late 1960s, yet another album of <u>Portrait</u>.

There were other topics dealing with moral decay, including several very new ones particular to the epoch such as the arrival of divorce, abortion, the ubiquitous Brazilian "soap opera" [Telenovela] and AIDS. But they belong to another album. Suffice to say that a good deal of this portrait did and does deal with proper behavior and deviations from it in a largely Catholic nation, a nation obviously in a state of flux. But with deviation comes punishment, the essence of our next snapshots.

2 The Moral Example [O Exemplo]

This type of cordelian "folheto" is in simplest terms a didactic story-poem which presents a moral lesson. One of the most important types of poem in the cordelian tradition, it is fundamental to understand the worldview of the cordelian poet and his public, the people of this Portrait. These are the poems which give examples of "punishment inflicted on man by the divine, punishment of people disobedient to the laws of the Messiah."[22] "Disobedient" can cover a broad range of actions from petty thievery to gossip to adultery but especially any action which is a consequence of lack of belief in the divine or making fun of those who do share such beliefs.

The literary form called the "example" [o exemplo] has its origins in religious and moral traditions from the Middle Ages in various European Catholic countries when writers (both religious and noble) treated social customs and the vices and virtues of man. The means used to transmit the message were among the most varied: sermons from the pulpit of the church using stories, fables and legends (many of oriental origin) and books of stories with similar origins to the sermons. An example was a work in prose of stories and fables with a moral message at their end in verse, Count Lucanor ["El Conde Lucanor"] by Don Juan Manuel (Spain, 1282-1300s). Later came the important Fictional and Nonfictional Stories of Profit and Example ["Contos e Histórias de Proveito e Exemplo"] by Gonçalo Trancoso in 1585. These are just two cases in point.

The moral story sometimes used a fable narrated in prose or a story in verse which illustrated the moral concept that the author wanted to express. This form of writing came on the one hand from the Latin exempla, thus the name "example," and on the other, from the oriental fable or story. The evolved form found in Brazil's "cordel" is dynamic. Its structure (with variations) is as follows: the sinner is converted into a monster or monstrous animal for mistreating family members or for being an "unbeliever," making fun of religion, faith or someone associated with the faith. The sinner has to wander the earth as punishment, suffering greatly, but also inflicting horrible pain on others instead of living happily on the road to God's paradise.

Sonia Brayner in an article "The Fantastic in the 'Literatura de Cordel'" talked of the business of the metamorphosis into an animal:

> The metamorphosis is a result of the evil associated with a temperament "so evil" that from his/her infancy he challenges the family structure: sister, mother, father. The transformation can also be the result of disrespect

to any entity held as divine or quasi-divine, like the case of Father Cícero. As one sees, the transformation is the form of punishment assumed by the transcendent or by some threatened social institution. (. . .) The aspect of religious punishment is fundamental. This is the aspect of fear that is desired in the readers, and is always accompanied by a moral element.[23]

So these stories are an example to the fearful reader to stay on the straight and narrow, for if not, punishment is sure to follow. But it is the unusual form that makes them so popular and abundant in this portrait: a fictitious story with wild, fantastic turns of event, yet with a veneer of reality or at least realism to make the "moral whopper" (as Candace Slater called it in her Stories on a String . . .) [24]more believable.

Perhaps the most famous of all these stories in modern cordel is Rodolfo Coelho Cavalcante's The Girl That Beat Up her Mother and Was Turned into a Dog on Good Friday ["A Moça que Bateu na Mãe na Sexta Feira da Paixão"]. The poet, in private, called such stories "nonsense," saying he would not waste time writing them if it were for himself, but in the same breath swore that his public demanded them, loved them and believed in them! He said the stories were reality for his readers. And even if one doubts the veracity of what actually happens, it is the idea that it could happen that sends chills up the spine of the humble outlander buying the "folheto."[25]

And the Bahian poet is not alone; his many colleagues, from the most traditional of old "cordel" to contemporaries living and writing in sophisticated Rio de Janeiro or São Paulo, echo the view in their story-poems. In a survey done in the late 1970s by this author, poets particularly from Juazeiro do Norte (the land of Father Cícero and religious pilgrimages, one of the places of Friar Damian's annual missions) waxed poetic in views about the "examples:"

They are really fine, providing examples and combating
the cruel evil of those who practice them.
(Manoel Caboclo e Silva, Juazeiro do Norte)
To defend the faith and the love one has in Jesus, Father
Cícero and Friar Damian, true live saint of the Brazilian
Northeast.
(Pedro Bandeira, Juazeiro do Norte)
People hear the sermons (of the Missions). The image stays in their psyche in
agreement with the details of the same. From one moment to the next appears

the fantastic story—poem. The people believe it. Give faith to it. Comment upon it. The poet writes about it.
(Abraão Batista, Juazeiro do Norte.)[26]

So these stories have a "moral." But they are important for the <u>way</u> the religious beliefs of Album I are expressed: the moral transgression takes place (sin) and certain punishment must follow (God's punishment) but under the strangest and most varied forms. What the sophisticated reader considers pure myth or humorous fantasy is a reality accepted by others. Accepted by all? Of course not, but the possibility of punishment for a moral wrong is the underlying factor.

A classic snapshot of the moral "example" is by the Bahian poet Rodolfo Coelho Cavalcante, <u>The Girl Who Beat Up Her Mother and Was Turned into a Dog (on Good Friday)</u>,[27] a prototype for the genre. The author claimed nearly one-half million copies printed and sold! In a particularly bad financial time for him from about 1960 to 1966, Rodolfo survived by selling trinkets and souvenirs in the markets and fairs of the backlands along with one story, <u>The Girl</u> . . . . He tells of filling a suitcase with copies of this poem and hitting the road for the little towns in the interior of Bahia State, living off just one title! The moral "example" is his forte, and over fifty per cent of all his titles (some 1700 by his own reckoning during forty-five years of "<u>cordel</u>" production) are moral lessons! They fit in with his psychic makeup, derived probably from his evolution from cradle Catholic to Protestant preacher to Spiritualist to the extreme, practicing a near puritanical morality as "The Evangelizer of '<u>Cordel</u>.'"

He begins <u>The Girl</u> by saying he will be telling one more example, that of the unbeliever and blasphemer with an empty heart who condemns religion! Those who make fun of God end up badly. Such is the case of one Helene Matias, daughter of an extremely religious mother, but a vain and false girl, the capital sins of "<u>cordel</u>." On a Good Friday in Canindé, Ceará, one of the Northeast's most holy places with its shrine to St. Francis, Helene tells her mother, "I'll be damned and turned into a dog if this so called Good Friday isn't a bunch of crap of our religion." Mom is startled and perplexed, and as the story pattern dictates, warns her daughter that such talk is the work of the anti-Christ, most especially on the day Christ was crucified! Helene reacts by giving her mom a good slap on the face, the old lady falls down in tears and swears that by God and the Virgin Mary and all the saints in heaven, Helene will be turned into an insolent bitch (dog) for such a grievous sin of hitting and disrespecting her own mother who in turn is a believer and respects God.

Helene makes matters worse by gnawing on some sun dried meat [charque]. One recalls no meat was allowed on Fridays and especially Good Friday. Helene then challenges God himself to turn her into a dog if He exists! In a flash it happens: her face changes, the bitch grows a tail, and Helene is a rabid, foaming at the mouth, horrible dog. With a human head and her own old features, she is "punished, a daughter damned for beating her own mother." Thus she begins her long series of wanderings and sufferings. She eventually repents, but the sin is too grievous for pardon (her mother and God are stern in this story), and her fate is to continue to wander, continue to suffer!

The poet, a former circus clown, writer of melodramas, primary school teacher and religious preacher, knew how to milk an audience. He would vary the telling of the poem in diverse printings, always mentioning the town where he happened to be selling his wares as the latest sighting of the girl, thus dragging them more into the story. And The Girl . . . was such a success that it produced a plethora of stories to follow, variations on an old theme.

So the poet and his many colleagues who produced "examples" were teaching, always stressing the evils of sin and the sure punishment to follow. But they were also entertaining, for the "art" of a good example was not the story line itself which was known and expected by everyone, but the "variations on a theme" and the poet's ability to dress up the story with some creative details and colorful language. The more monstrous the monster or animal, the more horrifying and evil its actions, the better the story. You did not have to believe the plot or the monster, although many readers did. The important thing was to have fun and accept the possibility, in fact, the inevitability of punishment by a severe but just God.

3 The "Phenomena"

Close relatives to the "example" are the "folhetos" called "phenomena" [fenômenos] or "cases" [casos]. These are once again didactic stories with a moral lesson, but are based either on real freakish births, natural phenomena but difficult to believe for their rarity, or outlandish events made to appear real by the poets. They are the "never before seen" persons or events. In either case, the freakish event or person is a result of God's punishment for a past transgression and is a sign of the Apocalypse. Liedo Maranhão describes these accounts as the stories of "people in the muck of sin without believing in the word of the Omnipotent God" or "God above, showing the phenomena."[28]

A perusal of titles explains best: The Two Children Who Were Born Connected Together, The Boy Who Was Born with His Head Turned Around, The Goat Who Was Born Half Goat and Half Person, The Pig that Gave Birth to a Little Boy in Santo Antônio de Jesus, The Girls that Were Born Stuck Together, Example of the Hairy Girl Baby in Paranatama. Two real life events made into stories were The Girl Born Outside her Mother in England and the most famous of such cases in Brazil in recent years, The Cowboy Who Gave Birth.

Above all, such events are news and appeal to that mysterious "darker" side of people, the same people who paid money to see the "freak show" in the old carnivals. Such stories in "cordel" provide the connection to the religious and moral vision of such people. The poet always makes it a matter of conjecture: surely this happened as a punishment from God. Someone must have sinned and sinned seriously!

The "phenomenon" that probably stirred most interest in all Brazil was The Cowboy Who Gave Birth, Phenomenon of Phenomena.[29] It was a story shared by "cordel" and the national media. Did it really happen? Was it a case of hermaphrodites in the backlands of Alagoas state? If it happened, why did it happen? Whose fault was it? The reader will find the answers when he considers the relationship between this "phenomenon" and the moral example.

It became big news in September of 1966. After the birth was reported in the local press in Alagoas, national magazines like Manchete and Fatos e Fotos (Brazilian magazines similar to Life or Look) and national television sent reporters to the scene. It was reported at the same time by the poet-reporter José Soares of Recife and several of his poet colleagues as well. Due to his haste to "scoop" other poets and the national press, Soares wrote a quick version with sloppy metrics and few facts, but that never stopped a poet from doing a story. In Soares' case it allowed him to quickly move on to a second printing due to the success of selling out the first.

He begins with the formulaic warning seen in most of the "phenomena" stories: the world is going to hell in a hand basket, the end is near. Why? Sisters are marrying brothers, daughters are shacking up with fathers. The way things are going, even religion is going to end! People want to undo what God has already done. Examples abound: an atheist made a deal with Satan, one girl married another in Minas Gerais, a pig was born with a gold tooth, and there is a bearded horse in Patos, Paraíba! And now there is this, an event he read about in the newspaper.

In Lages, Alagoas (a tiny town in the interior) a cowboy has given birth! Some say the cowboy was a woman, some say a man, and rumors run rampant. The mother of the new baby is Joana da Conceição, but because Joana's own mother had wanted a boy, her parents decided to call her João from birth and raised her as a boy. At the age of twelve, "João" drank sugar cane rum [cachaça] like all the other boys, rode wild ponies, dressed like a cowboy, and could drag down wild bulls like the best of them. "João" lived to cowboy and party, but did not like girls much, thus becoming known as the "girl-macho." But nature being nature and hormones, hormones, "João" fell in love with Pedro Augusto dos Santos, a fellow cowboy, and Pedro took "João" into the boondocks one fine day. Nine months later the baby was born, and the mother Joana is doing fine as is baby.

The locals are making fun of the whole thing, and Joana's mother is sure she is being punished by God for not leaving well enough alone. She was blessed with a baby girl and should have accepted the fact and raised her as a girl.

Doctors have come and examined Joana, and sure enough, she is all girl; there is no case of hermaphrodites. But the locals do not believe it and still think she's a freak. As for Joana herself, she has said in interviews that at seven or eight months she did not feel anything "special" aside from her stomach growing. She would try to hide it by tightening her belt more, but that was a bit painful.

But this is not the end of the story. One of the poets who improvised verse about the "Cowboy Who Gave Birth" added that you better be careful in Lages when you are around any of the "cowboys." One of the 'boys took umbrage and killed the poet with a long, northeastern knife used for cleaning fish, [a peixeira].

It was the poet's lead-in that makes the moral connection and follows the pattern of Northeastern traditional thinking: the birth was the result of sin, of mankind's arrogance and pride, trying to undo what God has already done, the greatest sin. But the story provided several days of mirth and entertainment, not to mention, speculation, for a public throughout not only the Northeast, but all of Brazil.

So now that Album III has told us how not to act, what should we do? The answer lies in the emulation of heroes and their virtues, the next album of snapshots in Portrait.

[1] It is good to remember that the concept of the moral foundation was well established by the master Luís da Câmara Cascudo as early as 1939 in his book Vaqueiros e Cantadores, Porto Alegre: Editora Livraria do Globo, 1939, p. 16.

[2] "O Mágico e o Fantástico na Literatura de Cordel," Sunday Supplement, O Povo, no author indicated, Fortaleza, March 25, 1970.

[3] Severino Simião, O Povo na Corrupção, n.p., n.d.

[4] José Costa Leite, Quem Tem Mulher Tem Trabalho, Condado, n.d.

[5] José Costa Leite, Os Prazeres da Juventude e a Traição da Mulher, Condado, n.d.

[6] Cuíca de Santo Amaro, A Mulher que Adulterou o Esposo, Salvador, n.d.

[7] Cuíca de Santo Amaro, O Crime de Brotas, Salvador, n.d. A variation of this title in another edition is The Woman Who Left Her Husband Unarmed.

[8] Cuíca de Santo Amaro, A Vingança do Homem de Brotas, Salvador, n.d.

[9] Cuíca de Santo Amaro, O Casamento do Homem de Brotas, Salvador, n.d.

[10] Antônio Apolinário da Cruz, Perto do Cabaré, n.p., n.d.

[11] Rodolfo Coelho Cavalcante, ABC da Meretriz, Salvador, n.d.

[12] José João dos Santos, "Azulão," A Era do Chifre, Engenheiro Pedreira, 1977.

[13] No author indicated, Editor Proprietário José Bernardo da Silva, O Namoro Moderno, Juazeiro do Norte, printing of 1957.

[14] Cuíca de Santo Amaro, O Namoro no Cinema, Salvador, n.d.

15   José João dos Santos, "Azulão," <u>Os Namorados de Hoje</u>, Engenheiro Pedreiro, n.d.

16   Manoel Apolinário, <u>As Maravilhas que Vê-se na Praia de Copacabana</u>, n.p., n.d.

17   José João dos Santos, <u>A Saia que Suspendeu</u>, Engenheiro Pedreira, n.d.

18   Rodolfo Coelho Cavalancante, <u>As Modas Escandalosas de Hoje em Dia</u>, Salvador, 1978.

19   Stanislaw Ponte Prete, <u>O Festival de Besteira que Assola o País—FEBEAPÁ</u>, 3rd. ed., Rio de Janeiro: Editora do Autor, 1966.

20   Rodolfo Coelho Cavalcante, <u>Os Resultados dos Cabeludos de Hoje em Dia</u>, Salvador, 1966.

21   Interview with the poet at his home in the Liberdade District, Salvador da Bahia, 1981.

22   Liedo Maranhão de Souza, <u>Classificação Popular da Literatura de Cordel</u>, Petrópolis: Editora Vozes, 1976, p. 47.

23   Sônia Brayer, "O Fantástico na Literatura de Cordel," <u>Boletim de Ariel</u>, Vol. 1, n. 2, 1973.

24   Candace Slater, <u>Stories on a String</u>, Berkeley: University of California Press, 1982.

25   Interview with the poet, Liberdade, May, 1981.

26   Declarations which appeared partially in the study already mentioned, "Os Poetas e Editores de Hoje em Dia", <u>Lore</u>.

27   Rodolfo Coelho Cavalcante, <u>A Moça que Bateu na Mãe e Virou Cachorra</u>, 25th printing, Salvador, 1975.

28   Maranhão, <u>Classificação . . .</u>, p. 50.

29   José Soares, <u>O Vaqueiro que Deu a Luz, Fenômeno dos Fenômenos</u>, Recife, 1978.

A Model to Live By: the Heroes of "Cordel"

Introduction

In one sense each album of <u>Portrait</u> could have been titled using a heroic character type from the cordelian universe: religious heroes, political heroes and the like.[1] But behind the types is a point of view. Since the life vision documented in "cordel" of tens of thousands of northeasterners, many now living throughout much of Brazil, is guided by religious and moral principals, in large part its life models, that is, its heroes, must be guided by the same principals. So it is not surprising that once again deep religious and moral ideals seen in these heroes will lead the Brazilian cordelian public down the right path. To put it in popular terms keeping in the spirit of this book, to keep on the right path one needs the "right stuff," and that is one way to define the heroes of <u>Portrait</u>. The deep, underlying virtues of the heroes of "<u>cordel</u>" are indeed "the right stuff:" honesty, integrity, fortitude [<u>firmeza</u>] and all the rest. And their opposites, lying, deceit,[<u>falsedade</u>] false pride [<u>orgulho</u>] are the "wrong stuff," the underpinnings of the villain who is also central to the challenge-response framework of "<u>cordel</u>."[2]

Having said this, it is therefore no surprise that the Brazilians who wrote, published, listened to and read the story-poems of "<u>cordel</u>" these last one hundred years have religious figures and leaders from the historic past among their greatest heroes, many the protagonists of Albums I and II. Jesus Christ is the "way and the truth," the greatest guide, and is followed by Mary the Mother, St. Peter, the apostles and saints, and especially those religious figures closest to the humble northeasterners, Father Cícero and Friar Damian. The wrong stuff? It is the devil himself or anyone following his ways.

But models for life reach beyond the realm of organized religion and morality, even though they must possess attributes flowing from the latter. So it is in other "traditional" stories of "<u>cordel</u>" where one can find the best possible document and memory of these models which comprise the heroes of <u>Portrait</u>. These heroes from the vast universe of "<u>cordel</u>"

come from a wide gamut of sources. Luís da Câmara Cascudo, the dean of Brazilian folklorists and perhaps the best of pioneer writers about "cordel," said the literature of the Brazilian masses of the Northeast consisted in three primary types: oral literature, traditional literature and popular literature. The heroes of "cordel" come from all three.[3] From the oral literature (to be seen in Album VI) comes the figure of the time-honored folk poet of the Northeast: the singer-improviser of oral verse [o cantador] who battles his opponents in a demanding poetic duel. From the traditional literature comes the broad phalanx of heroes of the chapbook literature of Europe which was the basis for the story-poems which comprise a large part of Brazil's "cordel:" heroes from the largely fictitious tradition of chivalry, fairy-tales of princes and princesses, romantic stories based on love and adventure, stories of animal heroes, and the stories of popular anti-heroes. And finally from Brazilian popular literature, one sees the entire heroic tradition created by the cordelian poets in Brazil since the late 1890s, original stories but based on the European models. One must include in this latter category, the original creations of the poets of the Northeast based on the "old" European or Oriental stories, and as well, all the real-life heroes depicted in the tradition of the current events and news stories in the chapbooks of eight pages, another important part of "cordel" since its very beginnings.

In almost all these stories good must win over evil, and the hero overcomes all manner of obstacles to achieve his (or her) end. The majority of "cordel" stories, some say as high as seventy per cent, which depict heroes are the long narrative poems of sixteen, most commonly thirty-two, and at times sixty-four pages called romances or histórias. These are the story-poems of love, suffering, adventure and a just victory to the good. The more obstacles, the more suffering, the more creative the evil opponent, the better the story. The hero wins by virtue of his own character and deeds, but also by virtue of belief in Jesus, Mary or another representative of the good. So, the religious-moral vision of the poet and his public remains intact.

The vast universe of our model-hero can be seen in the following fashion:

1. Heroes Recreated in Verse from Traditional Literature
   Charlemagne and the Twelve Knights of France
   Fairy Tales from the Oriental and European Traditions: Kings, Queens, Princes and Princesses, a Magic Peacock and Recent Northeastern Cordelian Adaptations
   The Animal Hero Adapted to the Northeast
   The Traditional Anti-Hero
2. The "Real-Life" Hero Remembered and Praised
   The Northeastern Bandit
   The Brave Man of the Backlands

1 Heroes Recreated in Verse from European Traditional Literature

Charlemagne and the Twelve Knights of France

As strange as it may seem, medieval Europe and the knights of Christendom found a new home in the interior of Brazil's Northeast at the end of the nineteenth century. Many of the same heroes of the French national epic, <u>The Song of Roland</u>, found their way into the homes of the humble outlander via a circuitous route. A modified prose version of the French epic (by way of Portugal and including many of its cast of characters) was put into prose in the "popular novel" in Spain and Portugal. The popular prose version arrived in Brazil and became primary reading on the ranches and plantations of the Northeast interior: <u>The Story of Charlemagne and the Twelve Knights of France</u>.[4] The poets of "<u>cordel</u>," Leandro Gomes de Barros the best known, took it upon themselves to transcribe the epic stories of Charlemagne from this prose version into the simple six or seven line strophes of "<u>cordel</u>" at the beginning of the twentieth century. Thus Charlemagne himself, but more so his favorite knights Rolando and Olivier, became known to the humblest of poor outlanders and came to epitomize their notion of the heroic. Luís da Câmara Cascudo, the dean of Brazilian folklorists, tells of encountering outlanders with the given names of Roland and Oliver, this in his younger days early in the twentieth century in his native state of Rio Grande do Norte and other states throughout the region.[5]

The cordelian poems about Charlemagne and his knights came to be sold in dozens of printings with many titles and had sales numbering in the hundreds of thousands over the century. They became the backbone of the heroic cycle of "<u>cordel</u>." Based only slightly on historic reality, they came to embody "the right stuff" in "<u>cordel</u>:" above all, the Christian paladins battling insurmountable odds in the person of evil "Turks" (as the Moslems, Moors, Saracens etc. came to be known) with the dream of converting them to the true faith of Roman Catholicism! And with the name of Our Lady on their lips, they became humanity's champions. Refusal to convert to the true faith (the only faith!) on the part of the evil Turks became the catalyst for armed combat either for forced conversion or to the death. The rewards were great: Christian baptism and the saving of one's very soul! Such lofty goals were mixed with the fantastic: battles facing thousands upon thousands of enemies, including giants, and the inevitable subplot of complicated love with cases of mistaken identity and incantations thrown in. (Out of such fiction, the novels of chivalry in the fifteenth or sixteenth centuries in Spain and Portugal, Cervantes created his great parody <u>Don Quixote de la Mancha</u>.)

Portrait retells one of the prototype stories for "cordel," The Death of the Twelve Knights of France.[6] The emperor Charlemagne, king of the French, has twelve knights who excel in his service, three of whom are his favorites: Roland, Ricarte and Oliveiros, the first his nephew and most beloved. Galalor, one of the original twelve, is "cowardly, vile, and a traitor who sold out to the Turks for a farthing, but who suffered a tragic death because God is just."

In a time of relative peace, the emperor sends Galalor to the kingdom of Saragossa in Spain with the purpose of christianizing the two local Turkish kings Marcírio and Belande (recall that Spain is still in the hands of the Moors). He wants them to "leave their idols and to adore Jesus." The mission begins well. Galalor acting as ambassador from the court of Charlemagne is received by the two kings, and the normal exchange of questions and information (an epic poetic tradition) takes place. But the two kings discover immediately that Galalor is a traitor: "By his appearance they could tell he lacked integrity." He agrees to set up an ambush of Charlemagne and his knights at Roncevalles Pass where the hidden Turkish armies can easily attack and cut them down. Here the poet is moved to complain,

> "Oh damned Galalor
> Man of evil destiny
> You were born of noble blood
> But avariciousness consumes you
> Already rich, you sold out
> Muddying your good name."

Using "black treason," you committed against God the most vile of all offenses, selling out your comrades. You will pay for this later! You are of the ilk of Judas who sold out Christ the Redeemer and even Adam who sold out his creator because of greed!

Galalor returns to Charlemagne with presents given by the Turkish kings to the leader of Christendom and lies ("cordel's" first and foremost sin, [falsedade!]), saying the Turks want to be Christians. The emperor sallies forth with five thousand troops heading to the rendezvous of Roncevalles where the Turks await him with no less than ninety thousand soldiers. Roland, Oliveiros and the rest of the Twelve Knights are in the advance troops while King Charlemagne, Galalor and others bring up the rear.

Battling valiantly, Roland sees the impossible odds and sounds his trumpet, the signal for reinforcements from the rear, but, alas, Charlemagne in the retro guard does not hear the signal. Roland plunges into battle once more after sounding the trumpet a second time, this time killing six thousand Turks all by himself! Twenty thousand more Turks arrive and charge

Roland and the remaining one hundred Christian knights. In the midst of pitched battle Roland discovers which of the Turks is King Belande and attacks, neatly slicing him in half.

Meanwhile Charlemagne is innocently passing the time with Galalor, playing board games. But King Marcírio, fearing the imminent arrival of Charlemagne, retreats to Saragossa and Roland, in the throes of death, wonders why reinforcements and the emperor have not arrived. But consoling himself in dying in good standing with the faith (he had confessed before entering battle), he makes his last act of contrition. The only bad part, aside from dying, is that he faces death alone without his comrades. There is time to address his wonderful sword "Durindana" and recall its mighty feats. He sounds the trumpet a third and last time, literally spilling his insides in the process, but this time Charlemagne hears the call. However, evil Galalor says it must just be a joke; Roland is just playing around!

Roland in a death scene rivaling the best from epic tradition (one recalls the <u>Iliad</u>), goes in and out of death, kissing his sword, remembering his battles and his comrades, and praying again. Praying in Latin (which the cordelian poet graciously translates into Portuguese), he gives up his soul, this "hero of the world."

At this point the poet, also following both erudite and popular epic traditions of formulaic change of scene, protagonists, and narrator, moves on to describe the Archbishop of Turpin who is joined while saying a mass dedicated to the Virgin. The soft sound of angels' voices reaches him, telling of the death of Roland. He rushes to tell Charlemagne the news as does "Valdivian," one of only two knights escaping the battle. All fall into tears, and when King Charlemagne reaches Roncevalles and discovers the body of Roland, he collapses to earth in heaving sobs, almost fainting from his overwhelming sorrow. In a litany of praise he recalls the virtues and deeds of Roland, "defender of the world, of Our Lady, of all humanity, aid of all Christians, pure guide of truth, strong column of the Church, the epitome of honesty." In this cordelian version of one of the most famous lamentations of the ages, Charlemagne prays, cries, praises, and complains of his and the world's own misery—to live without Roland is not to live at all! (This scene becomes a model for other heroic scenes of "<u>cordel</u>" and even of the Brazilian masterpiece, <u>The Devil to Pay in the Backlands</u>, arguably Brazil's best novel, written by João Guimarães Rosa in 1956!)[7]

Great fires are lit and the death vigil begins. But the emperor also prepares his vengeance, commanding that Galalor be found, bound and prepared for death. The next day the body of beloved "Oliveiros" is found, with no less than twelve lances stuck in his tattered body. Charlemagne's fury knows no bounds and he swears in an oath to the Virgin herself to avenge the deaths by killing Galalor and the Turkish kings. He catches up with part of the Turkish army at the River Ebro in Spain and in one fell swoop kills seven thousand Turks, wounding the rest. At this point one of the two Christian survivors of Roncevalles, Duke Trietre, tells Charlemagne of the real cause of the disaster, the treason of Galalor. Justice is quick; the dastard's limbs are tied to four strong horses and he is drawn and quartered.

The poem ends with the burial of the remains of Roland in the church of St. Roman, his sword Duridama at his head, his trumpet at his feet. Charlemagne commands the construction of a church in Roland's name on the site. The rest of the fallen knights are buried at Bordeaux and at Arles, and the emperor is left in his great sorrow. The poet ends with a humble formula, asking pardon for his "story of little art" and wondering where a poet competent to tell such a story could ever be found (once again one recalls the narrator of the Iliad and the hero Riobaldo in The Devil to Pay in the Backlands, both with similar questions).

Chronologically speaking, the story just retold in reality is only one of the series of cordelian poems treating the great emperor and his knights and armies versus the evils of the age, the vile pagans. Other stories are The Battle of Oliveiros with Ferrabrás, The Imprisonment of Oliveiros, The Battle of Charlemagne with Malaco, King of Fez, or Roland in the Lion of Gold, each greater than the last! Literally hundreds of pages of verse have been written both by the poets and hundreds more by scholars about the poets, but for the reader in Portrait it is the reality itself, the phenomenon of medieval Christian knights battling the infidel in far off times and places which matters. The heroic acts and virtuous souls become the model for one hundred years of Northeastern heroic poems in the "cordel."

Fairy Tales from the Oriental and European Traditions: Kings, Queens, Princes and Princesses, a Magic Peacock and Recent Northeastern Adapations

Just as the knights of the novels of chivalry of sixteenth century Europe would enchant the readers of Portugal and Spain (no less than St. Teresa of Avila was a fan, and Cervantes of course parodied such stories in his classic Don Quixote), so other heroes would fill the pages of popular novels and broadsides and eventually would become the heroes of the folk-popular literature of the twentieth century Brazilian Northeast. Princes, princesses, kings and queens, and all manner of evil enemies would populate the stories. Their titles are wonderful and endless: Story of the Soldier Robert and the Princess of the Kingdom of Canaan, The Secret of the Princess, Story of the Princess of the Beautiful Stone, The Princess Without a Heart, Princess Rosamunda or the Death of the Giant, or Story of the Princess Rose.[8]

This significant part of old "cordel" is comprised of literally hundreds of stories which came from the "traditional" popular novels of old Europe and were passed down in written form in prose and placed into verse by the early cordelian poets like Leandro Gomes de Barros or Silvino Pirauá. The most famous stories were treated in depth by Luís da Câmara Cascudo in his seminal Five Books of the People ["Cinco Livros do Povo"]: The Maiden Theodora, Robert of the devil, Princess Magalona, Empress Porcina and John of Calais.

Almost all the stories begin with a moral lesson (in prose in an epigraph before the poem begins or in verse in the first strophes of the poem): "A moving and sensational romance where cruel and ungrateful destiny dashes a young maiden upon the blackest path of existence. And she, fearless, overcomes all her suffering, all the treachery, thus being rewarded for her sacrifice and doing without." (Epigraph of The Triumph of Innocence or "Little Lady").[9] Other short examples are:

— One who is false never triumphs in life; one who is simple receives his recompense.
— In the power of God, destiny is like a book which only is closed with death.
— Faith in God brings happy results.
— The false person with his cynicism loses only when truth appears.
— Pride is the father of impiety, the twin brother of hate, and both engender evil and combat the truth!
— Love conquers envy; truth, lies; and justice, treason!
— Beauty and power may appear all powerful, but intelligence at times conquers them.
— The evils and power of money!

Many of these stories have their roots in the famous magical fairy tales themselves—popular variants of <u>Ali Baba</u>, the <u>Thousand and One Nights</u> or the Germanic tales found at a different time and place by the brothers Grimm. Snow White appears in a classic <u>romance</u> in Northeast Brazil, but without the seven dwarfs and instead in Asia Minor where a prince of Troy meets her (now a princess) and the two battle giants, sorcerers, Negroes and Indians, all the while in and out of magic spells that would make Don Quixote's head spin! Stories like <u>The Thief of Bagdad</u>, <u>Aladdin and the Magic Lamp</u>, <u>The Prince and the Fairy</u>, <u>Blue Beard</u> or <u>The Merchant and the Genie</u> deal with magic, promises, sorcery, evil villains, fairies, all in a complex and unbelievable series of events ending with a moral lesson—be faithful to your destiny and all will end well!

Perhaps the most famous cordelian poem of this type is <u>The Story of the Mysterious Peacock</u>,[10] and <u>Portrait</u> retells it. Its author, João Melchíades Ferreira, one of the pioneers of old "cordel," colleague and contemporary of Leandro Gomes de Barros and Francisco das Chagas Batista, is a major player not for the quantity of stories he wrote, but their importance. His <u>War of Canudos</u> is a seminal cordelian story of the journalistic vein, telling of the monumental battle in 1896-1897 between backlands religious "fanatics" and the Brazilian police and military who come to do them in. But he also penned one of the most famous <u>romances</u>, the <u>Peacock</u>.

It is a story of a mysterious peacock that began its flight in Greece and the story of a courageous young man who came, conquered and carried his true love off to happiness in Turkey. But his young maiden was a countess whose evil father was a "proud, arrogant count" who would oppose to the death the free choice of his daughter to love.

Our hero was called Evangelista, the son of a "Turkish capitalist," who hears of the incredible beauty of Creusa, the countess, and the fact that her father not only prohibits marriage but any contact with a possible lover ("a tough count, more arrogant than Nero"). She is allowed to show her gorgeous head in an appearance from the palace window once a year; the royal subjects then marvel at her beauty. Evangelista sees a photo of Creusa (poets are anachronistic and rather inaccurate when it serves them; the hero's home in Turkey is Mecca according to our poet). He falls head over heels in love and is determined to court and marry her; if not, he'll hang himself!

The only way to see Creusa is by stealth, so Evangelista manages to meet Dr. Edmundo who lives on "Workers Street" and who is a learned "engineer" who lives to invent "machinations." The learned doctor in effect invents an airplane, but in the form of a peacock: it is small, made of aluminum, powered by electric motor, with a gas tank and no horn, but lots of lights. With a tail, wings, neck, head and beak like a peacock, but also with a crank, key and starter button, "It flew like the wind in any direction." Best of all, it can be dismantled in a jiffy into a compact box. Dr. Edmundo also throws in at no charge a saw and an "enigmatic handkerchief" which if sniffed causes immediate fainting.

Evangelista uses the peacock to fly to the roof of the count's palace, the saw to make a hole in the roof, a long rope to climb down to Creusa's bedroom, and the magic kerchief over her mouth and nose to keep her calm. After three visits, each time declaring his good intentions to love and marry her, he makes progress with the heroine. Creusa at this point realizes what it is to love, what the freedom of love means, and how her mean father has actually been keeping her a prisoner instead of really just protecting her. There is a moment when she is forced by her evil father to try to trick Evangelista and identify him so they can catch him, but she confesses to our hero that this treachery really is coming from her evil father. Evangelist understands and realizes she is "innocent in her virginal role," and if she loves him, will carry her off to live happily ever after.

The count suddenly appears, angrily kicks his daughter but succumbs to Evangelista's magic handkerchief. Our heroes escape on the "monster with eyes of fire/ projecting its lamps" which zooms off in much more exciting fashion than the traditional flying carpet. The count's soldiers commanded to arrest the lovers grasp the truth: pride is an illusion; a father may govern his daughter but he cannot command her heart. The evil count dies in a fit of anger "for not being avenged." Evangelista and Creusa fly off to Turkey, get married and receive a telegram (!): it is from Mom who says Dad is dead, all is well, come and collect your inheritance. They fly off to Athens in the peacock, make a visit to thank Dr. Edmundo and are reconciled with Mom who says, "My daughter, you escaped captivity, and did right in fleeing and marrying in a foreign land. Take the inheritance, my son-in-law and inheritor." Such is the prototype for literally hundreds of such fairy tales in the rest of "cordel."

The stories are set in Scandinavia, Calais in old Normandy, Turkey, Egypt, the kingdom of Greece, in the Orient in the kingdom of Nicar, in Asia near Palestine, in a suburb of a dukedom, the kingdom of Orion, Germany, Milan, England in the times of Queen Elizabeth, Prague, Lisbon, in Turkey in the times of the emperor, in Alexandria, the Province of Arabia, the jungles of Africa, and Sodom itself!

But sources for the poets were still more varied; history, erudite literature and later the cinema would provide grist for the mill: stories like Helen the Goddess of Troy, Joan of Arc, The Story of Romeo and Juliet, The Lady of the Camellias, Iracema the Maiden with Lips of Honey, or The Robe. Many other dramatic stories from high culture were borrowed and recreated by the folk-popular poets of northeastern "cordel" and sold in the dusty markets of the backlands and the busy bazaars of Recife or Salvador. The names of the protagonists might change, the scenes might vary, but the great dramas and the moral vision and happy endings did not.

So this wealth of stories and their messages was put into the booklets of verse and sold by the tens of thousands of copies throughout the Northeast (and later wherever the Northeasterners would migrate throughout the twentieth century). But the matter did not end there: Leandro Gomes de Barros and his colleagues took the traditional story models, including even the episodic structure of the stories and certainly their moral messages, and created an entirely new genre adapted to their time and place in the world. Thus, the scene changed, the time changed, the names changed, but the essence remained the same. Stories like The Force of Love or Alonso and Marina, The Death of Alonso and the Vengeance of Marina, Story of the Sea Captain, Story of Mariana and the Sea Captain were originals written by Leandro imitating the old traditional classics. Story of the Indian Maiden Necy, The Fairy of the Borboremas, Story of Roques Matheus on the San Francisco River, The Fairy of the Borborema, Pedrinho and Julinha, Evil Paid for Good, Marriage and Shroud Made in Heavan, Sad Fate of Jovelina, The Romance of José de Souza Leão, The Story of Mariquinha and José de Souza Leão, and The Story of Zezinho and Mariquinha continued but with the drama taking place in the very backlands of the Northeast.

In the prototype Northeastern adaptation of such stories, the Story of Mariquinha and José de Souza Leão ["História de Mariquinha e José de Sousa Leão"],[11] a young cattle herder (read: poor commoner) flees a ferocious drought in Ceará state and finds work as a cowboy on the ranch of an evil rancher (read: evil duke) in another northeastern state. Our hero Joe falls in love with the rancher's daughter (read: princess), the two exchange love notes, and he carries her off into the sunset on his trusty horse. But he and she must battle thirst, horrible wild cats (read: dragons), and assorted other varmints in a great odyssey across the barren desert of the northeast interior. Finally, the hired thugs of the evil rancher (read: the evil soldiers of the king) come to do battle and José liquidates them all. Our hero then marries Mariquinha in a simple country chapel along the way, but being as good as they are, the heroes must return to ask her father's blessing. Joe asks for the blessing, but with his rifle in his hand. The father not surprisingly under the circumstances gives his best congratulations, they all go to celebrate the occasion with a Brazilian "cafezinho," and all ends happily ever after.

Just as pioneering poets like Leando Gomes de Barros, Silvino Pirauá Lima and a handful of colleagues created such stories from "old" "cordel" from the 1890s to 1920, their successors in a second and prolific new wave of cordelian authors would continue the tradition and create a modern variant on these old stories of love and the great adventures of their heroes overcoming all manner of obstacles to that love. Literally hundreds of variants on a theme were written, published in chapbooks and sold in the fairs, markets and street corners of the Northeast by dozens of authors throughout the heyday of the story-poems, from the 1920s to the early 1960s. These "John and Mary" story-poems in their own way continue the heroic tradition, but the hundreds of stories tend to resemble each other. After awhile, the reader finds it difficult to distinguish one from another (shades of the twentieth century television soap opera, a staple of contemporary Brazilian mass culture), but this in no way can take away from their great importance for at least forty years of poetic creation in the Northeast. They were best-sellers and a sure thing for the enterprising poet with a bit of imagination.

Examples are <u>Love Requited at the Bars of Prison</u>, <u>A Generous Citizen Deceived by His Consort</u>, <u>The Triumph of Love of Valerio and Violeta</u>, or <u>The Sufferings of Eliza or the Tearsf a Wife</u>. Variations on a theme is the best way to describe the hundreds of stories. In them one finds true love between husband and wife, true love between innocent, poor daughter and handsome young rich man, or between the rich daughter of an evil landholder and the poor son of an impoverished farmer. The villain is anyone getting in the way.

The Animal Hero Adapted to the North East

Variations from the old animal fables and classics like the <u>The Mysterious Peacock</u> (not really an animal but a story which would engender famous animal stories using the model) were heard and retold by generations of northeasterners via "<u>cordel</u>." Once again, the wonderful creativity of the bards would enable them to adapt the story of the animal hero to their surroundings. Because of fate and circumstance, some of these stories would be among the absolute best of all this folk-popular literature. Stories of magic wild bulls and wild horses would naturally become favorites in a region where cattle ranches were the mainstay of the colonial economy, the high and dry badlands and backlands, the infamous Brazilian "<u>sertão</u>." <u>The Mysterious Bull</u>, <u>The Mysterious Horse</u> and a plethora of variants would become famous and beloved to generations of outlanders when told by the magic pen of Leandro Gomes de Barros and colleagues.

<u>The Dog of the Dead</u> by the same Leandro would become a classic estimated to have sold a million copies! Strength, intelligence, fidelity and goodness are just some of the characteristics of man's best friend in this last and some say most famous of the <u>romances</u>.

<u>The Mysterious Bull</u>[12] by the poet Leandro Gomes de Barros is one of the most creative and <u>Brazilian</u> of all "<u>cordel</u>." It is the story of a bull that no cowboy on trusty horse was ever able to catch and pull down (the Northeastern cowboy does not use a lasso but throws the bull to the ground with a flip of his tail, a variation on U.S. bulldogging, but from the other end of he bull). Never was there underbrush and cactus that the bull could not run through, never a stream it could not leap in one bound, never a chase it which it tired, never a cowboy that could catch it! The narrator heard the story thirty years ago, and says it dates back to 1825, on the Santa Rosa Ranch in the backlands of the Northeast.

The bull's birth has to be told: its mother was called "The Mysterious Cow" because one night at the strike of midnight in the backlands, it was joined by two beautiful women and a talking bull which invited the women to climb on its back to take them home. The cow followed them and ever since has been known as "mysterious" or "bewitched," some saying it was the soul of a cow that died of hunger. Drought came to the backlands that year and the next, and the mysterious cow disappeared, that is, until August 24th, the day of the devil in those parts. On that day the cow gave birth to a young bull calf, black as coal.

A year later, with the return of the rains and subsequent roundup of the cattle, the old cow came in with her black bull calf, already amazing in size and appearance. An old Indian cowboy, wise in his ways, swears that there is no way that that old cow could be the mother of such an animal! At a year and a half it measures six hands, has huge horns a palm thick and hoofs making gravel of rocky soil. The cow and calf disappear once again for five or six years. Then a cowboy sees the bull and tries to catch it and bring it down, but is left in a cloud of dust. Thus begins the legend!

Cowboys come from far and wide and are offered wonderful prizes and wealth by Colonel Sezinando, the owner of the bull (fame, glory and booty, not unlike the prizes dreamed of by the Greeks camped outside the walls of Troy). Six cowboys at a time cannot catch it; word spreads that it must be enchanted! The names of the cowboys and their steeds are listed much like the heroes in a Greek epic or the knights in the Charlemagne stories. Chases last hours and even days, but with no luck. The old Indian cowboy Bemvenuto comes and goes in the story, always on its fringe, always mysterious himself, and declares the bull enchanted, son of a genie, nursed by a spirit from Egypt, and raised by a fairy in the local Borborema hills!

The rancher Colonel Sezinando forms the mother of all roundups, this time sending forty-five of the best cowboys of the region to catch the bull. But Indian Benvenuto mysteriously and conveniently says his horse is sick and he cannot join the chase. The cowboys on their sturdy mounts all run to the chase, tire and fail.

Suddenly a famous cowboy from Minas Gerais arrives on the scene, having learned of the fame of the magic bull. He comes not for the sizable monetary reward, but only for the sheer joy and challenge of the chase and knows he will catch this bull. An incredible chase ensues: bull and mounted paladin crash through the roughest brambles, briars and cactus in the region from ten a.m. until three a.m. the following dawn. Stragglers find the cowboy and his horse lying exhausted on the ground, the bull nowhere in sight. Now Sergio the Minas Gerais cowboy hero believes the story—a bull as fast as lightning, quicker than a fish in water and surely enchanted! He cannot go home for the shame of it all!

The rancher buys a new horse with the moniker of "Dangerous." It has killed four cowboys who tried to ride it, but Sergio will try once again. An incredible scene right out of the classic Western film Monty Walsh ensues: the Minas Gerais cowboy tries to break the incredible bucking bronco, digging in his spurs, the horse jumping more than three meters high and literally bucking off the saddle and rider (one cannot help but remember the classic Strawberry Roan a song of the old American West). In unusual cordelian understatement, the cowboy says, "this one will do."

Rider and new horse sally forth once more, spotting the bull at high noon. This time the bull runs up a mountain, the cowboy follows, branches break, rocks roll down the mountain, and "Dangerous" tires. Then the bull slams into the heaviest underbrush and races up another mountain with horse and rider in rapid pursuit. The bull enters a valley, then a high pasture, and finally an island in a river, but suddenly breaks out again, and Dangerous collapses. Sergio finally must admit this is an enchanted bull, too much even for him. The poet tells us the path the bull left in his escape was wide enough for fifty-nine horses to pass through without touching!

Sezinando the rancher now gathers <u>sixty</u> horses and cowboys for the chase, naming each man as though he were one of the twelve knights of Charlemagne! The poet admits "there were even more whose names I cannot mention, for the one who told me the story could not recall either." Sergio from Minas Gerais leaves, totally defeated, but the rancher calls for the old Indian Benvenuto once again. He has vanished, coincidentally on a Friday night, disappearing on horseback with his wife. People say the Indian was really a sorcerer, that a fairy decreed him to no longer be a cowboy and turned him into a deer. Others say he was murdered, a result of the colonel's dirty work. But a little old lady on a neighboring ranch who witnessed it all gives the most likely story: at precisely midnight on a Friday night she heard voices at the Indian's house. It was the magic bull who said he had come to see Benvenuto. Then the bull, the Indian and his woman left. She says, "Out you devil!" [<u>Credo em Cruz!</u>]. It must have been the work of the devil!

Sixteen years pass with no word. On St. John's eve amidst a great celebration on the colonel's ranch with typical festive bonfire, a black bull suddenly appears in the front yard of the ranch house, stirring up the dust with his hooves. Dogs bark, people flee and the party comes to a halt. The next day Indian Benvenuto conveniently shows up asking the colonel if they ever caught that black bull. The colonel, now suspicious, says Benevuto should know; when he disappeared, so did the bull! Indian Benevuto says it's a secret; he can't tell, but the bull is back and they can try to catch him.

Then Sergio from Minas appears out of nowhere saying he got the colonel's message the bull was back, and he's ready to try again. The colonel says he sent no such message; something fishy is going on again. But then a cowboy from Matto Grosso shows up; he looks like the devil himself (shades of <u>Crossroads</u> or <u>The Devil Down in Georgia</u>). He says his boss heard about the bull and sent him to catch it. His horse is blacker than dark night itself, and other horses seemed to fear it, a huge monster of a steed at eight hands. Eyes the color of hot coals, hoofs like a chisel, seven circles marking it from head to foot, and seven signs of Solomon on its left side! (The sign of Solomon is a good luck symbol in the backlands, to ward off bad luck and lightning, but this animal is depicted more like the Beast of the Apocalypse!)

Fifty-nine cowboys accompany the new rider, the devil himself if he exists, and discover the bull nearby. Bull, horse and rider fly off in fury, the fifty-nine and the colonel following, saying "Satan's hand is in this (shades of <u>Ghost riders in the sky</u>)." They come upon a crossroads, the devil's meeting place in Northeastern folklore, but instead of crossing, cowboy, horse and bull disappear into the road in a blinding flash of light, and an eagle and two vultures fly from it. Those who witnessed the event swear the earth opened up in the middle of the crossroads and the bull, horse and rider leapt into the opening.

The colonel and the rest of the fifty-nine cowboys return home; the devil-cowboy and his horse have disappeared. They say the eagle is the bull, changed by a fairy from inside the earth who also turned the horse and rider into the two vultures. Colonel Sezinando can take no more and sells his ranch and leaves the backlands. But today on nights when there is thunder, the old mysterious cow is seen at the crossroads as well as two women, talking, gnashing their teeth, and crying, this where it all took place. This story for all its power and glory may be the best of its kind in all "<u>cordel</u>."

The Traditional Anti-Hero

An important final part of the heroic tradition coming from Europe is that of the anti-hero, in its simplest sense, the hero without the trappings of the traditional "super" hero. This hero becomes just as much a champion as Charlemagne, but is really the poor man's hero: he is poor himself, but brainy and street smart, surviving by his wit. Some say he is just one step behind the devil. He was known as Pedro de Malas-Artes in Portugal, but became Pedro Malazartes in Brazil. And he engendered a plethora of cordelian figures, foremost among them Cancão de Fogo and especially the very northeastern João Grilo or John Cricket.

The model was from European popular tradition, really a universal figure who through his wit, his tricks and his bedevilment entertains and survives all odds. He becomes the "pícaro" in Spanish tradition, the famous Lazarillo de Tormes. In Portugal he is often the butt of the joke, a bit dull in the head, and easily fooled (is this the origin of the Brazilian Portuguese jokes?) But in Brazil in the Northeast he is once again the trickster, the deceiver, and always the underdog. He becomes known by many given names and types as well: he is "someone who uses his head" [quengo], or "a pallid, sickly looking (hence yellow), but clever rogue" [amarelo], who will literally die of hunger if he cannot find a way to persuade or steal a bit from others more fortunate.

The consummate anti-hero of "cordel" is John Cricket [João Grilo], a true rogue as described above, but made famous beyond the humble cordelian literature by a well-known adaptation and recreation in Brazilian drama, cinema and television by the renowned playwright Ariano Suassuna: The Rogues' Trial ["Auto da Compadecida"]. The author took some of the major cordelian masterpieces and made a classic play of them in 1955 in Brazil.[13] It is the story of this most northeastern of popular anti-heroes that Portrait chooses to summarize: The Deeds of John Cricket.[14]

Born a Christian, smart but ugly, John came into the world precociously at seven months, and there was an eclipse of the moon to mark the event! Small, thin, with the swollen stomach of the northeastern undernourished child, with skinny and crooked legs and a big mouth and lips, he was the talk of the town. His father died when he was seven, but in spite of it he lived from that time on joking and playing tricks on those he encountered.

In an early example of his mischievousness, a priest passes by his house and asks for water; John says there is none but he can have a drink of sugar cane water. After the priest drinks two cups, João tells him it was from a good sugar cane mill in spite of the fact there was a mouse floating in it! The priest yells and throws the cup to the ground breaking it into pieces. João scolds him, saying that cup was really his mother's bed pan. The priest vomits and declares that this child is the devil himself!

A bit later John Cricket decides to get even with the same priest who called him a little devil. He catches a lizard, puts it into a box and goes to confession to the priest. When the priest finds out he is confessing "the little devil," he raises a fuss, so John lets the lizard loose. It climbs up the cassock of the priest who jumps and hollers and finally must take off all his clothes to get rid of the lizard. Cricket replies: "So priests are men? I didn't know that; they always dress in a skirt like a woman!"

A second adventure is also motivated by the idea of taking vengeance when John remembers a past encounter with a Portuguese merchant. John approaches the Portuguese who is on his horse laden with two boxes of eggs to sell at market. Cricket asks permission to whisper a message to the horse, but puts a lit cigarette in its ear instead. The horse bucks off the Portuguese merchant, breaks all the eggs and Cricket is avenged again.

John goes to school at age seven and only lasts three years, but none can surpass him in cleverness, not even the teacher. He is a master of riddles (from the old European or Oriental popular literary tradition) and stumps the teacher. Later he robs some thieves who intend to split up their loot in a chapel (Grilo hides in a casket, dressed in a sackcloth, and scares the daylights out of the thieves who think he is a ghost from the other world). He thus fulfills the saying, "He who robs a thief, one hundred years of pardon" ["Quem rouba ladrão, cem anos de perdão"].

Cricket becomes known for his wisdom and is called by King Bartholomew, Sultan of Egypt, to solve some riddles (but the poet uses language and customs from the Brazilian Northeast: all drink a "cafezinho" and talk of drought in the backlands). The king has twelve questions for Cricket, and if he misses any one, it's curtains! Cricket answers them all and is rewarded with an easy life in the court with plenty to eat, having only to answer questions once in a while to earn his keep. On another occasion in court he puts a smart aleck duke in his place: the duke tried to charge a desperate beggar for "soaking" a piece of bread in the good smelling vapor of the duke's stew as it was cooking. By letting the duke just hear the sound of the coins he would fine the beggar for his infraction, analogous justice is done! (Such questions, riddles and situations were adapted by no less than Cervantes in Sancho Panza's island reign.)

A final episode is when Cricket is called to another rich kingdom to astound with his intelligence. Expecting a richly dressed, fine, wise man, the nobility of the kingdom see only a ragged Cricket, and although accepting him in the castle, they pay him no respect. Teaching them a lesson for their hypocrisy (refusing even basic courtesy to a guest because of his appearance), Cricket exposes their falsehood and they end praising him as one with the wisdom of Solomon!

Just as delightful is playwright Suassuna's adaptation of this same John Cricket in a modern morality play in a tiny town in the Northeast when Cricket tricks his former bosses, then an evil landholder, avaricious clergymen, and even a northeastern bandit. Called to account for his lies and tricks in a trial in heaven before Jesus himself, he outsmarts the prosecuting attorney (the devil) with the help of a good lawyer (the Virgin Mary herself who takes pity on the poor), and thinks he has outwitted the Mother of Heaven herself by persuading Jesus, with her support, to let him go back down to earth for a second chance at life. The play ends with his comeuppance and a lesson: you can't fool the Mother of God who happens to be the world and heaven's best lawyer!

Another of the great classics takes the trickster and combines him with the stories of Charlemagne. In The Gambling Soldier ["O Soldado Jogador"][15] Ricarte (by coincidence or not, the same name as one of the twelve knights of France) in this story is a gambling soldier who must attend an obligatory mass for military personnel. But he gets caught looking at a deck of cards in mass and is arrested. He explains in his defense before the commanding officer that since he is a simple soldier without rank (even though an inveterate gambler), he cannot afford a daily mass missal, so the deck of playing cards serves that purpose. Accused of blasphemy, he defends himself by explaining the symbolic religious significance of each card, the Ace the creator, the King, Jesus Christ, the Queen, Mary, and so forth. The reader is left wondering, is he sincere and a believer, or is this a consummate conman? Brazilian folklorist Theo Brandão collected dozens of international versions of the same tale amassing more than five hundred pages of manuscript, thus proving its universality. And no less than T. Texas Tyler in the U.S. wrote a country and western version in the late 1940s which was recorded and made into a national hit by Tex Ritter called "Deck of Cards."

"Cordel" abounds with the clever tricksters like John Cricket or even "Master Vulture" seen in Album I—the anti-hero who happens to be a smelly, vile vulture but a very Catholic defender of the faith who perseveres against the Protestant upstarts in a masterpiece of cordelian humor! Such are the heroes from the fictitious mode of the folk-popular poetry. But there are many more, and this second type of hero comes from the real life experience of the Northeast and its cordelian public.

2 The Real Life Hero Remembered and Praised

There is another kind of hero for the poets and public of <u>Portrait</u>, a hero found to be sure in hundreds of booklets of verse throughout the twentieth century, but in those story-poems more closely linked to real life. This is the role model coming from the daily existence and experience of the Northeasterner, once living in the heart of the Northeast, but now perhaps a migrant in the Amazon region, or in São Paulo or Rio de Janeiro in the industrial south-center or even Brasilia the new capital. The main fact about this hero is that he or she exists in real life as well as made a memory in the poems. And although this hero may come from a multitude of facets of life, his characteristics were already modeled in the traditional heroes previously seen in <u>Portrait</u>. The same virtues abound, and the same vices are in the famous villains of modern "<u>cordel</u>."

The form and format of these cordelian heroic stories is incredibly varied. Closest to the "traditional" heroes is the figure of the northeastern bandit [<u>o cangaceiro</u>] once accurately presented in almost journalistic fashion, then made myth. Less based on known real-life models, but yet fashioned on a "type" from Northeastern ranch life is the figure of the "brave man of the backlands" related to the stories of love, suffering and adventure already seen. But a third type is the real person, the personage, [<u>vulto</u>] as the poets call him, a known figure in local, national or even international life. This may be a famous local popular type like "Big Birth" [<u>Nascimento Grande</u>], a colorful giant of a man in old Recife, or Cosme de Farias who spearheaded literacy drives in Bahia, a national political figure like Getúlio Vargas who became associated with the hopes and aspirations of the masses, or more likely today, a soccer star or a singer or actor from the ubiquitous television soap operas [<u>novelas</u>].

This latter group will be described and detailed in other albums largely because they appear more likely in a journalistic function as an event of the day, but clothed in the garments most often of the traditional hero (or at times the villain). Thus the great Getúlio Vargas, "Father of the Poor," or Tancredo Neves, "Martyr of the New Republic," will appear in Album VII "In politics we hope, but do not trust." And the arch-villains Mussolini, Hitler or Juan Perón will appear in Album VIII "There is a big world out there", and Pelé, Mané Garrincha, Roberto Carlos, and Luís Gonzaga will have their place in Album VI "But we have our distractions." In one way or another, all are admired, and occasionally the poets will wax heroic in their descriptions, using terms and formulas from the traditional stories of fiction already seen.

The Northeastern Bandit

Closest to the old heroic spirit of folk-popular poetry from Europe and the early models from the Northeast in a huge quantity of stories is the northeastern bandit [o cangaceiro] and his "cousin," the "brave man of the backlands" [o valente]. These stories at times will use story line, description of characters, and religious and moral underpinnings for heroes modeled from traditional "cordel."[16] Portrait sees first the "cangaçeiro," the northeastern bandit.

The heroic bandit is a vast theme in the poems: he is a combination of backlands bandit, gunslinger, criminal, and battler for justice and the poor of Brazil's Northeast. In recent "cordel" he is less bandit and more of a true epic type, larger than life, a true "knight" or paladin of the backlands. Instead of armor and sword, he may wear the leather leggings, vest and hat of the northeastern cowboy, but now with metal "Signs of Solomon" pinned on the upturned brim of his northeastern style leather cowboy hat. He may sport bandoleers cross his chest, a heavy revolver in his belt on one side, a razor edged knife on the other, and he may tote a Winchester 44. (The story-poems' treatment of the bandit forms a somewhat loose analogy and comparison to folk heroes Pancho Villa and Emiliano Zapata of the Mexican "corridos"). This bandit hero (or anti-hero at times) is referred to throughout the poems by epic epithet: King of the Bandits, King of the Backlands, Terror of the Northeast, Lion of the North, Master of Death, or in the case of the infamous Lampião who was blind in one eye, "The Blind Rooster." He is truly a folkloric and modern cousin of the medieval knights of Charlemagne, of Roland or Oliver. The scene of a Charlemagne pouring out his tears and soul upon the loss of his trusted and dear paladins is repeated in a poem of that "Robin Hood" of the Northeast, Antônio Silvino, who cries for his lost (dead) companions. And the same scene is repeated once again, and by no coincidence, when Riobaldo laments the loss of his beloved fellow bandits and his love in the great modern Brazilian novel The Devil to Pay in the Backlands ["Grande Sertão: Veredas"] by João Guimarães Rosa.

It is the folk narrative process of idealizing reality, of converting it into myth and legend, that is seen most in this hero of "cordel." The bandit in point may be an historic figure who really lived and practiced terrible acts, or an entirely fictitious hero based on old stories. No better example of the first is the most famous bandit of all, the greatly feared Lampião ("Flash of Light") who literally terrorized the Northeast for over twenty years until 1938 when he and his consort Maria Bonita were mowed down in a bloody ambush by law officers, a scene reminiscent of the climax of Bonnie and Clyde in American lore and cinema. The real Lampião, a truly bloodthirsty bandit who lived only by the code of violence and vengeance, has been converted into a romanticized hero, made folkloric and mythic, an altogether different image than that of his fierce and bloodthirsty real life.

A similar phenomenon took place with the real life bandit Antônio Silvino of Paraíba who originally stole, robbed and fought those who got in his way but now is a cordelian Robin Hood robbing the rich (who else? the poor in the Northeast have nothing to rob) and giving to the poor.

According to folklorist Câmara Cascudo, the bandit was originally an errant criminal robbing citizens, sacking small towns in the interior of the Northeast and consequently being pursued by the law. Once caught, and it took years, he was either imprisoned or shot to death. But the problem is that the bandit according to the poor public of "cordel" invariably was a victim of society, forced to enter the "dark side" by a basic lack of justice in the backlands. The story for Antônio Silvino and Lampião is much the same: a father or relative is shot in cold blood, and there is a lack of response or refusal to seek justice by local law officials in cahoots with the perpetrator of the act. The victim, Antônio Silvino or Lampião, ends up taking the law into his own hands and punishing the killers by death. He then, in turn is inevitably pursued by those protected by the "law" and becomes a new victim. The bandits always seem on the verge of "leaving the field," always pine for home and family, and always simply want peace and justice.

But reality intervened: Antônio Silvino was caught, tried and imprisoned by the police in Pernambuco state, served a long jail term as a model prisoner, rehabilitated his life and put his sons through school. Lampião, however, met the bloody end just described, riddled with bullets on a small ranch in Sergipe state. The heads of him and his paramour Maria Bonita were severed, put in kerosene cans and taken on a macabre odyssey throughout the Northeast, this proving to unbelieving outlanders that the bandits really were dead. The heads were later put on display in no less than the famous Nina Rodrigues Museum next to the Medical School of Salvador da Bahia where they were viewed by the public for over thirty years until civic disgust and outcry finally forced a burial.

One of the largest themes in the story-poems with a vast bibliography, the stories of the bandits are among the most colorful of the poetry. Sociologists and some political scientists see the bandits as victims of society or as incipient social revolutionaries, victims of class justice. But folklorists see them as embodiments of the hero of ages past in some cases, and anti-hero in others. They are central figures in Brazilian literature, cinema and modern television drama, but are almost always idealized, made myth and often are portrayed with little resemblance to the cold, hard reality they represented in the Northeast: local men facing backlands justice and the great task of surviving in a cruel, violent world. They were depicted variously as victims, as doers of justice, as courageous, strong, men of integrity fighting evil. But the reality was that they lived a severe code of "with me or against me," honoring and protecting sworn friends and coldly liquidating enemies when attacked and cornered. (Was Roland different? Did Charlemagne sees the infidels in a different light?) Victimized or making victims of others? Hero or villain? Hundreds of the story-poems registered, documented and sang their deeds, first of all in a journalistic fashion contemporaneous to their lives, later in poetic fiction made larger than life by poets and a public in need of real-life heroes to match the heroes of other times and places in their fictitious world of romance.

Because the literally hundreds of stories of each major figure, either Antonio Silvino or Lampião, cannot possibly be done justice in a few pages (or perhaps in many), Portrait chooses a modern cordelian story, pure fiction but highly representative of the bandit stories, to speak for all. The Encounter of Lampeão with Antônio Silvino[17] is by the poet José Costa Leite of the interior of Pernambuco state, a wonderful poet who worked across the decades, and is still working as an old veteran of the poetry at this writing. In his poem Portrait hopes to capture the essence and the flavor of this real life modern hero.

The poet says this story is for those who like to read stories of the "brave men," of men who will slit their enemies' throats and wipe the blood on their hands! He describes Silvino first, a man from the Pajeú region where men are men, where they ride Brahma bulls instead of horses and the weakest are weaned on cougar's milk! Lampião on the other hand was the "terror of the region," wicked since birth, and did not fear to trade life for death. Both are perverse, worse than Satan himself! Such men never die in their sleep!

But then the poet uses legend: Silvino who is a good and just man became a bandit because a rich rancher killed his father, and the local police did nothing! Such is law in the backlands: you live with a gun in your hands, the strong are right.

"Crime, robbery and death,
That was the law that existed.
Talk was only of bandits,
And no one could resist or escape.
Bullets zoomed from one side,
Blood poured from the other." [p. 2]

So Silvino took up the gun, avenged his father's death and began to kill people; police, soldiers and bounty hunters followed him in endless pursuit. He could not get an honest job but had to rob the mail, banks, trains and ranches to survive. His fame grew in the backlands. He mysteriously escaped capture and death, often due to the prayers or incantations he had learned (recall The Mysterious Bull and Indian Benevuto).

Meanwhile Lampião hears about Silvino and wants only to slice his throat with his foot-long knife. His rifle flashed in so many battles at night that he became known as "Flash of Light" [Lampião]. His sidekick was his woman, Maria Bonita, the wife of a simple shoemaker, fancied by the bandit for her beauty in a casual meeting and carried off into the sunset on the back of his trusty steed. His gang has sixty-two men, "the kind that drink blood" and fight a cougar hand-to-hand, never running from a fight. To live is to battle, to face fate, to confront death, and if you die, that is fate, no more. He becomes renowned in battles in six states!

The poet, in a similar switch of narrative as that of the poet who told of the death of Roland, turns to the meeting between these two terrors of the backlands. Silvino is holed up at the ranch of a friend, and they eat local delicacies like corn bread and other northeastern treats, talk and head off to sleep in their hammocks. But Lampião and his troops arrive in the middle of the night, and following cordelian custom, announce themselves, loudly banging on the ranch door, saying "Open the door, it's Lampião" (since the earliest "cordel," adversaries will bang on doors, announce their intentions as a preliminary to pitched battle).

So the epic battle begins, a real shootout! Bullets whiz in all directions; smoke fills the house. Maria Bonita drills three men with one shot (the poet says she is worse then Lampião, smiling when she cuts an enemy's throat and watching him roll in pain on the ground). Silvino leaps on Lampião and the two enter into hand-to-hand combat, "like two beasts foaming at the mouth amidst gnashing of teeth," no one guessing which one is braver." Lampião pulls his knife three hands long and says, "Silvino, prepare to die." Silvino, fast as a cat and possessor of magic prayers, stabs Lampião, but his knife will not penetrate. Lampião in turn, knowing just as many magical prayers, stabs at Silvino, but his knife bends on contacting Silvino's stomach. Both facing "cold steel" leap like monkeys, but eventually reach a standoff, regarding each other like one python ready to devour the other.

They see each other as undefeatable and recognize each other as the greatest bandit of all, so all ends well when Antonio Silvino and Lampião give each other a big Brazilian embrace [abraço]. Wounds are wrapped to heal, the dead are buried, and all drink a nice, hot, strong and sweet Brazilian "cafezinho" to seal the friendship! Such is the fictitious encounter of the two most bloodthirsty bandits of the Northeast, but between the lines the traits of the hero remain: great strength in battle, a complete lack of fear, great respect for one's enemy, no holds barred in a life and death struggle, but eternal friendship to the deserving. No greater respect could be given a worthy and noble enemy.

The Brave Man of the Back Lands

The brave man of the backlands is the hero of hundreds of poems in a special story type in the poetry; he is a true northeastern hero with attributes of the traditional hero already seen in cordelian fiction. The most famous of all the brave men of the backlands is the hero from the story The Brave <u>Vilela</u> ["O Valente Vilela"].[18] Vilela dominates through his strength and dexterity in the epic battles in the backlands. But he is a different arch type than that of the famous bandit like Lampião. Like the bloodthirsty bandit, he begins life as a killer with an evil disposition, but in the story he is not depicted as an assassin per se like Lampião, but as "a man condemned to exile for his crimes, a man hiding from the law, desiring only to live in peace, and incapable of surrender to the same. He is a man who will defend his freedom even unto death" (a statement by Luís da Câmara Cascudo about Vilela in his classic <u>The Flower of Tragic Romances</u>, introduction).

Vilela in this poem represents the most admired traits of the courageous man of the backlands: the common man, married, faithful to his wife, with incredible courageousness and almost superhuman traits. As the reader shall see, Vilela will listen to the plea of his wife to not kill the sheriff's lieutenant sent to arrest or kill him and who commits suicide after losing face to Vilela. Our hero repents of his crimes, does penance for forty years in the backlands, is saved, dies and becomes a saint! He is thus an example, an ideal model for his courage, his repentance and his devout contrition for all he has done in the backlands. He is called the "divine bandit" by no less than Câmara Cascudo and is a fitting climax to this album of the traditional heroes of <u>cordel</u>.

The poet tells the story of a man so brave even the law itself was afraid of him. Of foul temperament, he killed a brother when he was ten in a fight over a toy, the son of his godfather a few years later at age fifteen while hunting, and his brother-in-law at age eighteen. The local police sent a force of thirty-six men to arrest him, and not one survived to tell about it. Yet another force was sent, larger than the last, and they were gunned down as well.

Finally a brave lieutenant [<u>alferes</u>] promises to bring Vilela to justice. After a long journey into the backlands he arrives at Vilela's ranch and challenges him from outside the ranch house door (the customary beginning of the battle in "<u>cordel</u>"). They both brag and trade the customary insults (a back and forth challenge and response that is the key structural element of the poetic duel between oral improvisers of cordelian verse to be seen in a later album, and for that matter, for most of the bandit or brave backlands stories).

The insults are similar to those just seen in the battle between Lampião and Antônio Silvino. The lieutenant beats on the door of the ranch house, demanding to be let in, saying, (read left to right):

The Lieutenant says:

"My revolver breaks any lock;
My knife opens any bottle.
I bring 180 armed men,
Born to fight, raised for a ruckus,
Men who drink blood
Like others drink punch." pp. 92-93.[19]

The Lieutenant responds:

"Vilela, I've eaten bacon
With more hair on it than you;
I'm going to rip the fingernails
Right off your hand.
Open the damned door
And come on out to the field of honor."

Vilela answers:

"Nobody gets me out of my house
I fight on my feet, I fight lying down
I fight leaping over crevices,
Bullets bound off me like popcorn.
I fight with clothes, I fight naked
Bring on your 180 men.

Vilela says:

Better be quiet Lieutenant
And cut out all the hot air.
A man who has killed a hundred
Might as well make it a 101.
I haven't eaten yet today,
So I'll break my fast with you.

The lieutenant retorts,

"Vilela, you're fooling yourself;
Your crimes consume you.
You may be the terrible tiger,
But I'm worse than a werewolf.
Talk is cheap;
I'm also a man."

Vilela then appeals to a softer side of the lieutenant, telling him to go home, raise his family, take care of his wife and child. If not, they'll be left alone. The lieutenant concludes, "Vilela, this time I'm serious. I'll either take you tied up to jail or in a hammock to the cemetery." Vilela responds,

"Lieutenant, a bull on the loose
Licks whatever it wants to.
I'll never go to prison;
I'd rather die first . . . ."

The lieutenant has brought one hundred and eight troops from the king, "our emperor" to fight Vilela, but when he turns around, he discovers all have fled. He is alone to face Vilela.

So a ferocious duel begins between the two. Bullets whine through the air, smoke covers all, and Vilela leaps to escape the flying lead. Even the bullets that seem to hit him somehow bounce off his leather clothes (he has the magic of Lampião). Guns now empty, the brave rivals face each other with cold steel, the true and final test of backlands bravery. Clashing knives give off sparks like a blacksmith's forge. The lieutenant trips and falls and Vilela in a flash has his knife at his throat. The lieutenant says it was because he tripped, not because he was less a man, and prays to almighty God to have pity on him, a family man: "Free me from swallowing such bitter bile." Vilela is ready to cut his throat, but suddenly hears a voice, "Don't kill the man, my husband, have pity and let him go."

Vilela is really irritated and says,

"Woman, get out of here;
All you are is a pain in the neck.
If the tables were turned,
Do you think he would let me go?
When I heard the footsteps
I knew it was you.

So you've left the house
And your duties and the baby.
This is a man's business
So just stay out of it . . .

She responds,

"I never saw anyone
With such an evil temperament.
How can you kill someone
Who never offended you?
Kill me instead. If you kill him,
Who will take care of his children?

Vilela says,

"I can't understand women,
They are sneaky
And don't play by the rules;
When it comes to women
Arguing with their husbands
They are damned stubborn.

> But when they want something,
> They all turn soft and whiny.
> Okay, let the damned lieutenant go
> And let him get the hell out of here.
> And tell him
> My woman was his lawyer!"

The defeated and humiliated lieutenant leaves, sad and lifeless. He is so disgusted with his fate that he believes he has no alternative but to commit suicide. Vilela, also upset that the fight was not allowed to come to its natural conclusion, but feeling responsible for the death, disgustedly leaves the ranch. He finds a hidden corner of the backlands, becomes contrite, does penance for forty years and dies a saint. The poet ends in great epic fashion,

> "Good greetings my readers,
> My story has come to an end.
> The lieutenant was valiant
> And died a brave man.
> But more valiant was Vilela.
> He died, became a saint and was saved."

The incredible epic overtones of the story, the link to the famous battles of cordelian bandits like Lampião and Antônio Silvino, Vilela's wife as the woman lawyer for the helpless (reminding of the role of the Virgin Mary in The Punishment of the Arrogant Soul, a cordelian classic used as the basis for Ariano Suassuna's The Rogues' Trial), and finally the traditional, orthodox repentance, contrition, and penance leave the violent killer who was Vilela reformed and a saint. He will go on to become the model for other heroic backlands heroes in countless cordelian stories. Valiant Vilela thus indeed becomes the "divine bandit" and is a fitting climax to Portrait's album of the traditional heroes of "cordel," models to live by.

---

[1] This is why the research team of the Casa de Rui Barbosa in Rio de Janeiro, in their important classification of Popular Literature in Verse, decided to use the model of the heroic in their series of books on "cordel." See <u>Literatura Popular em Verso. Catálogo</u>, Rio de Janeiro: Casa de Rui Barbosa, 1961.

[2] This is in agreement with the vision already cited in Luís da Câmara Cascudo in his <u>Vaqueiros e Cantadores</u>.

[3] Cascudo's is a longstanding theory, but it is summarized in "Da Poesia Popular Narrativa no Brasil," in: <u>25 Estudios del Folklore</u>, México, D.F., UNAM, 1971.

[4] Thanks to the kindness of researcher Joseph Luyten, we have a Xerox copy of the version in prose published by the Garnier Bookstore of Rio de Janeiro. It was this prose version that came into the hands of pioneer cordelian poets like Leandro Gomes de Barros or Silvino Pirauá Lima. It was such poets that converted the prose into sextets and septets in the old romances of "cordel" and through an elementary sales network spread them throughout Brazil's Northeast in the final days of the 19th century and beginning of the 20th.

[5] Facts revealed to us in an interview with Professor Cascudo at his home in Natal, Rio Grande do Norte, September, 1966.

[6] Marco Sampaio, Editor José Bernardo da Silva, <u>A Morte dos Doze Pares da França</u>, Juazeiro do Norte, printing of 1941.

[7] See our textual comparison of "cordel" and the masterpiece of João Guimarães Rosa, "Grande Sertão: Veredas e a Literatura de Cordel," in <u>Brazil/Brasil</u>.

[8] The seminal work on the topic is still Luís da Câmara Cascudo's <u>Cinco Livros do Povo</u>, Rio de Janeiro: Livraria José Olympio, 1953.

[9] Francisco Guerra Vascurado, Editor José Bernardo da Silva, <u>O Triunfo da Inocência</u>, Juazeiro do Norte, n.d.

10 João Melchíades Ferreira, "Proprietors," the daughters of José Bernardo da Silva, <u>Romance do Pavão Misterioso</u>, Juazeiro do Norte, printing of 1975.

11 João Ferreira Lima, Editor Proprietário José Bernardo da Silva, <u>História de Mariquinha e José de Souza Leão</u>, Juazeiro do Norte: Typografia São Francisco, n.d.

12 Leandro Gomes de Barros, Editor Proprietário José Bernardo da Silva, <u>História do Boi Misterioso</u>, Juazeiro do Norte: Typografia São Francisco, n.d.

13 We pointed out the texts of the romances adapted and recreated by Suassuna in our <u>A Literatura de Cordel</u>, Recife: UFEPE, 1974, chapter 4.

14 João Ferreira de Lima, "Proprietors," daughters of José Bernardo da Silva, <u>As Proezas de João Grilo</u>, Juazeiro do Norte, printing of 1975.

15 <u>O Soldado Jogador</u> was annotated in Álbum I.

16 See Luís da Câmara Cascudo, <u>Flor dos Romances Trágicos</u>, Rio de Janeiro: Editora do Autor, 1966.

17 José Costa Leite, <u>O Encontro de Lampião com Antônio Silvino</u>, Condado, n.d.

18 Attributed to Francisco das Chagas Batista and also to João Martins de Atayde, the author is not indicated; Editor José Bernardo da Silva, <u>O Valente Vilela</u>, Juazeiro do Norte, Typografia São Francisco, n.d.

19 This strophe and succeeding strophes were taken from: Curran, <u>Antología Bilingüe da la Literatura de Cordel</u>, Madrid: Editorial Orígenes, 1990.

Album V

Life Is a Struggle and Life is a Saga

Introduction

The most basic day-to-day reality of the masses of Brazilians who write, print, sell or read "cordel" is that they are poor and are from among the most underprivileged of Brazil's social classes. But at the same time, ironically, they have produced one of the most entertaining self-portraits of Brazilians, that is, of themselves and their lives in the booklets of verse: memory and record of much of the Brazilian national reality.

The folk literatures of the world always deal with the plight of the poor, for it is the poor who compose, sing or recite such literatures. The Mexican song-ballad [corrido] for instance has as a major theme—"about misery," ["de la miseria"]. "Cordel" is no different, and this topic in particular is a key to Portrait. The poets have a formulaic phrase and even a formulaic tone of voice when they talk about the vicissitudes of life: "Life is getting difficult" ["A vida está ficando difícil"]. The northeasterners say this in almost a sing-song tone and a weary look in their eyes. Portrait's snapshots reveal this reality; it is as much the essence of the protagonists of this book as their faith, their moral view and their idea of the heroic. Their poverty in effect defines them, but so does a richness of spirit seen in a will to survive. From its very beginnings in the late nineteenth century, cordel dealt with the difficulties in life. Above and beyond other factors in a day to day eking out of daily bread was the question of how expensive it is to live. This important theme is reduced to one word in Portuguese: "carestia" (the high cost of living). Poets from Leandro Gomes de Barros' times in 1910 to the most contemporary of recent days in the 1980s and 1990s, poets hailing from the Northeast to Rio and São Paulo, all echo the theme.

The theme is always framed by a consideration of climatic events and calamities, by economics, and very often by politics, the latter of necessity another album of Portrait related to the evolution of the twentieth century in Brazil. And it really cannot be separated from all the poems dealing with the rich and the poor, more "philosophical" stories with a more resigned tone than those dealing directly with the cost of living. The tone of the latter stories varies greatly: from a stark, dismal lamentation to sharp, biting, sarcastic, or humorous commentary on the times.

In any case, it is this topic and the hundreds of stories which treat it which give a very realistic dimension and in one sense a truly accurate image of the protagonists of <u>Portrait</u>. One reads the stories and cannot help but be drawn in emotionally by the detailed descriptions of the daily struggle for life, for survival of the poets and their public. The Northeast is the poorest region of the potentially rich country called Brazil, and Recife, the main center for the story-poems for fifty years of the twentieth century, has been compared to Calcutta because of its poverty. Behind all is the difficult nature of life, but between the lines is the same vision of hope and faith that dictates that somehow, sometime, someone will make things better.

1 Difficult Times in the Early Days: the Chronicle of Leandro Gomes de Barros

One way to look at the difficulties of life is through humor. In one of his classic poems, The Power of Money, the High Cost of Living, Incredible Crisis ["O Poder do Dinheiro, a Carestia da Vida, Crise para Burro"],[1] the pioneering poet of cordel in 1909, Leandro Gomes de Barros, says that money rules the world and is surrounded by ambition; it is the reason for killing and justice for a price. (Read strophes left to right.)

"There are very serious questions
Which go before the tribunal,
Questions which require much paper,
Paper which carries the weight
Of legal evidence,
The main kind being notes of $500 . . . .

So with money,
You can accomplish anything,
Without it nothing.
Ugly girls find boy friends,
And university graduates
Become thick as flies!

To prove his point Leandro tells the hilarious story of the Englishman whose dog dies and who wants to have a burial mass in Latin and with litanies for the family pet. When approached with the idea, the local priest laughs in the Englishman's face, that is, until he learns recently departed has left a will and in the will, gold coins for the priest saying the mass. "What an intelligent animal, what a noble sentiment," says said vicar, and quick as a flash, the dog gets buried and in Latin to boot. A particularly overbearing and hypocritical bishop hears of the fiasco and is quick to condemn the priest, that is, until the former is told that part of the gold goes to the diocese. "What an intelligent animal, what a noble sentiment," says said bishop and laments, if only ten more had died! Judas sold out Christ for a few coins and Holy Mother Church can always find an angle!

The poet shifts gears in another booklet of verse to describe the real plight of people around him in the early years of the twentieth century. In The High Cost of Living ["A Carestia na Vida"][2] Leandro Gomes de Barros talks of hunger, the cost of food constantly going up, the day worker making only 600 mil-reis (less than a penny each) a day. The only people with money are sugar mill owners, big businessmen and bandits. The poor man is like a dog, led wherever his owner drags him.

In The People on the Cross [O Povo na Cruz][3] the poet talks about the sad situation of the poor Brazilian:

"Hunger eats his flesh
Work wears out his arm

When the poor man dies
The only thing he leaves

Then the government gets hold of him
And has to divide him up:
Customs, the state, the governor's office,
Each one gets a piece.

Are orphans and a wife,
And the only inheritors are
The judge, the scribe
And the gravedigger."

In Nostalgia from the Past [Saudades do Tempo Passado],[4] Leandro Gomes de Barros tells of the plight of the average person. Taxes are killing him. Rio de Janeiro (Brazil's national capital in 1910) gets its share first; São Paulo is protected, but poor Pernambuco and Paraíba (poverty stricken northeastern states) lose out! But one hundred years ago when there was a monarchy, it was not this way. Now that Brazil has governors and mayors, everything has changed, and this is the way it has turned out!

Taxes, as hated then as now, drove the poet wild. In the Ten Cents to the Government [O Dez-réis do Governo][5] published in Recife in 1907, the poet says they tax everything now, and it won't be long until they try to tax the rain, the sunshine, even the dust and wind. Before the elections they always promise to better things, but afterwards, everything goes up one hundred per cent.

"This world has gone so wrong
And things are so bad now
That the guarantee for the poor man
Is getting kicked and thrown into jail
The kids don't even know
What a full stomach is."

"The work week has six days
Whoever wants to stay out of trouble
Has to give two to the State
Two and a half to the mayor
And better not complain
And be unhappy."

The poet's conclusion is in One Stick with Too Many Ants [Um Pau com Formigas][6] published in Recife in 1912:

"They call this the century of light
I call it the century of fights
The age of ambition
The planet of intrigue
Many dogs after one bone
One stick and lots of ants . . . .

"So since the Republic
Everything causes us terror
Belly clubs don't go to school
But they have a diploma
The bandoleer is the law
The rifle the governor." . . .

"The rich man wins the election
The poor man wins only intrigue
He sacrificed himself for the other
And the winner now ignores him
The poor man ends up saying
This is a stick with too many ants."

The chronicler's conclusion: the rich man brags, the poor man keeps quiet, and God lives far from here.

So this litany of problems for the poor was chronicled and in effect documented for the ages by the cordelian bard Leandro Gomes de Barros at the beginning of the twentieth century. There is nothing new under the sun because for the next eighty years the poets of cordel would never cease to repeat the same complaints of the world. Time may pass, governments come and go, the fortunes of political messiahs wax and wane, but there is one constant: the misery and poverty of the poor and the always increasing cost of living.

In the 1940s poets like Rodolfo Coelho Cavalcante and Cuíca de Santo Amaro would repeat the same theme in the capital city of the northeastern state of Bahia in story-poems with the same title: The ABCs of the High Cost of Living [ABC da Carestia].[7] Their stories are like sociological treatises on the times. Cavalcante, perhaps the most visible of cordelian chroniclers for almost fifty years from his house in a proletarian section of old Bahia, said "The poor man lives crying/ The rich man gloating/ Just what he always wants." There are strikes in public transportation, and the trolley system, a foreign-owned entity, is the latest: "And thus the Brazilian/ Lives subject to the foreigner/ With no rights to complain." Beggars line the streets and the rich man ignores them; the poor invade vacant land and build slum shanties [invasões] only to be ejected by the lawyers of the rich landholders. The only solution [jeito] is to get down on your knees and pray to God.

Rodolfo's competitor and colleague, Cuica de Santo Amaro, called the "Hell's Mouth" of cordel in Bahia from the 1940s to the 1960s for his role as folk gadfly, says it all but with a twist of topic in Office Workers' Debts Never End [Dívida de Funcionário Nunca Termina].[8] Paychecks come late if at all; you have to buy the basic necessities on time, and when you do get the paycheck, taxes and union fees take most of it. Everything goes up except your wages: food, rent, even a casket to get buried in. Men beat their wives out of frustration. Wages have got to go up!

In the 1960s, 70s, and 80s the Brazilian military regimes promised they would bake a big Brazilian economic cake and share the slices with all. The regime would do this via utopist huge projects for Brazil (called "pharoaonic" by the Brazilians), and they, in effect, produced the "Brazilian Miracle" which changed little for the poor. Poets in Greater Rio like Azulão, Gonçalo Ferreira da Silva, Apolonio Alves dos Santos and others continued the lamentations of bad times in brilliantly satiric poems dealing with the modern age. The titles tell the story: <u>The Mysterious Cow that Spoke of the Present Day Crisis</u>, <u>The Sufferings of the Poor Who Pay "Social Security" Tax</u>, <u>The ABCs of the Price of Beans and the Tumult in the Lines</u>, <u>Life of the Poor Man Today</u>, <u>The Invasion of Inflation</u>, and <u>Gas Prices Rising, the People Starving</u>. All tell of the plight of the poor.

And as if economic misery brought on by inflation, high costs, and unemployment were not enough, there were the natural disasters to deal with, an incessant cycle of no rain or too much rain, drought or flood. The annals of <u>cordel</u> are full of poems treating floods and other natural disasters for the last one hundred years, with titles like <u>The Tragedy of Floods in All of Rio de Janeiro</u>. All manner of man made disasters are chronicled as well, traffic wrecks dealing with trucks, but more so with buses and trolleys or trains that the masses use for transportation. And of course the underlying tone is that all this, just maybe, is really God's punishment for a sinful humanity! Drama! Tragedy! Life! Death! These are the elements of a great cordelian story. And together with economic misery and natural disaster, crime is a constant in the life of the poor. The more horrific, the more repelling, the better the story.

But the greatest of the tragedies of life, the most gripping of the stories of <u>cordel</u> and the portrait of its people from the very beginnings of its existence until the present is the relentless role of the great droughts in the dry Northeast and the astounding ramifications for all Brazil. This story alone represents the odyssey of millions of poor Brazilians and in many ways is the on-going heroic story of <u>cordel</u>. It is a topic <u>Portrait</u> treats in the second part of this album: "Life is a Saga."

2 The Droughts

Introduction

There is an immense bibliography of articles, books, films and television programs, documentary or fictionalized, of the "drought cycle" of Northeastern Brazil and its long-range effects on the region and its peoples. The key word is "immense," too immense to treat here except in summary form. Suffice to say, the best memory, document and record of this national disaster will be the story-poems of <u>cordel</u> itself, and thus a key part of <u>Portrait</u>. To appreciate the plight and then the flight of Northeasterners, truly a national odyssey made into saga by the story-poems, one first needs to know the basics of the geography of the Northeast and then its weather patterns.[9]

The area is divided into three climatic zones, the wet coast [<u>zona da mata</u>] where abundant tropical rains provide the basis, along with fertile land, for the plantation economy which exists to this day. This is the sugar cane zone of the Northeast. A second band of land adjacent to the coast receives far less rain, but still provides good pasturage for livestock and fair crop growing. This is the pastoral zone [<u>agreste</u>], often hilly and heavily populated as well. The third zone is the most famous, the dry backlands [<u>sertão</u>] which is to the west of the pastoral zone. This later zone is the sub-region of the Northeast that has engendered many of the highlights of Brazilian history and culture. A large area in the interior often filled with brush and brambles and in some areas by tall cacti, it is the area of the heroic and mythic Brazil: the land of the courageous man of the backlands able to withstand extremes in climate and a life of hardship in order to survive. It is also the land of bizarre religious leaders called "religious fanatics" by the unbelievers who made the area famous with bloody religious sacrifice at "Pretty Rock" [<u>Pedra Bonita</u>] in Pernambuco in the early 19th century and especially at a godforsaken backlands villa called Canudos in 1896 in Bahia state. After a national war was fought in 1896 and 1897 to eliminate the Canudos fanatics and their charismatic leader "Good Jesus Antonio Conselheiro," things quieted down for awhile. But the twentieth century brought a more lasting leader revered as a modern saint—Father Cícero "The Miracle Worker of the Backlands" of Juazeiro do Norte, Ceará, and his successor the Capuchin preacher of missions, Friar Damian.

Along with the poor masses searching for a ray of hope in wild-eyed, self-proclaimed messiahs and in truly reverent religious leaders, the area engendered another phenomenon, the bandits of the Northeast. Isolated ruffians became folk heroes as far back as the late 17th and 18th centuries with Lucas da Feira, O Cabeleira and others. But banditry came into its own in the very late 19th century and the first four decades of the twentieth with the leaders Antônio Silvino and the infamous Lampião. It was just a coincidence that at the same time as the bandits roamed the Northeast, <u>cordel</u> reached its high point of production.

So it was that an accumulation of the most diverse phenomena came to affect life for this part of the Northeast: an unjust landholding system with most land held in the hands of a few people, a semi-feudal labor system in place by default after slavery was finally outlawed in 1888, local political bossism [<u>coronelismo</u>] and justice where the rich and powerful controlled all life, an official religion weakened by vast distances, few priests and trained leaders to provide education, and perhaps most of all, the insane effects of weather.

In much of the region it always was and still is a question of feast or famine. There are two seasons in the Northeast, winter (June to October) and summer (December to March). "Spring" and "Fall" are barely noticeable. Winter is characterized normally by heavy rains to nourish the land and crops; summer is dry, a natural period of sunshine and heat which ripens the crops and brings good weather for harvest. But both seasons are regularly out of kilter. The region is devastated by periodic floods and droughts, more often the latter. The most famous is the drought of the "two sevens," the killer of 1877. Statistics are unreliable and vary, but most believe that up to one million northeasterners actually died in the devastation of that drought; the worst hit the inhabitants of the state of Ceará. Many of those that did not die fled. The cycle had always existed, but it came to a head at that time.

It was then that massive movements of northeasterners began to migrate from the Northeast, on the one hand to the dream of the luxuriant, rain soaked Amazon rain forest and the rubber plantations which provided work, but always to the Northeastern coastal cities in the wet coastal zone where it was hoped life would be better. Even more important would be the move to the mythic, utopist, rich South East, to the Mecca of Rio de Janeiro or São Paulo. A penultimate chapter would be the boom times in the new city of Brasília from 1955 to 1960 where northeastern labor helped build the utopist capital designed by avant-garde architect Oscar Niemeyer and brought to fruition by the progressive politician Juscelino Kubitschek. The last and on-going saga is the exodus to the West, to the El Dorado of Matto Grosso and Rio Branco or to the North, Amazonas, Pará and Roraima. In these vast lands the migrants either homestead or squat on previously forested land and hope for better times.

Out of this economic and social movement came arguably one of a handful of high points of Brazilian culture: the literature and subsequent artistic creations via film, music and television portraying this the latest of Brazilian odysseys. The Novelists of the Northeast, a group of politically and socially motivated writers including José Lins do Rego, Graciliano

Ramos, Raquel de Queiróz and Jorge Amado, made the region and its problems known to all Brazilians (and many foreigners via translation) from the late 1920s to the 1960s. There were a handful of previous literary works which paved the way, Euclides da Cunha's Rebellion in the Backlands ["Os Sertões"] which chronicled and made famous in 1903 the conditions of poverty, hopelessness and messianic utopist solutions for the poor at Canudos and José Américo de Almeida's Cane trash [A Bagaceira] which was an early account of the migrant workers from the backlands who became seasonal "slaves" on the sugar cane plantations near the northeastern coast.

To many, this was the high point of Brazilian culture until very recent days. Many works of literature became classics in Brazilian film, first in the art medium of New Cinema [Cinema Novo] in the late 1950s and 1960s and later in the commercial films and television dramatic adaptations of the 1970s and 1980s up to the present time. Graciliano Ramos' Barren Lives [Vidas Secas], the story of the drought as it affected a poor backlands cowboy and his family, is a classic among such works adapted to the crude realism of early black and white films. Jorge Amado's Marxist novel Red Harvest [Seara Vermelha] which combined religious fanaticism, the drought and banditry in an epic tale of the region was important. His Gabriela whose main protagonist is a victim of the droughts turned happy heroine in Bahia is an example of the slick, commercial film of the 1970s. But these named novelists' cohorts each contributed as well—Lins do Rego and his nearly photographic portrayal of the sugar cane region along with novels about the bandits and Raquel de Queiroz with stark portrayals of the drought in her native state of Ceará.

Brazil's sophisticated tradition of erudite poetry also portrayed the drought, perhaps most effectively in João Cabral de Melo Neto's masterpiece Severino's Life and Death ["Morte e Vida Severina"]. The TV version of the same won national and international acclaim, in part by virtue of its incredibly beautiful poetry set to music by a rising star in Brazil, the composer-singer Chico Buarque de Holanda.

Buarque de Holanda himself would assure that the middle and upper class urban Brazilians would not forget the plight of the poor northeasterner when he wrote the classic song "Pete the Laborer" ["Pedro Pedreiro"] in the mid-1960s. This poem-song probably best explained the reality now turned myth of the Northeastern migrant to university students thirsting for social equality and justice in times of military dictatorship and repression. However, a true folk-popular singer of the Northeast, Luís Gonzaga, the "father" of northeastern "country" music [forró] and known to generations of Brazilians, epitomized the myth in what became for most Brazilians the "northeastern national anthem," the song "White Wing" [Asa Branca].

The reader of <u>Portrait</u> needs to know the myth to understand this album: when the drought comes, the northeasterner must flee with his family, often with all they own and can carry on their backs, to search for work in a better place. He begins a long, painful and even dangerous odyssey, walking or packed in a truck like cattle to market, or occasionally with a third-class ticket on a riverboat or country train. His destination may at first be close by, the rainy greenness of the coastal plantations, or far away, the rubber plantations of the Amazon, but more likely, the huge unfriendly cities of Rio or São Paulo. After suffering in his odyssey to get to the "promised land," he finds work, probably a menial job at a construction site, is exploited by greedy capitalist owners, but manages to get by. His dream is to return home to his beloved North East when the rains come and eek out a living amongst his own. The reality is different: the rains do not come or come late, and he gradually adapts to a slum dweller's life in Rio or São Paulo. Not part of the myth, but ironically a result of it, he marginally enjoys the advantages of the big city by uniting with his own in "the little North East," a part of every large city he inhabits. But his heart is sustained by ever more nebulous and idealized memories of all that was dear to him in the old North East.

The real chronicle, the most believable, the most accurate, and the most heart wrenching, is by the protagonists themselves and is portrayed in the story-poems of "<u>cordel</u>." Thus is explained the title of this Album, "Life Is a Struggle and Life Is a Saga." Its protagonists are heroes without the trappings of heroes; they are the poorest of the poor, bedraggled, starving, and desperate. But they are survivors and by the mere act of living have defeated the evil enemies of drought, unemployment, poverty, misery, starvation and hopelessness in the Northeast. The final ironic chapter in the saga is that the new life may be worse than the one they left, but it is their lot.

The second part of Album V then is a report in narrative poetry in the booklets of <u>cordel</u> by the protagonists themselves of what amounts to one of the singularly most important of Brazilian sociological phenomena of the times: the movement of peoples from a rural to an urban setting and the vicissitudes of life it entails. A final part of the album is the story of where this odyssey has left them today at the beginning of the 21st century and the life they live as marginalized people in Rio de Janeiro and São Paulo.

Because of the immensity of the saga, one must prepare bite-size portions: from the backlands to the northeastern coast, from the North East to the Amazon, and from the North East to the southeast Mecca of Rio or São Paulo, all resulting in the evolution from farm to city. The story has been a constant in <u>cordel</u> from its beginnings to its most recent stories and is a true portrait of twentieth century Brazil.

The Backlands and the Drought

The poets occasionally will wax lyrical in their praise of life in the arid backlands as the bard João Martins de Atayde did in his "Sighs of an Outlander" ["Suspiros de um Sertanejo"][10] but more often they will lament "difficult times." As early as 1920 in a posthumous edition of his poem The Drought in Ceará [A Secca do Ceará],[11] the poet Leandro Gomes de Barros talks of the reality of the drought with its consequences of hunger and famine, where even the cattle die.

For the next eighty years new titles will tell the same story: The Drought and the Horrors of the North East, Story of the Suffering Refugeess of 1958, When There is Drought in the Back Lands, The Worst Drought in the History of the North East, or All the Northeast Is Saddened When There is Drought in the Back Lands. The poems all relate the same sad reality, but at different times throughout the twentieth century.

The Move to the Amazon

One of the few options in the 1920s was to go the Amazon as a hired hand on the rubber plantations. The previous local source of labor, Indians or mixed bloods [caboclos], had been decimated by the hard work, brutality and disease. The demand for rubber was ever increasing with the invention and mass production of the automobile in the United States, so there was a need for rubber tires; this was before the advent of synthetic rubber. The need grew even more a few years later when there were problems of trade with Europe due to World War II and the disruption of normal commerce by Hitler's submarines. So a national ministry called The Department of Coordination of Economic Mobility created a special organ: SEMTA or Service of Mobilization of Workers for the Amazon [Serviço de Mobilização de Trabalhadores para Amazônia] with the sole purpose of recruiting workers for the rubber plantations [seringais] in the Amazon Basin. Thousands of desperate northeasterners volunteered and their story is told in cordel.

One poem with S. Araújo listed as author shows on its cover a rubber worker with a rifle in one hand, a bandoleer across his chest and a hatchet and rubber gathering bucket in the other. It tells the story from his perspective and is paraphrased here: The outlanders of the North East were living okay, but advertising came with all its promises of gold, food and medicine for anybody wanting to migrate. (An American reader can only recall the Dust Bowl of the 1930s in the United States, the Okies, and Steinbeck's Grapes of wrath which told of promises of paradise in California with its orange groves and agriculture and all the jobs for penniless migrants who had lost their land, unable to make payments and or pay taxes). All you needed to do was to sign on the dotted line and be registered. There were guards to keep an eye on you at the disembarkation point—a cruel trick! Each recruit got five cruzeiros for food for his family and all suffered on the trip by land to Iguatú, state of Ceará. There you were issued a straw hat, a pair of pants, a shirt and sandals and sent on to the coast at Fortaleza.

In Fortaleza you were taken to the SEMTA office. You signed up for two years and were given a hammock, clothes and twenty cruzeiros. Guarded like criminals and treated with disdain, you went by boat from Fortaleza to Belém in the State of Pará near the mouth of the Amazon River with only jerky and squash to eat. (It is no coincidence that it was exactly at this time that the Guajarina Press in Belém, Pará, came into its own as a major "northeastern" press of the cordelian poetry.) You lived like a prisoner in Belém and did not even get a chance to look around the city, but were herded aboard another ship, given twenty more cruzeiros and more bad food and shipped to Manaus, the capital of Amazonas State. There you received 200 cruzeiros, got on board another boat and shipped up river.

Once you arrived at the plantation, the suffering really began: sickness came, people died from jaguar attacks, snakebite and fever. Your clothes were worn out and it was too expensive to replace anything because you had to buy even your food in the company store. It was all exploitation. Some tried to get other kinds of work, but it never worked out. You could not save enough money for the passage home. If you finally got sick enough, yes, then they would send you home. I'm telling this in fear of getting caught, of being censored, but I've got to tell the story. Life goes on, and we owe the government work and . . . . [12] And so it went in the Amazon, but the larger stories would continue.

Sufferings of the Northeasterner in the South

By far the largest internal migration in Brazil took place after the rubber boom days and involved the massive flight of northeasterners to southeast Brazil, to the cities of Rio de Janeiro and São Paulo and farms of the same states. Estimates are that one-third of the megalopolis that is São Paulo is made up of migrants from the North East. The city is called the "largest northeastern city in Brazil outside the North East," much like Liberdade District in São Paulo is called the largest Japanese city outside of Japan. Northeastern Cultural Centers have become the gathering place for homesick migrants and their descendants with a regular weekly bazaar, food, music and dancing. There are radio stations dedicated solely to an immense audience of northeastern culture, and they abound in São Paulo.

In Rio de Janeiro migrants are also a significant part of the total populace of Greater Rio including the Baixada Fluminense, the industrial zone outside of Rio itself. Their traditional gathering place on Sunday morning is the Northeastern Fair in São Cristóvão in the north zone of the city which serves similar purposes to the cultural centers of São Paulo. The fair is the nexus and symbol of "saga and struggle."

In the mid 1970s Raul Lody of the National Campaign for Folklore wrote a wonderful article describing the Fair.[13] It is poetry in prose and truly captures the spirit of São Cristóvão. The fair is "the commercial side, but also the emotive and social side: the encounter with people from home, the spoken accent of the North East, leather sandals, the 'flat heads,' [cabeça chata], the smell of rice and liver [sarapatel], the oral poets and the poetry of cordel. The fair is above all an encounter, a way to forget homesickness for the backlands, of the green beaches with coconut palms, of manioc flour, and of the rhythm of the oral improvisers of verse, since, every Sunday is the day of the Northeast at St. Christopher's Fair." Lody details cordelian poets, folk woodcut artists, oral poets, small trios and bands, the whole range of northeastern cooking, describing each food, and northeastern folk medicines and curatives. He lists the merits of each. He tells of games, fortune tellers, photographers, of the types and merits of each type of sugar cane rum and roll tobacco. One sees why the migrant stories focus on the fair. Lamentably the fair has decreased in size since those days and has changed in character as well: what most abounds today is the blaring music of competing northeastern country music [forró] bands.

Even plazas in Rio's South Zone—a middle and upper class residential zone for Brazilians and tourist Mecca as well—wax and wane as places to hang out for the "flat heads" [cabeça chata] from the Northeast as cruel Rio de Janeiro natives [cariocas] came to call them. After all, it is northeasterners who are the doormen, night watchmen and often the maids the South Zone depends upon to keep ticking. This author of <u>Portrait</u> witnessed wonderful performances of <u>Bumba Meu Boi</u> (a folk play-dance from North East and Northern Brazil) and performances of oral poets [<u>cantadores</u>] in the Largo de Machado in the Flamengo district in the 1960s. And the poets recited and sold their verse as well even in Copacabana in plazas just two blocks from the beach.

The immediate reasons for the migration to the industrial Southeast may have been drought and its consequences, but the long-term causes were the endemic social inequalities and lack of opportunities to make a living for the lower class in both the rural and urban Northeast. The flight and plight is a major story in <u>Portrait</u>. This is the odyssey often told in heroic terms of the journey itself, the struggle to survive once in the big city, the process of adaptation, acculturation and confrontation of serious social prejudices, and finally the continuation of the dream of the return.

There are many stories which treat the journey, in reality a filthy, bone-jarring, seemingly endless nine or ten days spent riding in the back of a two-ton truck with wooden slat sidings, thus called a "parrot cage" [<u>pau de arara</u>]—a pejorative metaphor which by extension came to refer to the migrants themselves. Such stories are either by the poets who made the trip themselves or by those who have only heard of its miseries and write "don't do it" stories of reprisal. The shining stars of <u>cordel</u> in the São Cristóvão Fair in Rio de Janeiro were all originally migrants as were lesser known luminaries in greater São Paulo. Some indicative titles are: <u>The Sufferings of the Northeasterner Traveling to the South</u>, <u>The Crying of the Northeasterners in Rio, the "Pau de Araras,"</u> <u>Poverty and Confusion and the "Pau de Araras" from the North</u>, <u>The Northeasterners in Rio and the North East Abandoned</u>, <u>The Northeasterner in Rio</u>, <u>The Drama of the Migrant</u>, <u>When There is Drought in the Back Lands</u>, and in São Paulo, <u>A Family of Hillbillies in São Paulo</u> and <u>The Migration of the Northeast to São Paulo</u>. The stories come in all flavors and all refer at least in passing to the myth, the utopist dream of the return to the Northeast once the rains return or prosperity is attained, but there is great divergence from that point of departure.

In the now classic <u>Sufferings of the Northerner Traveling to the South</u> [Os Martírios do Nortista Viajando para o Sul][14] one is able to feel the pain and sense the struggles of the journey by virtue of Cícero Vieira da Silva's (penname Mocó) blend of narrative and lyric verse. The poet begins by telling of the horrible high cost of living in the Northeast so that even if you have a job, it is not enough to live on. But you do not even have that. You face real hunger each day with a wife and children asking for a simple piece of bread. You are out of work and walk the streets each day knocking on doors asking for any kind of job. After days of rejection, you decide there is only one solution—make the journey to Rio. Your wife says the whole family will die of hunger, but you assure her you will find work (the classic unskilled job of bricklayer's or mason's assistant), send money within a month, and she can do laundry and ironing to at least keep bread on the table for that time.

The poor husband and father goes to a relative and gets a loan of 2000 cruzeiros to be paid with 3000 in one month!; he buys a ticket on a <u>pau de arara</u> truck for 1700 and has 300 for provisions. Dried beef, crackers, matches, tobacco, hard sugar candy [<u>rapadura</u>], sweet rolls, manioc flour and a bottle of <u>Bode Seco</u> sugar cane rum will get him to Rio and hold him over until the first paycheck. He chars the meat black over a fire at home, throws it all into a knapsack and is ready to go:

> "He says goodbye to the family
> And blesses his tiny children
> With a heavy heart
> He gives them a million kisses
> Leaving a sprout of nostalgia
> His love to take root."

The kisses turn to tears as he climbs aboard the truck which leaves "cutting the dust/ of the long, strange road" (the poet uses the same adjective to describe the long road to the South as the heroic backlands poems use for the epic "great crossing" of the dry backlands desert). The poet indeed makes this poem into an epic. Riding like cattle in the back of the truck, the migrant faces sun, dust, dirt and cold rain and wonders when it will all end. The farther he goes, the sadder and more homesick he feels.

The truck pulls off the road at night and parks; he either sleeps on the ground or sets up his hammock, tying one end to the branch of a tree and the other to the slats of the truck. He tries to sleep but can't because of his sadness; he comes to realize he is in search of something that will never be certain (one wonders if Chico Buarque de Holanda read this poem before composing <u>Pedro Pedreiro</u> when Pedro looks for something "greater than the world"). The unnamed migrant spends the night thinking at the side of that deserted road (another important but coincidental parallel to "Pete the laborer, thinker, thinking" ["<u>Pedro Pedreiro, penseiro, pensando</u>"] by Chico Buarque).

Sick and exhausted, the poor migrant can scarcely get his stiff joints to move in order to climb down from the truck when it rolls into São Cristóvão in the North Zone of Rio after nine or ten days on the road. He walks down the main street of São Cristóvão without even a cigarette in his pocket, his cardboard suitcase in his hand and his clothes the color of mud.

He "walks mistrustfully/ like a bird that cannot fly," looking for someone, anyone from home that he might recognize, but there is no one.

He asks for work at a construction site and is told that not even the Virgin Mary would get a job there because things are so bad. The foreman is firing, not hiring. But desperate and persistent, he finally gets work as a mason's assistant after three months, but finds that social security deductions take half his pay. He works eleven months, not missing a day, but is fired just before completing a year on the job (one year guarantees more permanent benefits). With the tiny severance pay he does receive he grudgingly heads back North, swearing never to return to the South. But within a month he is broke again and prepares to repeat the journey.

Cícero Vieira ends with:

> "He who has traveled to the South
> Reading this book will embrace me
> This happened to me
> And it happens to everybody
> The reality is you travel
> And the day you arrive
> You can only tell the same bad luck story."

BEGIN SIDEBAR. We knew well Apolônio Alves dos Santos, the Paraíban poet living in Rio, having done both written interviews via the mail and oral tape recordings with him in Rio de Janeiro, and having made many visits to his cordel stand in the Northeastern market in Rio de Janeiro. Neat, pleasant and prosperous looking, Apolonio (now deceased) made a good living for years in Rio. That is, he managed to convert his shack in the Rio slum of Benfica into a comfortable home. However in our last interview in 1990, he was disillusioned, telling how he was robbed of a "lousy" chicken he had purchased for dinner in the slum [favela] market. He decided to leave Rio, go back to Guarabira, Paraíba, where he had relatives, one of whom with a printing shop who had printed his stories over the decades. We heard later that Apolonio was back in Rio, disillusioned with the North East he had hoped to return to, a true first-person testimony of "Life is a Struggle." In a recent visit in 2000, we heard the sad news of his death. END SIDEBAR.

Apolonio tells the story in The Northeasterners in Rio and the Northeast Abandoned[15] when he launches into a scathing attack and socio-political analysis of why the migrations came about in the first place. In short, the large landowners in the Northeast were greedy for even more land and oppressed the poor small farmers living and sharecropping on their lands. This includes the sugar mill and plantation owners who forced the formerly independent small farmers to work for shares or as hired laborers [alugados], forced to buy their necessities in the company store. The money at the end of the week was not even enough to go to local market day [fazer feira]. So they make the trip to Rio.

The poet says that the construction job is hard. It's the pick [picareta] or the wheelbarrow [carrinho de mão]; take your choice. The migrants live in distant workers' slums [subúrbios] and have to get up at midnight to catch the train into Rio's Central station and then buses to sites. (Portrait will shortly see a famous rendition of the train ride.) They can either do that or live closer in one of the famous hillside slums of Rio.

But the good news is that you do have a job and the Thirteenth Month Benefit (a bonus of one month's pay at the end of year) and you are not in effect a captive to the company store like back in the Northeast. Apolonio waxes poetic, almost euphoric in describing the credit available to someone who has a job. If one is careful, he can actually buy things now and again, furnish his modest house and live decently.

He concludes in first person: I lived this, I know what it all means, I was a victim. Believe me, it's better to go to Rio and live "subject to the gringo." The northeast migrant is a good worker, not afraid to sweat, and the government knows his labor is needed for Brazil to progress. So the South gets stronger each day, the Northeast weaker and abandoned. It's all true, it's all correct, so please buy my folheto!

Perhaps the most well known cordelian story about the daily routine of the poor in Rio de Janeiro is the cordelian classic, The Early Morning Train [O Trem da Madrugada][16] by another fine migrant poet from Paraíba in Rio de Janeiro. Azulão whose real name is José João dos Santos, was born in Paraíba state in 1932 and came to Rio at seventeen. He worked in civil construction, but wrote cordel and was an improviser of verse [cantador] at the same time. By 1949 he was a success on the folk poetry radio station in Rio, so he returned home, married his sweetheart and returned to live definitively in Rio. He worked as a doorman and wrote cordel and was the first poet to sell his poems at São Cristóvão in 1952. By the late 1980s he had written more than two hundred cordelian stories, was called upon for poetry performances in the universities in greater Rio and had recorded programs on television. In 1989 he was also a civil servant, an officer in the office of the Secretariat of Culture in the mayor's office of Nova Iguaçu where he had lived for thirty-two years in the Engenheiro Pedreira district. Azulão would experience a great thrill and then disillusionment when he dabbled in Brazilian politics as a candidate for the PTB or workers' party, a story Portrait will tell in Album VII "In Politics We Believe but Do Not Trust."

The Early Morning Train tells in a tragic-comic way the life of the poor commuter (often a northeasterner) living in the Baixada Fluminense, the flat, swampy area of Rio de Janeiro state outside of Rio proper where the large mass of workers live and commute to jobs in the city. The story-poem is funny and meant to entertain the cordelian public who hear it recited in the market and who buy it because they live this reality. But it has an undercurrent of the sufferings the poor commuter faces daily.

Beginning with jokes about the oversexed punks who use the jam packed conditions to pinch and touch women on the train and the hopeless ways the women try to defend themselves with stick pins and umbrellas, it describes every aspect of the train ride. It could apply to most bus lines from the suburbs as well. The train gets progressively more crowded at each stop; people are stuffed like sardines in a can, with stale air and body odor exacerbated by summer temperatures in Rio. The poor washerwoman's bag of freshly washed and ironed clothes for "madam" and "doctor" in the South Zone of Rio is stepped on in the melee. But the crowdedness has its ironic side—the pickpocket has made his move, but cannot get off of the train! And woe to all if the train breaks down, for vandals will break windows and glass in the doors to get air. In the end it is a tragedy for all, for if the cars go out of service, even fewer are available for the poor commuter.

Azulão describes small commerce on the train: all the vendors and what they sell—coconut candy, combs made from steer horns that will not break even in curly hair associated with blacks [cabelo pixaim]. The vendors are always on the lookout for the cops [o rapa] who check for proper licenses to sell. There is almost a festive atmosphere of venders trying to outsmart the inspectors!

Azulão closes by telling of the poor soul so exhausted from the work day that he falls asleep on the night train home, wakes up at the end of the line, and has to stay on board in order to make it back into work in the city the next morning! And if you don't believe it, Azulão sardonically says, "Come and get to know the suburbs of Rio." He is one of many modern urban social protest poets [poetas de contestação], and this is just one subtle reminder of that fact to the Brazilian and foreign tourists who may frequent the northeastern fair but would never get on that train!

Such is the cordelian account of life for the northeasterner in the South. But there is another aspect that is extremely important in the chronicle: the humorous stories written by the northeasterners themselves of the hillbilly in the city. Often written by wily veterans of the saga like Apolonio Alves dos Santos or Azulão in Rio de Janeiro with a customary tongue in cheek style, the accounts tend to describe the follies of the hick in the city.

One needs to know that this same self-deprecating humor already existed as a staple in cordel in the North East when the country bumpkin came into even a small backlands town for the fair. There are many original titles from the Northeast itself: A Conversation Between Two Hillbillies, A Marriage Down on the Farm, The Hillbillies in Church, or Joe Hillbilly's Goof ups in Town. There is a famous scene from one of the masterpieces of the Northeastern Novel when the great Graciliano Ramos describes his main characters, Fabiano and his country wife, coming into town for market and church. The wife starts the long walk into town in high heels which make her look like a bird and cowboy husband Fabiano is in a tie which literally seems to choke him to death. Leandro Gomes de Barros joked of the hillbilly afraid of the military draft during World War I and to avoid it married the first female in sight, for better or for worse. So such stories go back a long way.

But the stories of the hillbilly in Rio or São Paulo are a bit different. In many of these stories the migrant at least part of the time is laughing at himself. He and his friends have been there; they have lived the odyssey of the journey, the early struggles and the immense shock of dealing with the city. The poet may write using incorrect "hillbilly" speech and pronunciation indicated by spelling to make fun of the way they talk in the country. And there are many misunderstandings caused by different semantics between country and city. But there is also in many of the stories an undercurrent of being made fun of, of the deep prejudice shown in the attitudes the city dweller has about the migrant population. Yet today the native of Rio or São Paulo [o sulista] has strong feelings about the "nortista," the Northeasterner in town.

A "classic" in this story type is Azulão's Joe Country Bumpkin in Rio [Zé Matuto no Rio de Janeiro].[17] The poet tells of Joe who was born in the backlands in the interior of the Northeast. Warned by his mother of the evils of the world and the big city, he decides to see for himself. He believes in the myth of the northeasterner who arrives in Rio, gets a job as a day laborer and eventually gets rich.

Azulão does a masterful job of converting the hillbilly speech to cordelian poetic text indicating country pronunciation through his spelling. Dialogue is in country or matuto speech, narration in standard Portuguese.

The migrant's journey is familiar: the sad goodbyes as he boards the pau de arara truck and the cold he soon gets from the dirt, rain and change of climate as they pass through Bahia state on their way south. The truck breaks down six times alone just in crossing Minas Gerais state! Zé tries to save money by eating just snacks and arrives in Rio semi-starving after fourteen days of travel. Sitting on a bench in São Cristóvão Square, Zé is approached by a policemen and is sent to Copacabana "where there is always work." He squabbles with the bus driver who wants his fare; Zé says the guard told him to do it, so he won't pay. He gets off at one of the busiest, most dangerous stops in Rio, on Barata Ribeiro street after the tunnel from Botafogo, and is almost run down by the traffic. He spends his first night sleeping on the ground in busy Copacabana, eating bread and bananas to save money.

Humor takes over when he sees the ocean for the first time calling it "oh what a helluva pond" [ó açude danejo]—the only bodies of water in the N.E. interior are such man-made reservoirs. He thinks if the backlands had this much water there would be no sadness or misery. He is amazed by all the people on the beach, some who actually go into the water (contrary to some beachgoers in the Northeast), and is amazed that they actually bathe in plain sight of others! His reaction—"How immoral! What a lack of respect!" ["Que safadeza! Que farta de arrespeito"]—is funny to the hillbilly reader. Not liking the high brow ways of Copacabana [os luxos,] he decides this is not the place for him.

A helpful street vendor sends him to Rio's Central Station where trains come and go to the poor suburbs, thinking he will be amongst his own there. The 1999 Academy Award nominated film Central do Brasil has the same setting. He urinates against a tree by the station, is arrested by a guard, but is freed once the guard hears his explanation: from where he is from in the country there's always a place to do such things! Zé goes into a cafe and orders the plate of the day; he gets macaroni and says he didn't order worms but beans! He sees soldiers marching in the streets (was the poem written during military regime days?) and says it's just like Lampião and the bandits in the Northeast. If there is a revolution thousands will die!

He goes into the Central Station, then to the underground section, but cannot find a ticket booth. He then spies a mannequin in a tailor's shop, thinks it is a real person and says, "Except for lacking two arms, you look just like my aunt." He tries to get closer to talk to the mannequin, bumps into the showcase window, breaks the glass and is cut. A guard sends him to the station pharmacy, but suspects foul play.

Zé now has only one desire: to get on the quickest train going back up North. The guard explains you cannot get there by train, so you will have to return to São Cristóvão Square and catch a pau de arara truck. Ze says he will even walk to the truck if he has to and hopes to get a free ride back North by signing on as a driver's assistant. The ticket agency in São Cristóvão plaza says he better wait until the next day, which is fair day, because there will be a better chance to make a deal. In misery and near hysteria, Joe tells his plight to northeasterners in the fair who were formerly migrants just like him. They take up a collection and buy him a ticket home. In route he sells his hammock, his hat, his suitcase and even his trusty northeastern fisherman's knife just to eat. He manages to arrive home ashamed, disgusted and half-starved, but is relieved when his mom serves him a huge plate of northeastern beans. Grateful to be home, he swears [dá figa] at the South, vowing never to return.

In a way these stories are just as eloquent as Luís Gonzaga's "White Wing" [Asa Branca] if not as clever or sophisticated as Chico Buarque de Holanda's "Pete the Construction Worker" [Pedro Pedreiro]. They express in language the protagonists themselves understand and sentiments they feel the great struggle and the great saga that continue today at the beginning of the new millennium. The poor Northeasterners will continue to leave the backlands and will travel even farther than their predecessors—to the "new Mecca" of the West and southern Amazon or perhaps ironically to the gold-laden far North of Roraima near the Venezuelan border, past the played out Serra Pelada gold mine of Pará State.[18] But the homesickness, the nostalgia and mainly the memories and pride of their backlands will not disappear. This chapter of struggle and saga is an indelible part of their story and our Portrait.

[1]   Leandro Gomes de Barros, O Poder do Dinheiro, A Carestia da Vida, Crise para Burro, Belém: Guararina Edta., 1909, p. 2.

[2]   . . ."O Dinheiro" . . ., p. 12.

[3]   Leandro Gomes de Barros, O Povo na Cruz, Saudades do Tempo Passado, Encontro de Leandro Gomes com Chagas Batista, Recife, n.d.

[4]   Leandro Gomes de Barros, "Saudades do Tempo Passado" in O Povo na Cruz . . ., p. 10.

[5]   Gomes de Barros, O Dez-Réis do Governo, Recife: Typografia Murania, 1907.

[6]   Gomes de Barros, Um Pau com Formigas, Recife, 1912.

[7]   Rodolfo Coelho Cavalcante, ABC da Carestia, Salvador, march, 1947.

8   Cuíca de Santo Amaro, <u>Dívida de Funcionário Não Termina</u>, Salvador, n.d.

9   Our sources for this introduction to the drought and its social foundations are: Manuel Correia de Andrade, <u>A Terra e o Homem no Nordeste</u>, 2nd. ed., São Paulo: Brasiliense, 1964; Gilberto Freyre, <u>Vida Social no Brasil nos Meiados do Século XIX</u>, Recife:IJNPS, 1964; Raimundo Nonato, <u>Memória de um Retirante</u>, Rio de Janeiro: Irmãos Pongetti, 1957; and Stephen Robock, <u>Brazil's Developing Northeast</u>, Washington: The Brookings Institution, 1963.

10   João Martins de Atayde, Editor Proprietário José Bernardo da Silva, <u>Suspiros de um Sertanejo</u>, Juazeiro do Norte, printing of 1962.

11   Leandro Gomes de Barros, <u>A Secca do Ceará</u>, Guarabira, PB: Pedro Baptista e Cia., 1920.

12   The paraphrased poem was by S. Araújo, Salvador, n.p., n.d.

13   Raúl Lody, "Feira de São Cristóvão o Nordeste na Guanabara," in <u>Revista Brasileira de Folclore</u>, Rio de Janeiro, year 13, n. 8, jan/april, 1974, pp. 47-48.

14   Cícero Vieira da Silva, "Mocó," <u>Os Martírios dos Nortistas Viajando para o Sul</u>, n.p., n.d.

15   Apolônio Alves dos Santos, <u>Os Nordestinos no Rio, o Nordeste Abandonado</u>, n.p., n.d.

16   José João dos Santos, <u>O Trem da Madrugada</u>, Engenheiro Pedreira, n.d.

17   José João dos Santos, <u>Zé Matuto no Rio de Janeiro</u>, Engenheiro Pedreira, n.d.

18   I am still waiting to see my first <u>folheto</u> about a Northeastern migrant in the United States.

Album VI

We Have Our Distractions

Introduction

The <u>Portrait</u> of a people and its way of life must include their diversions, what they do to have fun. Even the harsh reality of the Northeast is not all drudgery all the time. Like the rest of the Brazilians, the northeasterners who write, publish, read and believe in "cordel" share much with their fellow countrymen. Foremost are the local and national festivals and holidays, both secular and church related. Carnival in Recife, João Pessoa, Fortaleza, Maceió, and especially Bahia has a flavor all its own, and these are the cities where a major urban presence of the story-poems existed for much of the twentieth century. And the beaches of the Northeast are famous for being the most beautiful with the most pleasant water temperature in Brazil. The cordelian public, most of them originally country folks, often dreamed of taking a dip in the ocean [<u>banho de mar</u>] on visits to the coast and often wrote humorous stories about the first visit to the sea.

The old fairs and markets were primary sites to visit and a place to socialize on a trip to the small town in the interior or even the large coastal city: the São José Market in Recife, the Mercado Modelo in Salvador, the fair in Feira de Santana in Bahia, and the famous fair in Caruarú in Pernambuco State, among others.

Religious festivals, local saints' days and major feasts of the liturgical calendar were and are highlights each year. St. John's day is a major feast and holiday in the Northeast on the 24th of June, and St. Peter's on June 29 is a close second in importance. Christmas and Easter are of course major events to celebrate as well. More important for many are the local festival days seen in Albums I and II, like Bom Jesus da Lapa on the São Francisco River in Bahia, Bomfim in Salvador, Father Cícero's Juazeiro do Norte in Ceará, São Francisco de Canindê in Ceará and the festival of the Virgin of Nazareth in Belém do Pará, a neighboring state to the Northeast with many migrants from the backlands and a famous cordelian press.

The national "religion" of soccer [futbol] is just as celebrated by the humble public of "cordel" as by all of Rio's social classes in the Maracaná soccer stadium, particularly with the arrival of the transistor radio and television. Many well-known poets like José Soares in Recife and Cuíca de Santo Amaro in Salvador da Bahia started their careers selling single-sheet [folha volante] poems with accounts of local matches reported in verse. Local soccer favorites in each state, national favorites like Flamengo, Fluminense, and especially the Brazilian national team with its ups and downs in World Cup play are all faithfully documented in "cordel." Stars are venerated to the point that one of the most well-known recent poetic duels [peleja] in "cordel" is the imagined duel between Mané Garrincha and Pelé.[1]

Local folk traditions as well, aside from market day or the weekly fair, are the scene of dozens of cordelian poems. Events or happenings like the rural "rodeo" [vaqueijada], folk dramas like "The Bull Play" [Bumba Meu Boi], local dances [arrasta-pés] and northeastern music [forró] are all documented and are favorites in "cordel" literature.

With the national satellite network developed by the military regime in the 1960s and 1970s television became ubiquitous with a presence even in the backlands, so television programs became part of the diversion in the poetry. The national network news programs like Repórter Esso, later called the "National Journal," soccer and the Brazilian soap operas became a major source of entertainment, at times to the detriment of "cordel" itself. TV and the transistor radio provided topics for poems but eventually took away sales and market for the poets.

But when one speaks of a portrait of the twentieth century as a whole, there are two major factors of diversion for the traditional cordelian public: the booklets of verse themselves, for they are not only entertainment per se but document everything else that is entertainment, and their country poetic cousin, the oral, poetic duel of two poet-singers [cantadores] which dates back to the middle of the nineteenth century in the Northeast and is in many ways one of the precursors and pioneering forces of "cordel" itself. So Portrait needs to see first of all these two sources of entertainment: the oral poetry of the "cantador" and the stories of "cordel" which serve primarily as entertainment for the buying public.

1 The Poet-Singer of Improvised Verse [O Cantador] and the Poetic Duel [A Peleja]

First a basic fact: one of the major types of booklets of cordelian verse is the oral poetic duel [peleja], either in imagined versions written directly for "cordel" or recreations of real, famous oral duels of the past. The peleja comprises hundreds of known titles! No self-respecting traditional cordelian poet is without one, few or many in his list of writings. The duel of two poet-singers, improvisers of oral verse given a theme on the spur of the moment, takes many names: "desafio, peleja, repente ou cantoria." And a related cordelian poem is the debate, encounter or discussion [debate, encontro ou discussão], poems which debate an issue but may not be strictly speaking between two "cantadores" or even poetic duels.

The history of the poet-singer and the poetic duel is well documented by the scholars who pioneered such studies early in the twentieth century, people like Leonardo Mota, Gustavo Barroso and especially Luís da Câmara Cascudo (see the bibliography at the end of the text).[2] When Brazilian folklorists began to collect bits and pieces of folk poetry, and this was in the late 1800s prior to the existence of the modern tape recorder, they were first interested in the "cantador" rather than "cordel" itself which was considered a late-comer and really a hybrid form of popular poetry with some folk characteristics. "Cordel," after all, was in printed form in chapbooks with mostly signed authorship, and folk poetry then was considered to be oral, anonymous and long-lasting.[3]

But the scholars discovered that the "cantadores" quite often became "cordel" poets as well and that the metric forms in the story-poems in fact came from the "cantador" tradition. One must remember that this folk-popular poetry in its very beginnings at the end of the nineteenth century by pioneer poets like Leandro Gomes de Barros, Silvino Pirauá, João Melchíades Ferreira or Francisco das Chagas Batista was the result of the putting into verse in chapbooks the stories in prose from the European chapbook tradition and the creation of new story-poems in Brazil. But the poets of "cordel" also were from the oral tradition.

The "cantador" came first in Brazil, a true folk phenomenon and with distant ties to the European minstrel tradition. Scholars trace the poetic duel in the Western Tradition back to Theocritus and the poetic duels of shepherds in pastoral scenes in ancient Greece. Homer and then Virgil and Horace from the Roman tradition used the poetic duel as well. The tradition eventually passed to Medieval and then Renaissance Europe. The "tenson" or "débate provençal," the "questions and answers" [preguntas y respuestas] of the old Spanish song collections and the "poems of love and friendship" [trovas de amor e amigo] of Portugal are just a few of the antecedents. The tradition was passed on to America and became best known as the Argentine gaucho duel [la payada] and the Brazilian peleja of the northeastern "cantador."

The oral poet may have existed and performed all manner of poems and songs from colonial times in Brazil, but the "cantador" as we know and understand him is a nineteenth century phenomenon. So what did he sing? In the earliest days of colonization in Brazil, from the late sixteenth through the early nineteenth century, the Portuguese brought with them to Brazil a poetic tradition in the form of the oral ballad [romance]. These poems were both folk and learned in Portugal, were sung or recited throughout the frontiers of that new Brazil, but particularly in the Northeast since it was the first major area of colonization. But soon the songs, ballads and romances from Portugal were replaced with new poems about the first obstacles and struggles in the new land, in effect, Brazilian themes. So the early stories of poems of knights errant, faithful virgins and Christian crusaders gave way to poems about droughts, battles with Indians, religious and popular festivals and the adventurous life of the men of the backlands. Fierce panthers [onças] and jaguars, strong bulls, courageous horses and the cowboys who rode them came to dominate the songs.

It became the role of the "cantador" to sing and declaim these song-poems and these tales in the backlands, in the small towns of the interior and eventually in the major coastal cities. Originally a cowboy, a slave or perhaps a sharecropper who sang or declaimed songs and poems while working or at festivals, at an undetermined point in the mid-nineteenth century the "cantador" became semi-professionalized. What used to be done as a pass time during rare leisurely moments came to be a paid activity, albeit in a very modest fashion. It became custom for the wealthy landowner to invite well known "cantadores" to the ranch house for a celebration of a saint's day, a birthday, a wedding, or an anniversary as well as great traditional festivals like St. John's or St. Peter's day. The "cantador" became a Saturday night entertainment much like the local dance. He began to depend upon his skill as oral poet to earn at least part of his living. So in fact an itinerant poetic "class" slowly evolved and a few dozen "famous" poets became known throughout the Northeast. Curiously enough, the large majority of such singers were originally from Paraíba state, and the best known of early cordelian poets as well traced their roots to Paraíba (as well as the majority of migrant poets in Brazil's Southeast cities decades later).

The "cantador" became a "popular personage" [tipo popular], a sort best described by folklorist Luís da Câmara Cascudo,

> He is extremely proud of his station in life. He knows he is a symbol of
> superiority, a sign of elevation, supremacy, of dominion in his ambience.

A pauper, a wanderer, on the edge of starvation, he ostensibly presents an image of his own value and prestige, an image which contains the values of an unlearned and unpolished intelligence, but an intelligence aware of itself, reverenced and dominating.[4] ("Cowboys and poet-singers [Vaqueiros e cantadores], 1939, p.89).

This pride often bordering on arrogance came to fit the character of the "cantador" and of those poets who evolved to also write verse in the "literatura de cordel." As one northeastern poet described so well to this author in an interview in 1967:

Yes, I do believe I represent the aspirations of the poor masses because I am a rarity among the masses, and the man of the masses considers me to be a son of the muses. He understands me, he believes me, he applauds me, he listens to me, and he pays attention to what I say. I teach him to feel, to sing, to cry, to smile and to live.[5] (Mark J. Curran, A Literatura de "cordel," p. 45)

The original "peleja" of the mid-nineteenth century was a true poetic duel between famous singers. The original duels according to Câmara Cascudo were done to the musical accompaniment of a type of guitar with eight or ten strings [a viola] or with a sort of violin, [a viola de arco] ancestor to the "rabeca." The two poets would insult each other, each bragging of his talents and expertise and would debate using their knowledge of history, mythology, religion or geography, each one constructing his own imaginary, poetic "castle" or "making his mark" (one sees the inheritance from the oral epic tradition). The verses were full of hyperbole and braggadocio. At times there were lines or at least images which came from famous duels of the era, memorized by the singer for special occasions [obra feita]. But the good poet could always dominate the other through rapid and clever improvisation.

The old duels were in four-line strophes of seven syllables [quadras] with xaxa rhyme, but that meter has all but disappeared. A few of the famous singers were truly illiterate like the famous black slave Ignatius [Inácio] da Catingueira, but most knew the "classic" books of the backlands: a sort of farmers' almanac of the times [Lunário Perpétuo], the basic mass missal for Catholics [Missão Abreviada], and even "The Story of Charlemagne and the Twelve Knights" ["História de Carlos Magno e os Doze Pares da França"].

Perhaps the most famous duel, an integral part of Northeastern folklore to this day, is "The Duel between Roman and Ignatius" ["Peleja entre Romano e Inácio"]. A poetic duel now converted into myth in the Northeast, its participants were Romano Mãe D'Agua and

Inácio da Catingueira. According to the popular myth, the duel lasted eight days and nights and was a ferocious battle finally won by the semi-literate poet Romano who won by using "science" or facts from formal schooling to defeat the illiterate but brilliant slave Inácio. No one today believes the business about the eight days' duration, and in fact folklorists believe the duel may not even have ever taken place. What is for certain is that there were several versions or at least bits and pieces of the original version transcribed to verse in "cordel" by no less than Leandro Gomes de Barros, Francisco das Chagas Batista and João Martins de Atayde, the early cordelian masters. Câmara Cascudo believes that the original version of the duel was written by one of the best of the original "cantadores" of the nineteenth century, Ugolino Nunes da Costa.

Today when the "cantador" performs he is usually accompanied by a friend or rival, and they are in effect "in business" together. The competitive spirit is present in the duo when they perform the "peleja" or as it may be called today, the "cantoria." They are cognizant of famous, now legendary duels known to the masses of the Northeast, duels immortalized in the booklets of verse of "cordel" or in learned studies by scholars. Bits and pieces of those duels can still be heard in the "borrowed" verse of some of today's best "cantadores." But the fierce duel of old may be reduced to a "rhymed conversation," at times an almost choreographed performance between two poets who are friends and partners on the radio, TV and university auditorium circuit.

Today's themes are as varied as life, for the "cantador" improvises about what is happening in the present. There was a time when one poet tested another on geography, on the rivers and cities of Brazil, but today the poet who improvises with a clever turn of the tongue or a tongue twister seems to rule the day. Poets talk of the Brazilian national debt, the evil International Monetary Fund, the ups and downs of President Sarney's plan to deputize the populace to check on price abuse in the grocery stores, or more recently the debacle of the impeachment of Fernando Collor de Mello in 1990. But whatever the form or the topic, the tone of the old "peleja" remains along with certain formulas: the boasting arrogant challenge to the rival, the equally fierce response, the threat to "throw" the other poet off his rhyme and metrics with a difficult metaphor, meter or turn of the tongue. Much may be really memorized from classics of the past, but a quick mind and poetic gift of improvisation can win all.

Some believe the poetic duel of recent times and of today lacks the quality of the past, that commercialization has taken place, or that the radio, TV or public address systems have taken away the spontaneity and challenge of the past. But the medium remains and in fact may be more present than "cordel" itself in today's new millennium because it is performed live and still can draw a crowd. One can debate the quality of the poetic duel of today, which in effect is to debate what our times have to offer, but the medium does remain.

So the "cantador" is yet today a very real personage for the Northeasterner, whether performing at a combination roundup and rodeo [vaqueijada] in the Cariri region of Ceará, or on a public TV station or in a college auditorium in Rio de Janeiro or São Paulo. He may be a construction worker rather than a sharecropper or cowboy, and he may improvise on the radio instead of the veranda of the plantation owner's Big House [Casa Grande], but he carries with him the tradition of the past and the folkloric view of the present. And should the "cantador" ever pass from the scene, we now have a record of his presence through the recordings initiated by folklorists and available on disk, tape and even CDs. But more important is the written record of the verse of the "cantadores" in the booklets in verse of the literatura de cordel sporadically sold on the streets but available in all the great collections.

Because of the extremely large number of titles and poems, Portrait chooses to list some colorful and indicative titles now and the text from one of the most famous poems. Here is just a smattering of titles translated to English, first the cordelian "classics:" The Duel of Manoel Riachão and the Devil, The Great Duel of Black Lime with Ignatius da Catingueira, The Duel of Blind Aderaldo with Zé Pretinho from Tucum, The Duel of Joe Light with the devil, Duel of Bernardo Nogueira and Black Lime or the famous Great duel of Romano Elias with Azulão.

The earliest of the cordelian masters followed the tradition and invented their own duels with rivals in "cordel:" The Duel between João Atayde and Leandro Gomes de Barros, The Duel of João Atayde and José Ferreira Lima, The Duel of João Atayde with Raimundo Pelado do Sul, Duel of Joaquim Jaqueira and João Melchíades, or Duel of José Carlos with Manoel Tomaz de Assis.

And the tradition continued to the most modern day with well-known poets of "cordel" (many of whom were never "cantadores") writing their own imaginary or sometimes real duels with local singers or rivals in "cordel:" The Amazing Duel between Francisco Sales and Black Vision, Tremendous Duel between Francisco de Paula and João José (with the two "singers" shown drinking bottles of Brahma Choppe or Choppe Antártica beer in a local bar), The Duel of José Soares with Biui Silva, Great 'Singing Duel' realized by Manoel Camilo dos Santos in the Home of Monsenhor Silvestre, Duel of Costa Leite with Dila in Caruarú, or The Encounter between Blind Aderaldo and Rodolfo Cavalcante.

And dozens of imagined duels in the form of encounters, debates and discussions exist as well: The Encounter of Rui Barbosa with Castro Alves (Brazil's greatest statesman versus Brazil's greatest romantic poet), Duel of Garrincha and Pelé (Brazil's famous modern soccer stars), and even <u>The Country Bumpkin and the Playboy</u>, extolling the way of life of both. Common also are the encounters and discussions between country bumpkins and city dwellers, between sellers in local fairs and tax collectors, between Bible beating Pentecostals and traditional "old church" Catholics, and between sugar cane rum drinkers and tee totaling Protestants, the most famous being one of the oldest: <u>The Debate of Master Vulture with the Protestant Preacher</u> (seen in Album I).

The duel we choose to exemplify all is one of the old classics: <u>The Duel of Patrick with Ignatius da Catingueira</u> [Peleja de Patrício com Inácio da Catingueira][6] for it has many of the traits of the true old-time duel with good poetry as well. It is extremely difficult to capture the linguistic spirit and tone of the duel in English, but <u>Portrait</u> at least can give an idea of the content and atmosphere of a classic encounter.

The poem opens with the classic boasting in turn by each singer. Patrick says his poetic "blows" can knock out teeth and even knock your head off, and any singer who encounters him is already defeated. Ignatius says his baptismal name is Inácio da Catingueira but he was raised in Piancó and learned his trade in Teixeira (the cradle of the art of the poetic duel) and has left only carnage in his wake. The boasting continues for pages with Patrick adding that he makes fun of storms, that the owl fears <u>him</u> (the owl being a fearful predator of the night in Northeast lore), so Ignatius better prepare for the worst! Ignatius answers,

> "Calm down Patrick
> You are no lion
> For even the fierce lion
> One day loses
> Even its strength
> And a man finishes him off."

Patrick answers that when he was born the midwife [<u>parteira</u>] compared him to Samson and with the features of Roland! Ignatius answers, you better read the books and see what happened to Samson and Roland!

The battle suddenly turns into racial insult when Patrick accuses Ignatius of being a black man whom he will "tear into pieces." Patrick reminds Ignatius what Romano Mãe d'Agua did to him in a former duel. Ignatius says he was defeated by Romano's use of Sacred Scripture, and that Romano was really so afraid of him that he actually turned white with fear!

Patrick accuses Ignatius of being a common slave without education wanting to take liberties with his status in life. Ignatius answers that even though he was raised as a slave, he had good upbringing and manners and was well thought of by all. He says, if you, born a free man, are so educated and smart, where are your manners? Patrick says he was born poor but free, that he educated himself and has no trace of black blood. You can tell when he talks! Ignatius responds: What about that black skin of yours and that kinky hair? Those big white teeth and red gums? Hey, we look just alike, you sure seem to be like me!

Patrick says, Well, okay, I am dark skinned and I do have curly hair, but no man ever paid money for me. I'm not like you with grandparents who were slaves all their lives! Ignatius says, okay, but this forces me to marvel, hearing someone call himself "dark" when his skin is black as coffee! Your grandfather came to Brazil to be bargained for!

Patrick gives in, admitting that Ignatius knows their ancestors well, but says let's move on to a modern theme. Ignatius says all right, but don't get on your high horse and forget where you came from, after all, "He who lives in a glass house shouldn't throw stones" [Quem tem defunto ladrão/ Não fala em roubo de vivo]!

So the atmosphere of boasting, the pattern of challenge, response, challenge, response, and the racial theme of an era of slavery and preoccupation with social status based upon color is captured in this clever poem. Other tests of knowledge about sacred scripture, geography and mythology might handicap the great Ignatius, but quick thinking and courage allowed him to compete with others. One important aspect of the modern cantoria is absent in this famous poem—the poet who wins by using tongue twisters or a clever turn of phrase—but even this latter technique came from the famous old duels as well. Poetic talent, native intelligence and a sharp tongue made of such poets the heroes of the cordelian tradition. Such skills and poems remain to this day an important part of the poetry and an integral part of the entertainment of its poets and public.

2 "Cordel" Itself as Entertainment and Diversion

From the very beginning of Portrait the reader has seen that "cordel's" main functions for its public are first of all to entertain, then to inform and to teach. "Cordel" is essentially a narrative poetry with rare touches of lyricism. Motifs in the poetry converge when any given poem may cross boundaries and include one or more thematic types and may also entertain, inform or teach. A classic story of Charlemagne and his twelve knights battling the evil Moors exists first of all as an epic adventure story, but it also does tell however loosely of historic times and its basic underlying message is moral. But in this album of Portrait one sees specifically the entertainment function of the thousands of booklets of cordelian verse— how they entertain their public and how they document their public's other diversions.

Aside from the long standing entertainment function of the oral poetic duel [peleja] and its talented personage and participant, the singer and improviser of oral verse ["cantador"], it must be repeated that almost all of the "cordel" entertains. Although Albums I and II, the beliefs and manifestations of religion, exist primarily to teach and inform, they also almost always tell or retell a story, and this in itself serves to entertain. The moral stories of "cordel," the "examples" of Album III called "religious moral whoppers" by Candace Slater in her book "Stories on a String" the Brazilian 'Literatura de Cordel" above all teach and inform but they do this by also by telling an entertaining story or yarn (does one really believe that the young lady who beat up her own mother on Good Friday was turned into a dog?).

Album IV, "A Model to Live By," in its essence is storytelling in verse in a fictional mode, recounting the fairy tales, the stories of Charlemagne, the stories of love and adventure and even the retelling of the escapades of the real bandits of the twentieth century Northeast—all are meant to entertain.

And finally, Album V, "Life Is a struggle and Life Is a Saga" in essence recounts and tells the tale of the poor, northeastern migrants' efforts to escape intolerable living conditions in a drought-plagued Northeast and the long journey to the South East for survival. But one asks, why do the migrants want to hear time and again of the miseries of the drought and the stories of the difficult journey, the struggle to survive in a foreboding huge city and the jokes played upon them in their new lands? They already know the facts and do not need to be informed about them. But in the telling and the retelling they live a memory, they feel the nostalgia of home, the homesickness for relatives and friends not present. It is no different than going to the theater and seeing a tragedy or listening to a beautiful symphony in minor key (and one is reminded of the incredibly sad but beautiful violin solos of Schindler's List, telling of one of the greatest tragedies of all times). Entertainment is as large a part of the mix as learning what happened and the lessons from it.

Future albums will teach and inform as well—the story of Brazilian politics and history for one hundred years in Album VII or of world events in Album VIII. But there are dozens of cordelian poems that treat "cordel" itself, explaining what it is, why it is, telling the story of its renowned poets, lamenting the death of the most famous, and documenting forever the famous fairs and markets where the same poets have entertained an enthusiastic and waiting public for one hundred years. These too are the essence of the "cordel" as entertainment. The poet, who he is, what he stands for, and his role in relation to the public is a part of his total personae. He cannot be separated from the totality of what he does and what he produces, so the "cordel" itself and its role for its public is another aspect of entertainment.

The scenario of cordelian entertainment, the fair and marketplace, has held the key to the success of the former and its slow disappearance as of late (at Portrait's original writing; as already noted, "cordel" has had at least a minor comeback in recent years). Many story-poems exist to document forever the famous fairs and markets, perhaps the place most associated by the northeasterner with having fun and socializing with his neighbors. And finally, other manifestations of folk and popular culture which entertain are publicized and treated by "cordel" and sum up this album on how the people of the backlands and the rest of the cordelian public have entertained themselves for one hundred years. Portrait begins with the poet and his poetry.

The Poet and His Poetry

In the beginning as <u>Portrait</u> has said, poets were few. These were the pioneers who transcribed stories in prose from Portugal into the back lands' sextets and septets and printed them in the fragile booklets of the first "<u>cordel</u>"—people like Silvino Pirauá Lima and then Leandro Gomes de Barros, Francisco das Chagas Batista and João Melchíades Ferreira da Silva. Then came the first "entrepreneur" [<u>empresário</u>]—João Martins de Atayde who was from the interior but established his printing shop, stable of cordelian writers and sales network in Recife. Because of his dominance, the entire "<u>cordel</u>" in the region became known at that time as the "reefs" [<u>arrecifes</u>] or poems from Recife. Then came an entire generation of poets who traveled the fairs and the markets to sell their verse—Manoel Tomaz de Assiz, José Pacheco, José Cordeiro, Manoel Camilo dos Santos, Rodolfo Coelho Cavalcante, Cuíca de Santo Amaro, Minelvino Francisco Silva, among many, worked in the 1930s, 1940s and 1950s. Old veterans and new stars persisted in the difficult 1960s: João José da Silva in Recife, José Costa Leite in Pernambuco state, Rodolfo Coelho Cavalcante in Bahia, Manuel D'Almeida Filho in Maceió and others. Major writers showed up in the South, especially in Rio de Janeiro and sporadically in São Paulo.

But it was the 1960s when scholars, both foreign and Brazilian, really began to take interest in "<u>cordel</u>"—traveling to the interior to collect poems in the markets and fairs, interviewing the poets, and most important, publishing articles and books about them. As a result the poets themselves began to become aware, along with a middle and upper class urban public, of the importance of the "<u>cordel</u>" and its place in the cultural heritage of Brazil. At the same time major efforts took place to collect the "<u>cordel</u>" systematically, publish anthologies with facsimile editions, catalogues of titles and learned studies about the poets and poetry. The bottom line was an <u>awareness</u> of the poetry, both for its historic role and the real danger of its slow disappearance with the modernization of Brazil. Out of this awareness many new poems were written and published about the poetry and poets themselves. A plea for its survival was generalized. It is this story which dozens of poems tell.

One poet stands above all others in this new saga, creating visibility for "<u>cordel</u>" and defending its poets as well as their "cousin," the "<u>cantador:</u>" Rodolfo Coelho Cavalcante who wrote poems in Bahia from the early 1940s until his death in 1986.[7] Born in Maceió in the state of Alagoas, he lived a rough and tumble childhood dealing with an alcoholic father and running away from home frequently to escape the abuse. Eventually he traveled the interior with a brother putting on puppet shows, on one such occasion running into the bandit Lampião and his troops and being held prisoner overnight. Then he had his real apprenticeship as entertainer as a member of several tiny back lands' circuses, doing everything from crying the arrival of the circus from the back of a burro to becoming the main circus clown, handling fiscal matters as secretary and writing the mainstay of circus entertainments, a sort of melodrama.

From there he was sidelined in a brief stint as a protestant preacher and a grade school teacher, but dabbled in "cordel" in 1940 in Teresina, Piaui, writing out poems by hand and selling them in the streets, with topics, among others, about Nazi sympathizers during World War II. After a long journey through the backlands, still involved with circuses, he became established in Salvador da Bahia in the early 1940s where his career in "cordel" took root and bloomed. Printing poems and selling them in front of Bahia's Modelo Market [Mercado Modelo] and Lacerda Elevator [Elevador Lacerda], Rodolfo soon gained fame, first of all in a campaign to clean up the smut in local "cordel," but then moving on to greater things.

Inspired by a convention of Brazilian writers and journalists in Bahia in the early 1950s, Rodolfo decided to do the same thing for his "class," the poets of "cordel" and their "cousin" poets the "cantadores." The idea became a mission in which this "evangelizer in 'cordel'" spent every resource, financial, physical and emotional, which culminated in a national congress for the poets in 1955. From that point the dream grew and Rodolfo established the National Association of Cordelian Poets and Poet-Singers [Associação Nacional de Trovadores e Violeiros]. Another national congress followed in São Paulo in 1960, then a period of bankruptcy, sickness and exile to the tiny town of Jequié in the interior of Bahia, surviving by selling old coins, kerchiefs, pendants, and antiques but still doing his own "cordel." There was a revival in the 1980s when Rodolfo succeeded in getting the city of Bahia to install a permanent market stall to sell his and other poets' poems in front of the Modelo Market, a major tourist site in Brazil. He founded a new organization, the Brazilian Order of Poets of "Cordel," and soon gained national visibility.

In his stated production of 1,700 different titles of "cordel" and in his own four-page journals and in local conventions and congresses, Rodolfo did much to make "cordel" known to middle and upper class urban Brazilians throughout the Northeast and in Rio, São Paulo and Brasilia.

What can happen to a poet and the struggle to write, print his poems and survive is seen in an important poem by the important and really fine poet in Rio, José João dos Santos, "Azulão," who wrote such classics as Joe Hillbilly in Rio de Janeiro and The Early Morning Train, but now tells of his poetic odyssey in The Artist Unjustly Treated.

Azulão's poem The Artist Treated Unjustly [O Artista Injustiçado][8] may speak for generations of cordelian poets and poet-singers. He says he writes it directly for his public because they need to know the real facts. His theme is exploitation of all artists, but in particular the poets of "cordel," and his speaks from firsthand experience. He believes the poet is still respected in the original Northeast, but in the South he lives not only forgotten and poor, but actually persecuted. The worst persecutor is the license or tax collector [o rapa] who harasses the poet wherever he tries to sell his stories in the plazas throughout Rio de Janeiro.

Azulão touches on an age-old complaint: that Brazilians recognize as good only that which comes from outside of Brazil [moçambismo], a phenomenon which Brazilian intellectuals have attributed to a deeper problem—a national inferiority complex! But Azulão says it took the interest of the foreigners, specifically a "Frenchman" who went from one end to the other of Brazil recording "cantadores," researching "cordel," publishing articles and giving lectures (the ubiquitous Raymond Cantel from the Sorbonne who began cordelian research in 1964, amassing some say the largest private collection outside Brazil) to pull "cordel" out of the near bottom of the national cultural barrel. Azulão says Cantel's presence brought a veritable "invasion" of French and American researchers to the fairs to record and film the poets and "cantadores." Soon, Brazilian grade school, high school, and university teachers and their students sought out the poets for research papers, now recognizing "cordel" as a Brazilian "national resource."

Those Brazilians that previously looked down their collective noses became "experts" overnight, saying who was good or who was bad in the poetry. And as a result, pseudo-poets and "false artists" jumped on the bandwagon, brownnosing these "Johnny-come-lately scholars" and presenting themselves as the true and best poets. (Azulão can barely contain himself when he speaks of the former.) The worst insult: these "so-called poets" [poetaços]," this "plague," who dress up like cowboys and live "deforming" [deturpando] our poetry and shaming the Northeast!

Meanwhile, the real poets live marginally, unable to publish their poems, and the printing shops print "fantasy and phony decoration" instead of real cordelian verse. So-called "benefactors" have come forth in the press telling how much they have supported the poets and all they have done for them.

"They just want our poems
And to record our "cantadores"
To congratulate our performances
To applaud us, but they give no real value
They take advantage of our talent
And real money, we don't even see its color."

Azulão who is also a well-respected "<u>cantador,</u>" speaks specifically of this latter talent: they invite us to give a "<u>cantoria</u>" and want us to sing for nothing; they record the whole thing and pay us with beer, whiskey and rum. They think artists do not eat, do not need clothes, do not have to pay rent and are content with just being famous, even with tuberculosis and starving children. Well, the singers who work for nothing are idiots; with my belly empty I send fame and flattery to hell!

The poet concludes (and we paraphrase): I know these lines of verse may hurt, but they just want to make us museum pieces. The so-called help they say they have given us is nowhere to be seen. If just one-half the promises were true, I would be a rich man! Another exploited artist was Master Vitalino of clay doll [<u>boneco de barro</u>] fame of Caruaru, Pernambuco State. His pieces are in the museums and homes of the wealthy, and he is dead and his family poor. I hear there is a lawsuit in the works. I myself, says Azulão, have an L.P. of "<u>cordel</u>" poems, a big success with successive printings. The company tells me I had rights to only the first printing.

So that is why sometimes you will see me "let it all out," and get it off my chest. Here is what I will do:

> "When I see myself oppressed
> I use my pen to let it all out
> The lyre becomes the forge
> The poetry becomes my hammer
> I put this band of thieves to the torch
> And I melt them all in my forge
> That pack of thieves."

They will censure this poem and deny it all, but I have told how the "artist treated unjustly" really lives!

Azulão could be sure that the traditional public of "<u>cordel</u>" would hear or read the poem and agree with him. Solidarity amongst equals! A few other "rebels" have told similar stories, and they are true. The poet like his public and his poetry is a survivor.

The Market and the Fair

Equally important throughout the modern history of "cordel" are the booklets of verse the poets have written which describe the essence of the folk-popular ambiance of Brazil: the stories about the markets and fairs. Without the fair or market the poet could not exist, and the weekly market day and fair is probably the primary social "institution" of the cordelian public. In these stories one truly sees how this poetry is connected to something larger, to an entire way of life that in fact is fast disappearing in modern Brazil. Cordelian classics are the ABCs of Cayrú Plaza (the plaza in front of the Modelo Market in Salvador da Bahia in the 1940s and 1950s), What the St. Joseph Market Has to Offer (the São José market in Recife during the same period), The Northeastern Fair in the São Cristóvão Plaza in Rio de Janeiro (the 1960s to the present), and The Plaza of the Republic is Poetry (one of the main sites to sell "cordel" in greater São Paulo).

Rodolfo Coelho Cavalcante's ABCs of Cayrú Plaza ["ABC da Praça Cayru"],[9] is a classic written some years back and is a small gem which epitomizes how a market or a fair and all it comprises can be a major source of entertainment and pride in the Bahia of the 1940s. Portrait paraphrases and quotes a good portion of the poem:

The plaza is a place where journalists can document the traditions of Bahia, the folklore of its poetry, where "everything" is popular. The Cayru Market is where whites and blacks mix freely (the essence of Bahia's dream of mixture of the races), and is the scene of the "flea" market, folk photographer, soap box protestor, and troubadour.

There is Chico "the propagandist" with his p.a. system set up in the middle of the plaza, gathering a crowd in an instant and then making his magic and selling his merchandise. If you happen to go by at noon, you'd better close your eyes and ears or else you will lose lunch time listening to "your faithful servant" reading his verse! Police watch carefully, our "guardian angels" who defend, guard and deserve respect! Men, women and even small town crooks [malandros], people of all colors, travelers—they are our spectators. And quoting the verse,

"Suddenly you hear
The shout of "Get the thief"
It's the pickpocket in the market
Who just lifted something
All the people run after him
To get a close look
At the author of the confusion.

"Super hot!" "Fresh right now!"
Another shouts, "Have another one!"
Where are these shouts from?
It's the boys selling sweet rice.
And then the SNAKEMAN
Gives out a shout: Here we go!
And the people gather round."

"Nozinho "Cego de Fole"
Is playing "Joaseiro"
In front of him is "Benedito"
And nearby a singing poet
He is playing "Brother Samba"
And the great black kid arrives,
"Carioca the tambourine man."

"Lots of stuff, booklets of "Cordel,"
Magicians, singer-poets
Acrobats, glass-eaters
Hundreds of vendors
All in the happiest atmosphere
Like a symphony
Of Beethoven, my readers."

"Rodolfo Coelho stands
Under a shade tree
Declaiming Getúlio Vargas,
Juracy and The Brigadier,
Mangabeira and Adhemar,
The World Is Coming to an End,
Two for the price of one!"

One vendor has a voice so loud that he makes the Elevator Lacerda tremble. Others sell towels, woolen mattresses, material to cover sofas, and there is always the Bahian lady selling a bean-pepper-peanut oil snack [abará]. The street photographer [Lambe-Lambe] is there from sunup to sundown taking pictures of the people. There are sellers of roots and herbs, selling a remedy for toothaches and "body pain" and whatever ails you.

Hey, you can go hear the troubadour who will read you a story poem and not charge you a cent! The "common man" says to the poet,

"Hey I like it, Mr. Troubadour,
I like to hear your stories
Because they have a flavor
Something to console my sorrows
And then I saw two big tears
Roll down his face, dear reader."

Little commentary is needed, but the reader of this book who has had the good fortune to amble through one of the old markets or fairs of the Northeast or even the northeastern fair in Rio de Janeiro recognizes that this is the life of the cordelian public that is captured in all its essence in the entertaining story poem of "cordel."

The Praça Cayrú is now just a name, another former plaza full of life relegated to the noise, pollution and danger of a major traffic artery in the lower city of Salvador da Bahia. To be sure, the Modelo Market is still to one side, the Lacerda Elevator to another, but the small sailing boats' [saveiros] dock next door to the market is essentially gone, its market and fish fair a thing of the past, save for the wonderful descriptions in Jorge Amado's novels. Rodolfo's successors have a small poetry stand in front of the market entrance, but this marvelous scene of popular life in the 1940s described in the ABCs of Cayru Plaza is a thing of the past. One wonders, is it worthwhile to make an effort to keep such a thing going, or is its passage inevitable? One could say the same of "cordel." Portrait hopes to keep some of the memories alive.

3 The Humorous Story [O Gracejo]

But another type of booklet of "cordel" has sold by the thousands of copies and hundreds of titles over the ages—the funny or humorous story [gracejo]. It literally can be any eight page story sold in the market or fair that generically is considered "humor." The difference between this sort of poem and any story that may simply have a funny part or anecdote is that the former is from the very beginning written solely to entertain and make the fair goers laugh.

Liedo Maranhão, an expert and writer on "cordel" from Olinda, Pernambuco, says in his book Popular Classification of the "Literatura de "Cordel," ["Classificação Popular da Literatura de Cordel"] that these stories are written "to make the hillbilly laugh in the middle of the fair."[10] The poet José Costa Leite who is one of the great veterans of the poetry in Pernambuco is well-known for such stories. Old timers like José Pacheco were famous before him. Franklin Machado in his book What Is The "Literatura de Cordel"? [O Que É a Literatura de Cordel?] says the gracejos are simply any comical story in the form of a joke, anecdote or laughable situation meant to satirize life, thus, in effect, establishing a more "generic" definition for such poems.[11] But both he and Liedo Maranhão insist on distinguishing the "gracejo" from the "obscene" but non-malicious poems of another name, the stories of "putaria" or "safadeza." These latter poems are extremely rare but have caused printing shops to be closed down and poets and vendors to be chased by the law. These are the poems which Rodolfo Coelho Cavalcante found in the market in Bahia in the early 1940s, poems which insulted his own sensibility and the very existence of "cordel" according to the poet. They became his first cause célébre in Bahia in the 1940s (even though he admitted writing the more innocent "gracejos" with double entendre to make money and criticized his competitor Cuíca de Santo Amaro for selling truly pornographic poems with plain, brown covers to selected customers, these in addition to his "legitimate" cordelian stories). The "putaria" or "safadeza" poems are obscene, pornographic, describe the genitals and all manner of sex acts, and use vulgar or obscene language; these are the rarity in "cordel." Both scholars quote titles like The Dream of a Maiden. Liedo Maranhão apologetically includes its text, a "dream" a young lady has and tells to a girlfriend, describing all manner of sex by all sorts of folks. But he also admits that Cavalcante's anti-smut campaign worked and one can no longer find such stories (circa 1970).

Regardless of terms, language, definition, classification or scholarly arguments, all these poems make the humble buyer of traditional "cordel" in the marketplace laugh, and are a major source of entertainment for him to listen to, buy and take home for relatives, friends and neighbors to read. The line between a story which is a bit risqué and still considered a "gracejo" and a poem with no sexual allusion is sometimes fuzzy. Samples of double entendre stories considered "gracejos" are The Man With the Soft "Horn" [O Homem da "Gaia" Mole], Rosa's "Parakeet" and Vicent's "Turtledove" [O Periquito de Rosa e a Rolinha do Vicente] (respective sex organs), The Hillbilly Traveling Salesman Selling "Roll Tobacco" (read: penis) [O Matuto Vendendo Fumo Ambulante], or The Encounter Between the Seller of Roll Tobacco and the Old Lady that Sold "Tobacco" (read: his and her sex).

But in the broader sense famous "funny" poems need not be about sex at all. José Pacheco's The Fight Between the Dog and the Cat is such a classic. Apolônio Alves dos Santos' modern The Animals' Party [O Forró da Bicharada] follows in the tradition. The hillbilly poems that were described in "Life is a Struggle . . . Life is a Saga" in Album V are such cases, meant for the country bumpkin to laugh at the fair. The Statement the Hillbilly Gave to the Sheriff is a good example. Azulão's Joe Bumpkin in Rio de Janeiro, once again, is a classic.

Any story about "horns" or cuckolded husbands (Album III) will always bring a laugh, like The Man Who Was Born to Be a Cuckold, Mr. Mané of the "Big Point" or the Greedy Cuckold, or Azulão's classic The Age of the Cuckold.

The moral "examples" of Album III almost always have a humorous element, for who could believe the outlandish titles like The Girl Who Married Nine Times and Continued a Virgin. Highly moral, never obscene or "pornographic," such stories' titles were intentionally "borrowed" as models for the double-entendre "gracejo" stories like The Woman Who "Gave Tobacco" in the Presence of Her Husband (read: "had sex").

But whether making fun of themselves or others, the humor stories of "cordel" are among its most entertaining and important, and as long as they appear in the markets, one will know that the famous non-confrontational, "get along" attitude and accompanying "fix" [jeito] of problems by the Brazilians are intact and will keep Brazil a safer and less violent place.

4 Brazilian Soccer [Futebol]

A final important example of "cordel" as diversion are the hundreds of titles that tell of the national pass time of soccer [futbol]. In these story-poems one enters a sphere where the anticipation and the ecstasy of victory or the devastation of defeat rule the national psyche. God, Soccer and Carnival by the BBC is the title of one of the best film documentaries ever done on Brazil, and the title is not accidental. The diversity of Brazilian religion, the only real sport in Brazil and the national party do sum up much of Brazil. One could add the day at the beach, and the picture would be closer to completion. Gurus, pundits and scholarly theorists say that the Brazilian brand of social "democracy" with its mixture of race, religion and idealism is found precisely in Maracanã Stadium on Sunday afternoon, at the "Sambadrome" [Sambádromo] when the samba schools parade during Carnival and on any beach in the south zone of Rio de Janeiro in the hot summertime.

"Cordel" revels in portraying this national pass time in sports, soccer [futbol] as it is in Brazil. Poets are as much fans as their public, and in Brazil you root [torcer] for a team as much for social reasons as for the sport itself. One asks "Are you Flamengo?" as in the same breath you might ask "Are you Catholic?" or "Are you Brazilian?." And the answer, "I'm Fluminense" or "I live and die by Vasco" places you clearly in the mind of another Brazilian in regard to both the sports and social spectrum. The proof is seen in the soccer stadium, but also on the streets of the country on game day when people dressed in the team colors drive through neighborhoods honking car horns and waving huge team banners or run and shout in the streets after a victory.

Behind all this of course is the idea of having fun, of being entertained, but it is perhaps more complicated when seen as a reflection of the psyche of Brazil as a third world giant. There are dozens of books, news articles, weekly features and talk shows dedicated to one question: how goes the national soccer team and what are its chances in the next World Cup? Brazil, in short, believes that it is the best in the world at this sport, that only an accident of fate can keep it from winning the World Cup of Soccer held each four years, and that its style of soccer is truly national and Brazilian and is different from the rest.

You need a ball, something to represent a goal at each end of an empty space and time to play. All Brazilians, rich and poor, from the huge cities of São Paulo and Rio to the tiny field along the São Francisco River in the interior of Minas Gerais or a tributary to the Amazon, have the requisites. An empty field can be converted in the imagination of a boy in Piaui to a country Maracanã, the largest soccer stadium in the world built in anticipation of Brazil hosting and winning its first World Cup and to house the future new world champion (except for an unlikely accident of fate). The fates were simply acting just like Brazilians in 1950; they came late when Brazil was upset by little Uruguay in the world cup in the new Maracaná stadium in Rio de Janeiro. But Brazil eventually got its world cup (and more) as planned, beginning in 1958.

But this game is the game <u>par excellence</u> for a poor boy living in a slum or a tiny backlands village. You can play barefoot, you don't really need a uniform, and if you have to, you can roll up old rags or newspaper to make a makeshift ball [<u>bola</u>]. But if you are a bit creative and take up a collection, you probably have the means to get a real soccer ball. One of the national stereotypical notions is that Brazil is great at soccer because everyone learns playing in sand on the beach, and there is some truth to the notion. "<u>Futbol</u>" is ubiquitous on the beaches of Brazil where leagues are formed, portions of beach marked off, and any weekend produces literally hundreds of games throughout the nation.

The sport was imported by the British in the nineteenth century, was nurtured in private clubs for whites only, but eventually allowed blacks to play. Time passed, the sport grew along with the number of fanatical followers, and Brazil became an international power in the 1950s. Brazil was the first country to win the World Cup three times, thus, it had the right to keep the coveted Jules Rimet Cup. But as they say, "only in Brazil;" the cup was later stolen out of a display window in Rio possibly by an opportunistic thug-fan. Brazil has since added an unheard of fourth World Cup victory and is always a favorite to win. Consequently, its stars are superstars earning megabucks. There are many rags-to-riches stories, with Pelé leading the way, closely followed by Mané Garrincha, and then Sócrates, Zico, or a Ronaldo or Ronaldinho. After the third World Cup victory in 1970, a "soccer-brain drain" hit hard when big stars and coaches were hired away by Middle-East sheiks to play or coach for petrol-dollars, and even the snooty European leagues hired classy Brazilian players to bolster their empires, the most famous as of late being Barcelona with Ronaldinho and recent success in Europe.

But the World Cup is only every four years and takes place far from Brazil most of the time, so the really big annual affair is the Carioca Championship in Maracaná in Rio. Ever more hyped, ever more outlandish each year, <u>the</u> game in the Maracaná is a national spectacle with all the fans dressed in respective colors and carrying huge banners for each team. When the teams come on the field or score the elusive goals there are huge displays of fireworks and smoke bombs. It's Carnival all over again.

SIDEBAR This author experienced the Carioca Championship between long-time perennial favorite Flamengo and Bangu in the Maracaná in 1966. Seated in the lower deck "for safety" according to our host, we still experienced from afar the shouting matches, the brawls, the sudden balls of fire caused by burning rolled-up balls of newspaper thrown from the upper deck on anyone below, but mainly we witnessed the spectacle on the field. It was a dilly that year. The players entered the field by a tunnel from the dressing area and were welcomed by a roar of humanity. The game progressed but was unusual in that one of the stars, semi-crippled from a rough tackle, was forced to play almost the entire final period with a severe limp, unable to go out because of substitution rules. In fact in an amazing move, the referees called the game, so it actually never was finished, an extremely rare thing.

Most amazing to this author was the standing room only crowd in the "moat" surrounding the field. These were the cheap seats, and one soon learned why. A strange phenomenon took place throughout the game: a few troublemakers would begin to move, walk and then run around the oval. If you did not move with them, you had a fair chance of being trampled and possibly crushed to death. From afar it looked like a wave of red and white maggots oozing around the oval. And this was just a sidelight to the main event taking place on the field. The wild celebrating after the game was on the fringe of being out of control. Brazilian fans never ever need be accused of complacency and quietly watching the game, a complaint frequently heard after U.S. athletic contests.

We saw the great Pelé on another rainy day in the Maracanã, once again from afar and alas with no binoculars. The famous number 10 on the white jersey of Santos was the center of attraction in the contest held some years before Pelé bolted to New York and the Cosmos and added millions to the respective coffers. END SIDEBAR.

But it is the national team and the whole drama of preparation, anticipation, the games themselves and the aftermath that rule the stories of <u>futbol</u> in "<u>cordel</u>." Brazil <u>is</u> number one, the only team to win the cup four times in 1958, 1962, 1970 and 1994. The immortal Pelé and almost as good Garrincha starred in the first two wins along with a great cast, but it was the win in Mexico in 1970 that put the icing on the cake, for with the win Brazil was allowed to keep the coveted Jules Rimet Cup, proof of its superiority. <u>Portrait</u> chooses a description of that win as our example of all the stories, in part for the moment, but also because its author is one of the most celebrated in "<u>cordel</u>" for reporting on soccer: José Soares of Recife, Pernambuco, the "Poet-Reporter." Stories on soccer always guaranteed good sales and a bit of money in his pocket.

In <u>Brazil Campeão do Mundo 1970</u>[12] the poem reflects the game and also the era. At the height of oppression and censorship under a military dictatorship, President and General Garrastaçu e Médici was captured on international television at Aztec Stadium in Mexico with a transistor radio to his ear rooting for "his" national team. The regime had learned some time ago that the Roman axiom of Bread and Circuses could fit in a third world developing nation: give them carnival, football and Miss Universe and perhaps they would not mind total censorship and lack of a voice in society. People have stated that the only place one could shout <u>against</u> anything in Brazil during that time was in the soccer stadium. So the win also in a unusual way "proved" that the military could bring good times as well as bad and that Brazil was worth its salt on the world scene. José Soares' story summarizes all the games and the victory celebration, but his comparison of the "pretty" soccer of Brazil to that played by the ruffians from England in a way summarizes the entire epoch of the battle for world domination in the sport:

"England also
Was the devil of Europe
It invented a rough game
Saying Brazil was not up to it
But Jairzinho our detective
Arrested the thieves of the Cup . . . .

The English came to play
Armed with clubs
Our Captain Carlos Alberto
Settled that in a hurry
Not even respecting
'Ole Queen Elizabeth.

Although playing mainly a supporting role, Pelé still symbolized the team:

"My Pelé from Santos
Pelé that enters the fray
Pelé who "kills" with his heart
Pelé who plays with verve
Pelé who battles on the field
Pelé who enters the fracas."

There was carnival in the streets of Brazil, a tremendous celebration, but the poet could not forget the political moment as well in telling how the players themselves celebrated:

"In Everaldo's house
In Rio Grande do Sul
There was partying with beer
Port wine and <u>Pitú</u> (cachaça)
Shouting out "vivas" to Havelange
Zagalo and Garrastazu."

One notes that the president-dictator-fan was from Rio Grande do Sul.

"Cordel" tells much more. There are more bitter stories like the one when Flamengo—the national "people's" team—sells the great star Zico's contract to Italy, just another in the series of "soccer-drains" suffered by a too successful national program. But there are glorious stories praising King Pelé and Mané Garrincha, the latter the star who perhaps best embodies the struggle and the saga of the Brazilian national character.

Garrincha,[13] crippled since his youth, used a limp and awkward style of running to fool [driblar] the best players in the world, but was a tragic figure. Unable to handle success and life, he made a mess of marriages, fell into alcoholism and died poor and forgotten. Much like the bandit Lampião or even Brazil's best known president Getúlio Vargas, his real life foibles are forgotten in "cordel" which has now made him myth, greater than life. Garrincha although perhaps not greater than Pelé who has his own rags to riches story, seems more Brazilian.

---

[1] Antônio Teodoro dos Santos, Peleja de Garrincha e Pelé, São Paulo: Prelúdio Edta., n.d.

[2] Our introduction comes from these sources: Leonardo Mota, "Cantadores, 3rd. ed., Fortaleza: Imprensa Universitária do Ceará, n.d.; Luís da Câmara Cascudo, Vaqueiros e "Cantadores, Porto Alegre: Edta. Globo, 1939; and Gustavo Barroso, Ao Som da Viola, new edition, Rio de Janeiro: Departamento de Imprensa Nacional, 1950.

[3] See Câmara Cascudo, Vaqueiros e cantadores.

[4] Cascudo, p. 39.

[5] Mark J. Curran, A Literatura de "cordel", p. 45.

[6] Leandro Gomes de Barros, A Peleja de Patrício com Inácio da Catingueira, in Curran, Antología Bilingüe da la Literatura de cordel, Madrid: Editorial Orígenes, 1991.

7   See Mark J. Curran, <u>A Presença de Rodolfo Coelho Cavalcante na Moderna Literatura de Cordel</u>, Rio de Janeiro: Nova Fronteira-Fundação Casa de Rui Barbosa, 1987.

8   Azulão, <u>O Artista Injustiçado. n. p., n.d.</u>

9   Rodolfo Coelho Cavalcante, <u>ABC da Praça Cayrú</u>, Salvador, circa 1943, xeroxed copy.

10   Maranhão, <u>Classificação . . .</u>, pp. 87-90.

11   Franklin Machado, <u>O Que É a Literatura de Cordel?</u>, Rio de Janeiro: Códecri, 1980, p. 69.

12   José Soares, <u>Brasil Campeão do Mundo 1970</u>, Recife, 1970.

13   Flávio Poeta Fernandes, <u>A Vida de Garrincha</u>, Caxias, 1983.

Album VII

In Politics We Hope But Do Not Trust

Introduction

From their very beginnings the current event stories of "cordel" were "the newspaper of the poor" written by the "voice of the people" or the poet who always has been aware of his role as interpreter and spokesman for his public.[1] Some poets became "poet-reporters" who made their living in a rudimentary journalistic fashion by seeking out the events that "would awaken the interest of the people" and writing poems on them to sell in the marketplace. José Soares in Recife, Pernambuco, and Cuíca de Santo Amaro in Salvador da Bahia are cases in point, but most poets wrote these reports one time or another.

Modern times brought changes and a new awareness. In the 1950s and 1960s regional and national reporters for major news dailies, national magazines such as Manchete and Fatos e Fotos or Realidade, as well as television came to understand the poets' journalistic role and scholars came up with a name for it: "folk communication" with its "recodification" of national news into the simple six-line strophes of "cordel." They tried to explain what the poets already intuitively knew and took for granted: that the poet takes a major event that he has read of in a magazine or a newspaper or, more recently, seen on television, and "reports" it to his public in language and with a point of view familiar to them, thus retelling in his own way ("re-codifying") the message from the media. And it sometimes works the other way: the poet reports on local events for his own public and at times the major media pick up on his stories, "reporting" them to a middle and upper class readership.[2] Such a story was the "Cowboy who gave birth in the Alagoan backlands" in Album III.

But there is more to it than that. The hundreds of booklets of "cordel" which are journalistic in nature in their totality comprise what one could call a "folk-popular history" of twentieth century Brazil. In this writer's book History of Brazil in "Cordel" ["História do Brasil em "Cordel"], São Paulo, University of São Paulo Press, 1998, we saw how "cordel" is important as one of the sources for the learned historian in writing about his country. The reason is that from its very beginnings in the late nineteenth century there always was a part of the "cordel" that in fact reported on major events. But the poets did more than report; they gave opinions, they gave counsel, and they entertained at the same time.

A few scholars have always had the courage to recognize "cordel's" role; after all, its creators are poor, semi-literate, "uncultured" poets from a marginalized sector of society. Pedro Calmon, one of Brazil's important historians, wrote a book The History of Brazil in the Poetry of Its People in 1929 which traced events of the nineteenth and very early twentieth century, but dealing with poetry from the oral tradition and only very early "cordel." And another Brazilian historian said, "It's common to hear that Brazilian History needs to be retold. If Historiography decides to take up this task, it need not look down upon a comparison of the official version with the popular, because this confrontation will help to rewrite the true history of the Brazilian people."[3] Album VII tells that story with samples from the accustomed divisions of Brazilian history from the beginnings of "cordel" to the present, one century of national life.

But before getting to the stories, a few remarks will clarify what is found in them. Apparent from the whole is that the poets and their public have shown an amazing optimism. Because of their poverty and in many cases their basic inability to change their status in life, the cordelian readers have always looked for help from without. On the one hand, the basic search in the spiritual realm for a savior, a real messiah to alleviate their misery and better their lives, has been a constant in "cordel." That is why it tells the stories of Albums I and II, of looking to Jesus, Mary and the saints, and closer to home, to Antônio Conselheiro, Father Cícero or even Friar Damian.

But when it comes to the basics of job, home and food on the table, the only possible saviors are the politicians—the local, regional and national leaders who can bring funding to bear on the economic realities of Brazil. What "cordel" shows time and again is what one could call an "incredulous optimism," not really an oxymoron but closer to a paradox. Experience has taught the most humble reader of "cordel" that the politician—current or future leader—will say or promise almost anything to get elected. In most cases, in the minds of the cordelian public, the winner of the election then forgets those who elected him.

But yet, there are a few cases where the leaders do try to alleviate basic injustices and poverty, and they become the great political heroes of "cordel" who bear one message: there is hope. Some would say that this is one of the basic traits of the Brazilian people, the ability in spite of insurmountable difficulties, to survive and look to the future with optimism.

What also becomes clear from the cordelian chronicle is how much one can learn of Brazil, of its people with their hopes and aspirations, and of its major leaders and the flow of the most important of national events. The stories in their totality are a major reflection and document of a people and its way of life, thus an important album in Portrait.[4]

1 The War of Canudos and the Old Republic

The War of Canudos in 1896-1897 in the dry backlands of Bahia state was perhaps the first major event reported by a cordelian poet who was contemporary to it and a participant as well. But to understand the War, one needs to know what happened before it took place. The Old Republic had begun in 1889 and marked the real end of nearly four hundred years of Brazilian history since the time Portuguese explorer Pedro Álvares de Cabral discovered the country in 1500 and Portugal explored, colonized and ruled it. Colonization from the mid 1500s and growth under the Crown of Portugal took place until 1822 when Brazil became independent adopting the Republic as a form of government. But because the son of the Portuguese king was the person who declared Independence and expressed a desire to remain in Brazil (with his ironic "I'm staying"["Eu fico"] speech), little changed. In effect Brazil became a constitutional monarchy with the same royal family, the Braganças, ruling until 1889 when disillusionment brought change. Portugal's royal family and their descendents and its social-economic structure of class and slavery were no longer wanted. And besides, the United States and France provided models for the "new" Old Republic.

The Old Republic of 1889 would last for forty-one years and thirteen presidents, military men at first and then civil leaders of the "coffee and milk" regimes where the state of São Paulo and then Minas Gerais would alternate their man in the presidency. Times seemed to be good, material progress and national development were taking place, but some were getting along a lot better than others. This was revealed by an event that would in effect awaken the national consciousness to an awareness of the "other" Brazil—the northeast interior where extremely poor, uneducated and "fanatical" rabble would dare to challenge the power of local, then state militia, and finally the national police and army in a war to the death. Antônio Conselheiro, a self appointed leader and "messiah," led a ragtag army of poor squatters, backlands cowboys and ruffians in successful battles against the military might of the Republic, calling for a return to the better days of the Monarchy.

A soldier and participant wrote a major cordelian poem about the war years, but from later retirement days in João Pessoa, Paraíba: João Melchíades Ferreira da Silva's The War of Canudos.[5] His attitude as retired soldier and patriot is unwaveringly clear: in 1897 the Brazilian Army was led by a "warrior general" by the name of Artur Oscar against the rabble of a "bandit chief:"

"There rose up against the Republic
The bandit most cruel
Deceiving a great people
With an unfaithful doctrine
His name was Antonio
Vincente Mendes Maciel . . . .

To deceive the people
Ignorant people of the back lands
He invented miracles
Saying in his sermon
That he would change water into milk
And rocks into bread."

For the poet, the fanatical leader Antônio Conselheiro had created a band of hoodlums in Canudos just like the feared bandits Antônio Silvino or Lampião who would plague the Northeast in later years, and he describes the Canudos leader and his followers in the same language he would use to talk of bandits ten years later:

"The most perverse men
Of an unruly instinct
Deserters, horse thieves
Criminals and practitioners of witchcraft
They came to fill up the troops
Of the fanatic Conselheiro."

The poet goes on to tell of the third and final army expedition to Canudos in 1897 and the bombarding of the miserable place with heavy cannon until all was destroyed. The War was also reported by the journalist from Rio de Janeiro Euclides da Cunha who later wrote a book which became a national classic—Rebellion in the Backlands ["Os Sertões"]. It not only told the story of the war but opened the eyes of urban Brazilians to the "other Brazil" of poverty, misery, ignorance, blind faith and courage, the Brazil of the poor of the fringes of the Northeast.

The chronicle of the Old Republic would continue until its end in revolution in 1930 when the most beloved of all Brazilian politicians and presidents would begin to rule, Getúlio Vargas from Rio Grande do Sul state. But the thirty-three years between Canudos and that moment were amply reported and commented upon in the cordelian chronicle. The vicissitudes of fraudulent elections, political favoritism and nepotism (plagues to the present day in Brazil) would be reported upon and more importantly commented upon by cordelian poets of the time, perhaps the best being Leandro Gomes de Barros.

Leandro was a gifted poet and observer of the times who also possessed a great sense of humor and displayed it in stories which were highly critical but clothed in irony. He railed against corrupt Brazilian leaders and their cohorts in action, the capitalists from England who were in bed with the early presidents but brought capital, expertise and real accomplishments—for one, the building of the national rail system in Brazil.[6] The poet spoke of the high cost of living and bad times for his public, but his favorite topic was taxes. Taxes were imposed to pave and pay the way for the economic progress, and already the vibrant, progressive and relatively young São Paulo and old capital Rio de Janeiro were demonstrating their economic, social and political hegemony over the now poor cousins, the dilapidated states of the colonial sugar cane economy of the Northeast.

In one of his best satires, <u>Pots that Everyone Stirs</u>,[7] Leandro said:

"Brazil today
Is just like a cooking pan
Politics the cook
Is putting her on the fire
But a thousand hungry people
Are hanging around the flames . . . .

"Brazil is like an old donkey
With its old white tongue hanging out
So many trying to ride it
The old wreck has had it
Rio got up on the saddle
And São Paulo right behind it . . . .

"It's just like the politics
Of this current regime
Brazil is the pan
The state adds the salt
The municipality stirs it
But it's the Feds who get to eat.

"Poor Old Ceará
Has no one to complain to
He looks longingly at the burro
But he can't get on
Only when it finally stops running
Then maybe he can catch it.

"Bahia, Rio de Janeiro
São Paulo and Minas Gerais
They said it's our donkey
And belongs to no one else
But Porto Alegre says
It came from our corral."

Leandro can only conclude for all his colleagues of "<u>cordel</u>" in <u>One Stick with Too Many Ants</u> ["<u>Um Pau com Muitas Formigas</u>"],[8]

"They call this the century of light
I call it the century of fights
The age of ambition
The planet of intrigue
Lots of dogs and one bone
One stick and too many ants.

"So since the Republic
Everything causes us fear
Belly clubs don't study
But they have a Ph.D.
The bandoleer is the law
The rifle the governor."

The poet is talking of course of justice by those with the most firepower, the political bosses [coronéis] of the Northeast. This was a situation which the northeasterners believe brought on the age of northeastern banditry which symbolized the first thirty years of the twentieth century, for often the bandits were hired or used by the bosses in local battles for land and power. Portrait has already seen in Album IV the epic stories of the bandits Antônio Silvino, Lampião and Maria Bonita and how those real life criminals became bandits because of various injustices done to their families. They were made myth and today are the Robin Hood and Bonny and Clyde for generations of Brazilians.[9]

But at the same time there was also a beginning of political protest, violence and efforts at change. The "Salvations of the North" or regional political battles to wrest power from the old landed aristocracy-oligarchy by new urban, business interests flared up in the Northeast in 1910 and 1911. The best example was the "War of Juazeiro" reported in "cordel" in 1914 when an army of rabble in support of Father Cícero Romão of Juazeiro do Norte, Ceará, battled and then took control of Ceará State. But Cícero's people soon lost power and things returned to a shaky but familiar sameness.[10]

The Old Republic and its fraudulent politicians and elections would continue until 1930, but the 1920s brought signs and seeds of what was to come. A new wave of military officers called the Lieutenants [Tenentes] had become disillusioned with the lack of a role for the military in the governance of the nation in the 1920s. Their leaders demonstrated a new social consciousness and they helped to spark military revolts in Rio de Janeiro in 1922 and in São Paulo in 1924. "Cordel" faithfully reported on both. The old guard and the national army prevailed in both cases, but it was at this point that one of the most courageous and long-lasting of Brazilian politicians and leaders came upon the scene and forever became a part of the national memory. Luís Carlos Prestes, the "Knight of Hope" as Marxist writer and political activist (at that time) Jorge Amado so dubbed him in a biography of the period. Prestes escaped from the São Paulo uprising in 1924 to lead hundreds of followers on an odyssey through the West and North of Brazil, the journey eventually dubbed as "The Prestes Column." He tried to rally the poor rural masses to rebel in a Marxist inspired revolution, but he failed and fled to exile in Bolivia and then prison.

"Cordel" reported the infamous Prestes' Column particularly as it traversed the Northeast. But strangely enough, the yeast of revolution did not rise; the poor were too closely tied to the whims and favors of the landholders for their survival. The revolution did not "take," and cordelian poets characterized Prestes as a rebel, an anti-Catholic and contrary to the national needs in their stories about him. But as the national political chronicle would develop and attitudes would change in the 1930s and 1940s, Prestes would once again appear on the national scene, this time as conquering hero.

2 Getúlio Vargas—"Father of the People"

The leader who did succeed in capturing the political hearts of most Brazilians was a consummate politician from the most southern state, Getúlio Vargas of Rio Grande do Sul. He succeeded in breaking up the political monopoly of São Paulo and Minas Gerais, gained the support of the military and brought a breath of fresh air to a stale political atmosphere which dated back to 1889. Getulio would contest the fraudulent election of 1930 and rise up against the old regime in the same year with the support of disenfranchised politicians and states, including an important ally in Paraíba state, just coincidentally the homeland of the <u>cantador</u> and "<u>cordel</u>," Dr. João Pessoa, the local governor who was assassinated in 1930 by the status quo opposition. The act was considered the final desperate measure of the old regime to retain power, and the assassin was called a "perverse monster" in "<u>cordel</u>." The murder helped spark the revolution.

Getúlio ruled largely by friendly persuasion and by fiat, establishing a regime resembling Portugal's Corporate State of Antônio Salazar which had begun in 1928. He walked a tightrope between right and left, civilian and military, and succeeded outlandishly. When Communists threatened in 1935, he put down the rebellion easily. When right wing fascist Integralists reared an ugly head in the late 1930s, he found a way to eliminate them. At first neutral during World War II, he then became a partner of the Allies due to pressure by the United States, hemispheric economic ties and finally German submarine attacks on Brazilian merchant ships after Brazil had declared war on the Axis Powers in 1942. But Brazilian military generals who fought under Mark Clark in Italy in 1944 and 1945 began to wonder how they and their soldiers could risk their lives against tyrants in Germany and Italy while in effect tolerating a dictatorship under Getúlio at home. So they deposed him in 1945. These same "Defenders of the Constitution" would appear time and again in the twentieth century in such a role.

After a "vacation" on his ranch in São Borja for five years (even though theoretically elected a national senator), Getúlio launched an amazing public relations and political campaign to regain the presidency in 1950. But this time he wore the emblem of a "democrat" and using leverage he established by backing social and workers' legislation in his early terms, he won in a landslide. Now "Getúlio the Democrat" and workers' rights' president, he flirted with the left, trying to repeat once again the tightrope act of the 1930s. But economic woes and the particularly effective lobbying via the press of one of Brazil's political muckrakers, Carlos Lacerda of the conservative UDN (National Democratic Union) party, succeeded in making life difficult for Getulio. The great leader, the "Father of the Poor," committed suicide in the national presidential palace, the Catete Palace, in 1954, leaving a long letter explaining his plight.

"Cordel" had found its messiah! Getúlio became the sacrificial lamb who offered himself up for the benefit of the nation to protect the presidency and avoid civil war. To this date he is recognized as the most talented politician-president of Brazil, able to manipulate and control the myriad interests and pressure groups surrounding him, and father of social legislation and workers' rights in Brazil (a sort of Brazilian FDR). The poems of "cordel" adopted this charismatic leader and captured twenty-four years of national history in the process. For them, it was the first political victory for the poor in Brazilian history.

In an important book Getúlio Vargas in the "Literatura de Cordel"[11] the journalist and writer Orígines Lessa captured the Getulian odyssey in "cordel." From the early days it was the personae of Getulio that carried the day: charismatic leader, man with a pleasant smile for all, first a father figure, later a grandfather, and especially a "messianic" figure for the poor. Getulio was at least indirectly responsible for the codification of legislation for workers rights to organize and later social laws for all the people via FDR style social security plans. But Getúlio really became the people's hero when the opposition threw him out in 1945; cordelian poets printed literally dozens of titles from 1945 to the victory in 1950, all supporting the great leader.

Poems reported on and chronicled the entire Getulian odyssey. The Armed Revolt in São Paulo[12] in 1932, early in the Getulian presidency, told how his regime squelched a rebellion by old time conservatives wanting a return to "coffee and milk" days, but how Getúlio amazingly showed great mercy upon its leaders. Poems documented the Getulian New State [Estado Novo] which in effect prepared the way for his dictatorship from 1937 to 1945, telling of the infamous Cohen Plan contrived by the Integralists but adopted by the Vargas regime. It purportedly revealed a "communist revolt" which Getúlio used to initiate dictatorial state of siege powers. Later "cordel" reported Getúlio's crackdown on the Integralist party, a fascist leaning right wing group supporting Axis powers in the late 1930s. This was the final step to his absolute power. Getúlio closed the national congress and named his own "interventors" or state governors to run the country.

After World War II during which all protest or political dissension had been necessarily suspended by war powers acts, the unhappiness of those who had lost control—the old conservatives and the idealistic democrats who believed Getúlio had become a dictator and tyrant—came bubbling to the surface of the political pot once again. In 1945 Getúlio declared a complete amnesty to all past enemies of the regime as a sign he was not a dictator, so the Integralists and Communists came home to roost. "Cordel" chronicled the famous speech by Marxist Luís Carlos Prestes in a jammed soccer stadium in São Paulo in 1945, declaring him a returning hero.[13] Prestes, recognizing the power of the old right along with the ongoing threat of Integralist returnees, sided with Vargas as a lesser of two evils. But

Getúlio pronounced one too many personal dictums, and the democratic defenders of the constitution, the military, deposed him.

"Cordel" captured his departure from Rio, describing it more like a long needed vacation and rest than being thrown out of the presidency. Cuíca de Santo Amaro, the cordelian gadfly from Bahia and a long time admirer and supporter of Getúlio who claimed he had a personal friendship with him and was under his protection in the political hotbed in Bahia, wrote The Return of Getúlio to His Native Land,[14] quoting the president:

> "I am going to leave all politics
> Which for me is a pain
> I want to live on my ranch
> Sitting on the veranda with no tie
> Seeing all the happenings
> Up there in the Catete Palace."

Sit he did, but not with an idle mind; Getúlio immediately began planning his return, creating a revamped and fresh political machine for the great campaign of 1945 when he was elected a national senator and culminating in his presidential victory in October of 1950—the "We Want Getúlio" or "He Will Return" campaigns. It is worthwhile to quote Cuíca de Santo Amaro's paraphrasing of the old Apostles Creed (parody was a common technique in "cordel" in Bahia) because it summarizes what the people thought about Getúlio:

> I believe in Getúlio Vargas, All Powerful, and Creator of
> the Workers' Laws. I believe in Rio Grande do Sul and
> its Son, our patron who was conceived by the Revolution
> of 1930, born of a Holy Mother, invested in power by
> Washington Luís, and was decorated with the emblem of the
> Republic. He descended into Rio de Janeiro on the
> third day, paid homage to the dead [of the revolution]
> ascended into Catete Palace and today is seated in
> São Borja [Getúio's ranch in RGS] from whence he shall
> come to judge General Dutra and his ministers. I
> believe in his return to Catete Palace, in the communion
> of his thoughts, in his succession to President Dutra,
> and to his life everlasting. Amen.[15]

But the dream became a nightmare. After a few months of hiatus after his inauguration in 1951, the opposition began to rumble once again, among them Carlos Lacerda and cohorts, the same protagonists as in 1945, but this time with increased charges of corruption against the Vargas machine now accused of flirting with labor and socialism. The pressure got to Getúlio and he killed himself. There was a flood of cordelian poems lamenting his death, recalling his great days, but mainly placing him on the pedestal of messiah and also sacrificial lamb. It took some mental jumping jacks to do this while at the same time juggle the Catholic concept of eternal damnation for the sin of suicide. The poets wondered how Getúlio could be condemned to hell if he gave his own flesh and blood to save the presidency and the nation from civil war and chaos once again.

The justification was in Getúlio's own words in his suicide letter to the people when he declared his role as victim. Rodolfo Coelho Cavalcante vehemently declared that Getúlio did not really commit suicide, but was "murdered" by the traitors who opposed him. Like Christ himself, Getúlio was mistreated and oppressed, the proof being an assassination attempt months before. Who killed Getúlio? Not the poor, not the workers, not the oppressed masses, but the Doctors, the political traitors![16]

The poets wrote poems like <u>The Last Will and Testament of Getúlio Vargas</u> and in them they got even (an old cordelian trait) with Getúlio's enemies by employing a traditional story technique—sending good Getúlio to heaven where he pronounces from afar and in safety his last wishes:

— for Carlos Lacerda [one of the plotters of his assassination], death in hell
— for his political "son" Jango Goulart, the advice to leave politics and its nastiness [ironic in perspective because Jango would become president of Brazil years later]
— for the Brazilian people, the Workers' Laws and freedom
— for the politicians, the national treasury to misspend in their crooked election campaigns[17]

Thus "<u>cordel</u>" marked the end of the Getulian odyssey and prepared the way for ten years of chaotic Brazilian democracy highlighted by Juscelino Kubitschek and the founding of Brasília, an optimism but then pessimism regarding the strange Jânio Quadros, and then confusion about the reforming but threatening socialist Jango Goulart. With the latter's demise, Brazil then would enter a dark period of misunderstanding and hate, of idealistic and radical youth versus the traditional defenders of the constitution and democracy, the military.

3 Democracy and Chaos—1954 to 1964

Introduction

The period from 1954 to 1964 was one of the most chaotic but also vibrant in the sense of political action and the workings of Brazilian democracy. Getúlio's suicide in 1954 left as Vice-president Café Filho of the old PSD [Social Democrat Party]; in Brazil president and vice-president can be from separate parties. The constitution was respected, elections were held, and Juscelino Kubitschek was elected with João Goulart his running mate and vice-president to be, the latter a disciple of the great but deceased Getúlio Vargas. Kubitschek faced strikes by the Air Force, drought in the Northeast and political attacks by right-winger Carlos Lacerda who was now governor of powerful Guanabara state which included the city of Rio de Janeiro. But the new president was not to be denied and expanded Vargas' efforts of creating a national steel producing and automobile manufacturing industry, founded SUDENE ("Superintendency" for the Development of the Northeast) to deal with perennial problems there, but most of all headed the planning and construction of Brasília the new capital. Carved from an area really in the center of the country in eastern Goiás State, it would have a history of its own and symbolize the move westward, a longtime dream and version of Brazilian "manifest destiny."

But, if it could be possible, national politics was becoming even more complicated. Small deposits of oil had been discovered and fostered a new nationalism ("the oil is ours") and conflicts with international petroleum companies and western capitalism. The Cold War was at its height and Eisenhower sent John Foster Dulles to Brazil to get cooperation for CIA activity to fight the Red Plague. Left, right and centrists who guarded the constitution debated. Inflation and international debt grew once again (one recalls that "cordel" had told of President Affonso Pena who faced similar problems as early as 1909.)

But the 1950s were also good to Brazil. Its own avant-garde cinema became internationally known, Bossa-Nova arrived at the end of the decade as did the internationally acclaimed film Black Orpheus, and Brazil finally won its first World Cup in soccer, a great event highlighted by the play of a future world superstar, Pelé. But it was Brasília that galvanized the nation.

Created by Kubitschek with planning and architecture by Lúcio da Costa and Oscar Neimeyer, it used open space and modern materials of pre-fabricated concrete and glass to fulfill an original new vision. Literally created out of nothing, its construction involved building an original landing strip and transporting huge quantities of construction equipment by air. It was rumored that its founder had close ties to the concrete companies supplying the materials. As time went on, costs rose, money was printed to pay the national debts, and the old charges of corruption and cronyism of the Vargas regime were applied to Juscelino.

The huge economic expansion during Kubitschek's regime had a price and became the focal point of the 1960 election. A bespectacled former professor, Jânio Quadros of São Paulo, won the day with a national media campaign showing him with broom in hand to sweep away the corruption of the past. "Symbol, substance and style" was the cry of the day, but Quadros' regime soon became rather strange, then chaotic, and Jânio resigned after only seven months in office in August, 1961.

The regime had become famous for its unorthodox ways: Jânio often ruled by decree via handwritten notes passed on to cabinet ministers or congress. He adopted safari dress as the official government civil service "uniform" for the tropics, prohibited skimpy swimwear in the beauty contests, cock fights, bingo games and raffles and authorized horse racing only on Sunday. But his real downfall came when he actually tried to reform corruption in government and dared to touch upon the sacred cow of the Brazilian civil servant system. He also tried to follow a third-world political bent and on one occasion decorated Cuba's Fidel Castro with the Brazilian national medal. An effort at stabilizing inflation by adjusting currency brought a roar of outrage by the populace when prices of staples like bread, sugar and gasoline skyrocketed. Without warning Jânio resigned on August 25, 1961.

As "cordel" would often say, "the devil was on the loose." The resignation brought a crisis: Vice-president João "Jango" Goulart, a former minister of labor under Getúlio Vargas and a suspected socialist or even communist sympathizer, was in Singapore on an official trip to Communist China. The old "golpistas" of 1954 rose again and plotted with cohorts from the right with "Operation Mosquito" to blow up Goulart's airplane on its return to Brazil. Cool heads prevailed, congress debated, and Brazil, ever flexible, found its solution: change the form of government to a parliamentary system, thus in effect, taking power from the president and handing it to ministers and congress. Goulart had no choice but to accept and was inaugurated in 1961.

He did succeed as early as 1963 in turning the parliamentary system back into the old presidential system via a plebiscite vote. But his road was rocky. Determined to put into effect what he called the "Base Reforms," he forged ahead with the most controversial—what would be a national system of land reform—long heralded by the left as part of a national solution to rural poverty. Then Jango ran into a brick wall. Calling on all supporters, the regime organized a massive march in favor of the reforms in 1964 with 150,000 people marching in the "Central Parade" in Rio. The right answered with even larger protests, the most famous being "The March of the Family with God for Liberty" in São Paulo with an estimated 500,000 participants.

Protests increased as well as strikes. An enlisted man's revolt in the Navy in Rio added flame to the fire when Goulart refused to back the Navy's disciplinary code and punish the enlisted men. CIA involvement in the revolt was proved later, but the minor event caused Goulart to lose any support he might have had among neutral army officers and left a conservative, communist-fearing hard line in control.

But it was the old muckraker Carlos Lacerda who really sparked Goulart's downfall by mobilizing his own state police in Rio de Janeiro against the central government and evoking total censorship on April 1, 1964. Soon army rebels from the First Army in Minas Gerais began to march on Rio and powerful São Paulo General Armando Kruel joined the rebellion. The head of the national senate declared the presidency vacant even though Goulart was still in Brazil, and Jango fled into exile in Uruguay. The Protectors of the Constitution, the armed forces, temporarily moved in to take control and then by fiat among friends made it permanent.

Cordelian journalism played its part. The ten years from 1954 to 1964 proved to be another heyday for "cordel" with an atmosphere of complete freedom to report, approve or denounce events as they happened. No stories had the quantitative success of the suicide of Getúlio in 1954, but events still provoked stories sufficiently successful in which the poets fulfilled their role in the "newspaper of the poor" by the "voice of the people."

In 1955 the poets and public had things to worry about, like the newly elected Kubitschek-Goulart team being allowed to take power. The "golpistas" of 1954 who feared a turn to the left and wanted a chance at a return to national power for themselves were spearheaded by Carlos Lacerda, muckraking journalist responsible in large part for the old opposition to Getúlio Vargas in 1945 and now to Juscelino and Jango in 1961. Their backers had carried the day, so the Juscelino-Jango team entered office and eventually Brasília became a reality.

Nevertheless, Brasília now was the center of politics in the nation, and President Kubitshek's term came to an end. Jânio Quadros the ex-professor from São Paulo was elected and began his term in 1960,[18] and a seven month debacle followed. "Cordel" followed it from beginning to end, first optimistically as usual, noting that when Jânio revalued the national currency, he was in effect saving Brazil millions on the international debt. It also praised him for firing lazy public servants, many of them for doing nothing, but getting paid at two or three separate agencies (a famous tactic known to all Brazilians of the period, that of the famous "sign in book" [livro de ponto] where the triple-dipping public servant signed, left, signed yet again and again and received three salaries!). The poets recognize the great courage of Jânio who even required the large military attaché forces in plum posts in the exterior to be cut (perhaps skating on ice a little too thin). But his good intentions—raising the price of gasoline to protect the Brazilian oil company Petrobras and its employees— backfired when the cost of transportation caused steep increases in the price of foods like meat, bread, rice, coffee, butter and flour, not to mention bus and trolley fare increases passed on to the poor public. In spite of all, the poet is optimistic and believes good times are ahead. But they were not. Jânio Quadros resigned suddenly on August 24, 1961 after only six months in the presidency.[19]

One now sees in the previously ultra-conservative "cordel" verses tinted with the pro-labor, anti-capitalistic rhetoric of the age. Murmuring of U.S. intervention is mixed with a staunch defense of Jânio's third world independent policies. Yet an underlying fear caused by the Caribbean breezes from Cuba wafting south to Brazil is seen in a new cooperation between right and left. With Jânio gone, the plot by "golpistas" to murder his legal successor Jango Goulart squelched, the parliamentary system installed as a stopgap measure, the last democratically elected official in Brazil for twenty-one years would come into office in 1961—João Goulart from Getúlio's home state Rio Grande do Sul.

Jango had to walk the tightrope, proving to the right he was not a communist sympathizer and to the left that he indeed would be a strong pro-labor successor to Getúlio. He went to Washington D.C. carrying the anti-communist message but only received a "wait and see" response. Back home he had to do something to prove his progressive stance, so he proposed the Base Reforms, the keystone being an amendment to the constitution with the result that cash payments for land expropriation need not be made to the concerned landholders. Furor followed.

The interest of cordelian poets and public in land reform is entirely obvious; after all, they were traditionally from the land and had suffered no end of personal upheaval as a result of an unjust land tenure system. But the country was becoming radicalized. Leftist congressman Francisco Julião had formed the "Peasants Leagues" in the Northeast after visiting Cuba to see Castro's model. He incited hopeful squatters to move in on big plantations and demand ownership changes. The National Students Union which was heavily leftist as well and always in favor of populist causes volunteered for the Popular Culture Movement which advocated literacy programs for the poor, but in large part to help them gain the vote. With the large mass of rural voters without the vote because of illiteracy laws, (a fact only altered with the post-military Constitution of 1988), the left hoped to turn the political tide.

But there was opposition as well as support for the changes. The fact is that at this time both sides wrote "pseudo-cordel"—booklets in verse with blatant propaganda for one side or the other—in order to affect the public voice. One side attacked the Peasant Leagues in The Peasants League and Julião's answer:[20]

"Now the Peasant Leagues
Are taking property
Tearing up deeds
Humiliating the authorities
Practicing injustices
Crimes and barbarities.

"Coming from the depths of hell
One Francisco Julião
Seemingly expulsed
From a den of thieves
Today he walks the plazas
Trying to get the people's attention."

The poem portrays Julião as a crook, and worse yet for a cordelian public, a hypocrite, leading the poor peasants like lambs to the slaughter. It accused him of promising a rural labor union, land, bread and money when really deceiving the people for his own ends. The only ones he fools are the ignorant ones who dream of being rich without working, who want something for nothing! The poem registers an "old church" view that if there is poverty and injustice, it must be God's will. It counsels the people to have patience and carry their cross just like Jesus. It denounces Communism, land reform in Cuba and the difficulties of life that such a system would bring to Brazil.

The other side was just as vehement in condemning the right and its link to the Catholic Church in trying to keep the people down. But its rhetoric and propaganda were no less offensive and false than that of the right. Rafael Carvalho used the "cordel" style in São Paulo in a book of no less than 63 pages in length: The Peasants' Letter of Freedom ["Carta de Alforria do Camponês"].[21] In it he explains Francisco Julião's program to the prospective peasant reader in the market or fair. Carvalho shows a mastery of the basic concepts and turns of phrase of traditional "cordel" to present a Marxist solution that would never come to fruition. Highly idealistic, even utopist, the book shows how political activists took advantage of the medium to spread their message.

There were true cordelian poets who were active politically and still making a living from "cordel" who wrote poems during the Goulart regime. Azulão, in Rio de Janeiro, wrote Jango and the Reforms,[22] reporting on a desperate speech by Goulart on March 13, 1964, pleading his cause for the Base Reforms. It uses the reform and workers' rhetoric of the times, saying:

"The Brazilian needs
To take this cross from his shoulder
And to indoctrinate those
Who live blind without light
And say to the oppressors
The land belongs to those who labor on it.

"The worker with no name
Can no longer continue.
The son of the laborer
Can neither study nor eat
The bourgeois ruining
And the poor man dying of hunger.

Paraphrasing the poet: Brazil is in misery, and the worker is being exploited; he is without a roof over his head, is naked, hungry and with no land to plant. President Goulart's plan is a challenge to the large landholders, to the trusts and to the "sharks" to resolve this problem. The poet changes to first person narration with President Goulart explaining his proposal:

"I will do the Land Reform
By the taking
Of the lands next to
The roadways and other means
Which facilitate transportation
To any region of the country.

Ten kilometers to the side
Of all roads and roadways
Or along permanent rivers
Dams and railways
I plan to begin
Within sixty days."

Goulart repeats the litany of the times: Brazil is incredibly rich in mineral resources and agricultural land; what is planted anywhere immediately grows abundantly! He proposes not only reform, but punishment to those who refuse to cooperate, and he proposes sanctions imposed by the people and the Armed Forces. But land reform will have to be accompanied by reform of the monetary system, the international lending agencies, international exchange and foreign investment. And he promises the nationalization of five oil refineries as well.

The fact is that Goulart had neither the support of the political system nor even his own party in the national congress to carry out such reforms. His plan in effect caused chaos in Brazil.

4 The Military Regimes and Pax Militar

Out of necessity, much of this long period of military rule must be summarized by Portrait. In general it was at first a period of great hope—the defeat of the Communist threat! Then came the beginnings of government censorship, crackdowns on dissidents, sporadic and violent terrorist activities (including bank robberies, kidnapping of the U.S. ambassador and West German and Japanese diplomats as well), and severe oppression in the form of a squelching of student movements, closing of leftist inspired universities, and any opposition other than token. It was a time of government by decree from a manipulated congress which even had the pleasure of seeing the "bionic senators" created by the government to swell its ranks. But the macro economy grew, contracts and patronage went to the friends of the regime, and the rich did get considerably richer.

Only the poor seemed to be really worse off economically. The famous government symbol of the "big cake" to be sliced in pieces for all Brazilians never came to be. And the symbol of it all was the ever more corpulent minister of the economy Antônio Delfim Neto whom the poets of "cordel" would excoriate in the late 1970s and early 1980s when freedom of expression returned gradually to Brazil.

"Cordel" truly chronicled the times in this portrait of a people and country. The poets' initial reaction to the military takeover was seen in stories like The Victory of Democracy in Brazil and the End of Communism[23] by Rodolfo Coelho Cavalcante who would become the number one apologist of the military regime due to his visceral anti-communism and morally conservative ways. Patriotic to an extreme, rigidly moral and a victim of communist bullies who beat him and threw him into a canal to drown because he would not write poems for their candidate, Cavalcante was in lockstep with the ideals of the regime, including their plan of returning to the old morality.

He associated Goulart and the Base Reforms with the left. The poet includes among such enemies Jânio Quadros, Luís Carlos Prestes, Leonel Brizola, Francisco Julião and "all the others who agitated against the nation."

In another poem Cavalcante praises the moral stance of the new regime—cleaning up the immorality reigning in the country and returning to a better "moral" past—a view happily corresponding to his own ideals. In such story-poems the poet fulfills his own role as "moral guardian" and guide to his reading public, a role shared by many but not all the poets. Rock and Roll, the Beatles, long hairs and hippies, and Brazil's own new "rockers" Erasmo and Roberto Carlos, were signs for such poets of the laziness, corruption and drug using young generation. Cavalcante would counsel the youth to study, get a job and be good citizens.

But trouble came with the attempted assassination of the military "candidate" to succeed General Castelo Branco, the first military president of the 1964 "revolution." Terrorists planned for a bomb to kill General Costa e Silva while on a "campaign" trip at the Guararapes Airport in Recife, Pernambuco, on July 25, 1966. (This author had just arrived in Recife to begin doctoral research.) The event was reported by the poet Antônio Lucena de Mossoró in Tragedy at Guararapes airport.[24] Using terms like "terrorism by imbeciles," the poet says,

"The Brazilian Army,
Our army from Caxias,
Has the necessary qualities
To crush tyrannical acts
Practiced by such monsters
Opposing democracy."

The poet paraphrases the statements of the head of the Ninth Army in Recife: We will punish the terrorists, traitors to Brazil, preaching false doctrines of alien lands. The poet says it will do no good to oppose the generals, and fans of Fidel Castro or Miguel Arrais (leftist governor of Pernambuco until 1964) better be prepared to face the sad consequences.

No truer words needed to be spoken. The poet predicted the times: the government crackdown with Institutional Act #5 [AI—5] and its consequences which turned Brazil into an armed camp and oppressive dictatorship. With the censorship, never directed at such a modest, humble medium as "cordel," but definitely affecting it (a poet told us in the 1970s that politics was "a dangerous dish" to be served), there was little criticism of the ever more oppressive regime of Garrastaçu e Médici who was "elected" by colleagues after the sudden death by stroke of Costa e Silva in 1969. The poems instead treated the "Economic Miracle" and the good times of the late 1960s and early 1970s. The World Cup victory with General Garrastaçu e Médici with transistor radio plugged into his ear (like literally hundreds of thousands of "common folks") symbolized the good things the military regime could bring.

Poets would praise Médici's regime at its end in 1974 for creating new social benefits for the rural worker, the primary public for "cordel," via The Rural Foundation [Funreal], an agency proposed to give medical treatment and social security to rural workers just as already given to urban workers. Minelvino Francisco Silva, the "Apostle Poet" of Bahia, wrote in 1974 The Government of President Médici and the Thanks of the Workers.[25]

A deluge of poems would praise the "pharoahonic" projects like Itaipu dam, but especially the Trans Amazon Highway, in one sense the crown jewel of the military's plans for Brazilian expansion and a true opening of the West. <u>Onward and Upward Transamazonic</u>, <u>The Transamazonic Slashing Through the Forest</u> or <u>The People and the Transamazonic</u> praised the great national saga. Only in the 1980s would the disastrous results become apparent in "<u>cordel</u>" with poems about Chico Mendes and the rubber workers' fight to save jobs and lands, a campaign adopted by the environmentalists of the world in support of the larger issue of saving the Amazon.

A different breeze began to blow during the regime of the next military president, General Geisel of Rio Grande do Sul, the first Protestant to become a Brazilian president. "Cordel" published <u>The Departure of President Médici and Inauguration of the New president Ernesto Geisel</u> and <u>Only Geisel Created the Rights of the Poor to Participate in the Bread</u>, both expressing praise and optimism at the beginning of his regime. This would be the beginning of the political "opening," the breath of fresh air and very gradual return to democracy.

The Geisel regime accepted reform of the political parties and elections for mayors and governors of respective cities and states (never expecting that his party would lose). In fact the military only lost in São Paulo and Rio, but this would be a sign of times to come. José Soares reported the 1974 elections like a soccer game, his specialty in "<u>cordel</u>," with first ARENA (government) then MDB (opposition) scoring electoral goals.[26]

Strikes by students and especially a courageous new workers movement headed by Luís Inácio da Silva known by his nickname Lula, in 1979, 1980 and 1981 would change the direction of political winds during the final military regime, that of President General João Figueiredo. The wrong man at the wrong time for the defenders of the regime, Figueiredo would admit that he did not have the stomach to govern, even though he had faithfully served the military in diverse posts since the military takeover in 1964. He would face horrible economic times brought on by forces largely beyond his control—the doubling of oil prices not once but twice by the Middle East oil nations, the resulting inflation in prices and the cost of living, and the disastrous rise in interest rates owed by Brazil on the series of foreign loans used to prop up the regime and the economy after the oil debacle. Mounting dissatisfaction by the real power holders—Brazilian businessmen—due to bad times and general discontent would culminate during Figueiredo's regime.

The poets would comment on it all especially since IA # 5 had been abrogated in 1978 at the end of the Geisel regime, and freedom of expression was slowly returning to the nation. Once again a national amnesty was declared in 1979 for political enemies of the regime. All the old leftists returned and were hailed as victims and heroes. In addition, party reforms would bring the promise of elections on the state level in 1982 and the presidency in 1985.

Commentary would range from humorous to biting criticism. Poor President Figueiredo, a cavalry general, was billed as liking horses better than people and preferring to deal with the former. It was he who took the brunt of criticism for the previous fifteen years of brutality and repression.

The poets looking back from the present time of the early 1980s would write blistering attacks on the economic and social policies of the military. Azulão in Rio de Janeiro wondered why Brazilian money is worthless: whatever happened to all the gold found at Carajás and Serra Pelada in northern Brazil? And why is it that the more oil Petrobras finds, the more expensive its derivatives are for the Brazilian populace? One begins to hear the catchphrase of the next five years, fringe benefits [mordomia] for corrupt politicians who do nothing for Brazil.[27]

Trouble comes in the regime: steel workers strike in the industrial region, their leader Lula is imprisoned but is growing in popularity and power, as is his party the Workers Party [PT]. State elections are held and the opposition wins more seats. Leonel Brizola, an old enemy of the regime, a leftist-socialist sympathizer since the Goulart days, wins the governorship of powerful Rio de Janeiro state which includes again the city of Rio.

Azulão in <u>Brazil Crying</u> sums up and epitomizes the Figueiredo regime,

"After the man made
A horse of the nation
He saddled it, got on
Turned loose the reins
And let it run wild
Where the high cost of living invades
With the fury of a shark.

"So I ask how it is
That the poor live but do not eat?
A nation that does not eat
And has no government in charge
If the bad times continue
The people are going to explode
In a revolution of hunger."

So the last chapter for the military would be the unprecedented national campaign of 1983-1984 for direct elections for a new Brazilian president. The masses took to the streets in gatherings which seemed more like carnival than a political campaign. National television showed recording artists like Caetano Veloso, Milton Nascimento and especially Chico Buarque de Holanda who were instrumental in rousing participation and enthusiasm for a great campaign which resulted in the landslide election of PMDB candidate Tancredo Neves.

Dozens of cordelian poems were written and sold like hotcakes. The Neves story, from the campaign of 1983 to the election to his tragic sickness and death in 1985, is second only to the Getulian odyssey in the national political chronicle of "<u>cordel</u>." He was to take office on January 15, 1985, but on the eve of the election he became ill. Complications arose and after seven surgeries at the best hospitals in Brazil and with the entire country on its knees, he died, never sitting in the long coveted presidential chair in Brasília. Dying on the 21st of April, coincidentally the same day as the precursor of Brazilian Independence in 1789, Tiradentes "The Dentist," Tancredo was dubbed the "Martyr of the New Republic" and author of the "New Democracy" of Brazil.

5 The Return to "Normal"—1985 to the Present

Ironically, Tancredo Neves' running mate and vice president to be, Mr. José Sarney, had been a member of the government party, so few expected any of the reforms promised by Neves to come into effect. However, the poets in 1985 actually sympathized with José Sarney (perhaps because he was from the northeastern state of Maranhão) as witnessed by Gonçalo Ferreira da Silva in A Lot of Heat in President Sarney's Frying Pan ["Muita Sarna na Sarneira do Presidente Sarney"].[28] The poet first chides God himself as committing a "precipitous action" in taking Tancredo from the Brazilian people, and then admits Sarney's hands are tied by the economic mess left by Figueiredo. He believes that no one can govern in Brazil. The days of the "Economic Miracle" are over and a new cynicism is revealed:

> "Since miracles no longer exist
> According to an unbelieving people
> What is needed is a special formula
> Which may permit the president
> Through the force of magic
> To push the country ahead."

Sarney's answer to the Brazilians was extremely rational: "I'm no saint, so don't expect miracles." He promised to continue Tancredo Neves' platform and bring change and prosperity to Brazil. Sarney became a hero overnight when he modified the national currency once again, creating the "cruzado" (many recalled the military's efforts in 1966 when they created the "New Cruzeiro" but to no avail) and established a price freeze with a fiscal policy that enamoured the nation. Sarney ordered the fixed prices of all basic commodities to be published in a list in the national media and urged the public to check these prices against price-gougers in supermarkets and other stores. An infuriated public was filmed on TV shaking the lists in front of frightened supermarket managers and arresting the owners "in the name of the Brazilian people." For the first time, lower, middle and even upper class consumers felt that they had some real power. "Cordel" reported it all in a flood of stories like The War Against Inflation and the Power of the "Cruzado".

At the same time the national constitutional assembly was at work, sort of, in Brasília. Eventually producing a document the size of a telephone book with something for everyone, the new constitution became law in 1988. But one poet wrote The Letter of Tancredo Neves to the Constitutional Assembly[29] castigating the congressmen and their flurry of paperwork and proposals which were "inoperable and utopist." Congressional "dandies" dressed impeccably in front of the TV cameras offered proposals that embarrassed thinking Brazilians.

Then came the 1989 presidential campaign when young, handsome, devil-may-care, and adventurous but mainly rich Fernando Collor de Mello would carry the day. In one of the most hotly contested political battles of Brazil's entire history, Collor de Mello, with deep political roots from the right and financial connections to the media as well, was opposed by a true man of the people, labor leader Luís Inácio da Silva, or Lula. In a meteoric rise to national visibility and popularity by virtue of his leadership of the metallurgical union and the battle against the military regimes, Lula indeed represented something different. A northeastern migrant, one of twenty-three children, semi-literate in the beginning, he worked his way up the ladder by hard work and firm beliefs in the rights and power of the working class. Espousing a workers' socialism, he was diametrically opposed to Collor.

The Collor de Mello campaign echoed past politics: his main message was to bring an end to the corruption of preceding regimes, especially that of Sarney tinged by political privilege and the infamous political "maharajas" [marajás] who earned fantastic salaries while doing nothing. Collor de Mello's slogan and image was "The Hunter of Maharajas." Using the rhetoric of a reform candidate, but really representing the old right and always stressing his traditional roots and Brazilian Catholicism (he even arranged to be seen at a mass by Friar Damian the "saint" of the Northeast), emphasizing Lula's leftist roots and manipulating a national campaign via the media and TV Globo, Collor, the "beautiful" candidate, won by a whisker.

The campaign was reported by "cordel" and "cordel" imitators. Both candidates used poets, and when this was not possible, created their own "poems" for their causes. Lula's side wrote The Duel Between the PT and the Dictator Animal and Capitalist Monster and Things Are Different with Lula for President, stories with classical worker's rhetoric emphasizing the sufferings under the old bourgeois. Collor's side wrote The Victory of Collor and the Defeat of the PT[30] emphasizing Collor's Catholicism: "He is linked to the church; he goes to confession and mass."

The PT in turn wrote scurrilous stories telling of Collor's own corruption and inefficiency as governor of his home state of Alagoas. They told of deals to cronies and political patronage, all just as bad as the supposedly evil "maharajas" he was out chasing instead of doing his job as governor. Linked to the old government PSD and then Paulo Maluf, the military candidate who had opposed Tancredo Neves in 1984, Collor is associated with all the "shakers and movers" known to the masses. His link to TV Globo (his family controlled an affiliate in Alagoas) and how the powerful national network slanted news and even campaign debates in his favor are seen in <u>The Colorful Part of Collor that TV Globo Never Showed</u>. The national televised debate between Collor and Lula was similar to that of a clean shaven, handsome, John F. Kennedy and a 5 o'clock shadowed Richard Nixon—deja vu all over again in the national TV debates: Collor, smooth, well-spoken, almost "messianic," and Lula, bearded, rough spoken and a leftist! In spite of it all, the results truly showed the national sentiment: even without the huge political machine controlled by Collor and the financial interests, Lula almost pulled it off. He would have to wait for another day, and another.

After the usual presidential "holiday" with the national press, Collor de Melo instituted a radical new economic plan, called the "Cruzélia Plan," named for his female minister of finance, but it ended in failure and the revelation of a personal scandal involving her and a married federal judge. The results of the plan were chaotic and led mainly to higher unemployment than ever due to a lack of capital and money to pay workers. But this was the only the tip of the iceberg.

President Collor's own brother started the meltdown when he denounced financial irregularities in his brother's regime. In cahoots with his financial advisor, P.C. Farias, Collor and his cronies in the regime received kickbacks from the very private entities that had made bids in Color's great plan of privatization of the old government monopolies. All was revealed in "<u>cordel</u>" by Ulisses Higino da Silva in São Paulo in <u>The Hunter of Maharajas and the Tragic Reality of Brazilian Politics</u> ["O Caçador de Marajás e a Realidade Trágica da Política Brasileira"].[31]

Collor is eventually impeached and soon politics comes full circle. An interim president Itamar Franco fills out Collor's term, his main popular image that of a president of the nation accompanied by a beautiful young girl during the Rio carnival parade. Raising her arms over her head in that traditional "samba" stance, she revealed no clothing on below the waist! The poets say you laugh or you cry.

But sanity returned with the election (and now reelection) of Fernando Henrique Cardoso and yet another monetary reform—this time with the creation of the "<u>real</u>" and with real stability and hope (for awhile). Politicians and presidents will come and go. If Brazil will ever reach its dream, only God knows, but the poets will continue to document history, now with euphoric optimism, now with desperate cynicism, but always tempered with humor and "Brazilianness." And the document will remain—a political portrait of Brazil.[32]

1.   We have been seeing this phenomenon since 1966 in poems like <u>The Cowboy Who Gave Birth</u>, <u>The Man on the Moon</u> and a plethora of "news" stories, called "acontecidos" or poems of current events, by the scholars. That was when we formulated our thesis of the poet as "the voice of the people," or "representative of the masses" in this type of "cordel" which was in effect "the newspaper of the poor." This thesis was developed as a result of interviews with the poets in 1966-1967 and in another larger series of interviews in the late 1970s. We wrote about it first in a short study entitled "Bibliography of History and Politics in Brazil's 'Literatura de "cordel","" Tempe: Center for Latin American Studies, 1969; and various other studies culminating in <u>História do Brasil em Ccordel</u>, São Paulo: USP, 1998 (2nd. ed. 2001).

2.   There are a number of journalists and academics who have done articles and created theses as to "journalism" in the "cordel." Among them are Orígenes Lessa, Ricardo Noblat, Ernesto Kawal, Ossian Lima, Roberto Benjamin, and especially Joseph Luyten.

3.   Olga de Jesus Santos, <u>Cordel, Testemunho à História do Brasil</u>, Rio de Janeiro: Fundação Casa de Rui Barbosa, 1985.

4.   Our principal sources as to the academic view of history and politics in "cordel" in Album VII are those already cited from Luís da Câmara Cascudo and Pedro Calmon, and more recent sources: <u>O Álbum dos Presidentes, a História Vista pelo JB</u>, Rio de Janeiro, Nov. 15, 1989, Centennial Edition of the Republic, and the following invaluable sources by North American Colleagues: E. Bradford Burns, 2nd. ed., <u>History of Brazil</u>, New York: Columbia University Press, 1980; and especially two seminal works by Thomas Skidmore: <u>Politics in Brazil 1930-1964</u>, New York: Oxford University Press, 1967; and <u>The Politics of Military Rule in Brazil 1965-1985</u>, New York: Oxford University Press, 1988.

5.   João Melchíades Ferreira da Silva, <u>A Guerra de Canudos</u> in José Calasans, <u>Canudos na Literatura de Cordel</u>, São Paulo: Ática, 1984.

6.   Leandro Gomes de Barros, <u>Affonso Pena, a Orphã, Uns Olhos, O Que Eu Creio</u>, Recife: Imprensa Industrial, n.d.

7   Gomes de Barros, "As Panellas que Muitos Mexem" in <u>A Secca do Ceará, Panellas que Muitos Mexem (Os Guisados da Política)</u>, Parahyba: Typografia da Popular Editora, n.d.

8   Gomes de Barros, <u>Um Pau com Formigas</u>, Recife, 1912.

9   See the following books: Roberto Albuquerque and Marcos Vilaça, <u>Coronel, Coronéis</u>, Rio de Janeiro: Tempo Brasileiro, 1965; and Manuel Correia de Andrade, <u>A Terra e o Homem no Nordeste</u>, 2nd. ed., São Paulo, Braisiliense, 1964

10   See Ruth Terra, <u>Memórias de Luta: A Literatura dos Folhetos do Nordeste 1893-1930</u>, São Paulo: Global-Secretaria do Estado da Cultura, 1983.

11   Orígenes Lessa, <u>Getúlio Vargas na Literatura de Cordel</u>, Rio de Janeiro: Editora Documentário, 1973.

12   Thadeu de Serpa Martins, <u>O Levante de São Paulo</u>, Belém: Guajarina, 1932.

13   Cuíca de Santo Amaro, <u>O Discurso de Carlos Prestes</u>, Salvador, 1945.

14   Cuíca de Santo Amaro, <u>O Regresso de Getúlio à sua Terra Natal</u>, Salvador, 1945.

15   Santo Amaro, "Credo" on the back cover of <u>Deus no Céu, Getúlio na Terra</u>, Salvador, n.d.

16   Rodolfo Coelho Cavalcante, <u>A Morte de Getúlio Vargas</u>, Salvador, 1954.

17   Cuíca de Santo Amaro, <u>O Testamento de Getúlio Vargas e sua Chegada no Céu</u>, Salvador, 1954.

18   Manoel D'Almeida Filho, <u>A Espectacular Vitória de Jânio Quadros nas Eleições de 1960</u>, Aracajú, 1960.

19   Rodolfo Coelho Cavalcante, <u>A Renúncia do Ex-Presidente Jânio Quadros</u>, Salvador, 1961.

20   A.A.C., with pseudonym of "Iron Head," <u>A Liga Camponesa e a Resposta de Julião</u>, xerox copy, n.p., n.d.

21   Carta de Alforria do Camponês do Deputado Francisco Julião em Versos de Rafael de Carvalho, Editora Jotapê, n.p., n.d. xerox copy.

22   José João da Silva, "Azulão," Jango e as Reformas, Engenheiro Pedreira, 1964.

23   Rodolfo Coelho Cavalcante, A Vitória da Democracia no Brasil e o Fim do Comunismo, Salvador, 1964.

24   Antônio Lucena de Mossoró, Tragédia do Aeroporto dos Guararapes em 25-7-66, Recife, August 5, 1966.

25   Minelvino Francisco Silva, O Governo do Presidente Médici e os Agradecimentos dos Trabalhadores, Itabuna, 1974.

26   José Soares, A Vitória da ARENA, Recife, 1974.

27   José João da Silva, "Azulão," O Pacote, Engenheiro Pedreira, n.d.

28   Gonçalo Ferreira da Silva, Muita Sarna na Sarneira do Presidente Sarney, Rio de Janeiro, n.d.

29   Gonçalo Ferreira da Silva, Carta de Tancredo Neves aos Constituintes, n.p., 1987.

30   Zezé Folheteiro, A Vitória de Collor e a Derrota do PT, n.p., n.d. This is an example of a paid political "folheto" or propaganda poem, composed by someone favoring Collor's campaign and not by true cordelian poets in the marketplace.

31   Ulises Higino da Silva, O Caçador de Marajás e a Realidade Trágica da Política Brasileira, n.p., n.d.

32   The chronicle has to end somewhere and sometime. After the writing of "Portrait," the great and glorious moment of Lula Inácio da Silva came as he was elected President of Brazil. By 2004 he had to confront the same problems as usual, but in a world more complicated by war and international terrorism. But as perhaps anticipated and expected by the public of "cordel," Lula also had to face internal problems: accusations of corruption against him personally and his party the PT. In the past few years there has been a flood of new poems on the political situation in

Brazil, most treating the corruption of the "corrupt judges," "the big blackout" of 2001, and the recent tragic-comic episodes of the "monthly allowance" for opposition politicians and the "big shorts" of a politician stuffed full of money and discovered at an airport. Who knows what the future holds, but the bards of <u>"cordel"</u> will gleefully report it.

Album VIII

There Is a Big World Out There

Introduction

As humble or "small town" as "cordel" seemed to be and was in its northeastern beginnings, the poet as representative of the masses in his "newspaper of the poor" has never overlooked international events as they affect himself, his readers and his country. Thus this album of Portrait, a view of a people and a country, looks outside Brazil, but from a perspective which is totally Brazilian and cordelian.[1] The portrait would be incomplete without it.

From its very beginnings in the early years of the twentieth century "cordel" reported on major events and personages from outside of Brazil as long as they were of interest and pertinent to the reader as a Brazilian. Major international conflicts such as World War I, World War II and confrontations since then are the primary topics, but any newsworthy event such as the death of a statesman or a pope or the arrival of man on the moon is reported and commented upon according to the cordelian world vision. Early in the century it was the major news dailies that provided topic and perspective, but with the arrival of the transistor radio in the 1960s and then television, and today the Internet, the poets' horizons were broadened.

Once again, the totality of such cordelian stories is really a chronicle and a sort of popular history, for they report events in story-poems which are narrative in nature, but are also basically creative, that is, they mix fact and fiction. The poet above all entertains as he informs and teaches, but he does so in his selected medium—in verse—and using language and a world view common to his readers who by buying his verse allow him to earn a living. These stories were printed in fragile booklets and sold in the fairs, markets and on the streets in both the small towns and the major coastal cities of the Northeast, and eventually in Rio de Janeiro, São Paulo and Brasília as well. So a public from Manaus and Belém in the

Amazon, the entire Northeast, and the cultural-industrial-political centers of Brazil as well learned or would learn the news from their poets.

The opinions the poets expressed were and are formed by a curious amalgam of factors: the poet's interaction in the local community, his role as receptor of reports and images from the local, national and international media and as a believer in a system of values inherent to the Northeasterner. So, even though he is an independent voice, the poet will reflect in these poems what he knows to be and wishes to adhere to as a voice of his public's view of things, at least most of the time. So he will express his own opinion, but it is tempered by what he knows his public wants to hear. He will write his story-poem in the final analysis according to his own poetic talent and temperament as an individual artist. Thus, each poem reflects a slightly different voice, and that is good, for it is the variety of talent and voices that makes "cordel" so vibrant, interesting and entertaining.

The format of these stories is very similar to that of Album VII—In Politics We Hope But Do Not Trust. The issue or topic is usually presented in a challenge-response pattern, that is, a situation is presented and the protagonists will react and respond to it. Sometimes the challenge will be repeated more than once, but in the end, there is usually a victor and a moral victory for the Right and Good as well. Heroes are created and praised; villains are condemned and sent to cordelian hell. But the unexpected hero, the anti-hero is present as well. A love-hate relationship can be detected when the poet admires what all Adolph Hitler, Benito Mussolini, and Juan or Eva Perón did for their countries but divided or destroyed them at the same time.

But the principal protagonist of the story-poems on the world outside Brazil is the country, leaders, and heroes of the United States of America. They are presented time and again in two general ways: first with specific names and actions as in the poems about the assassination of John F. Kennedy or the arrival of three American heroes to the moon, Armstrong, Aldrin and Collins, and secondly in an indirect way, as in the actions of the nation called the United States and what it represents. The role of the U.S. in World War I and World War II and many conflicts since is that of defender, protector of freedom and democracy, but occasionally imperialist and conqueror as well. The wars in Iraq, especially during the administration of George W. Bush, will color and change the perception of the Americans.

Cultural events and leaders appear as well in this album, but less often. For example, the death of Elvis Presley was noted in "cordel" along with those of Brazil's own national cultural heroes. Hollywood icons like John Wayne, Elizabeth Taylor, and many others decorated the covers of cordelian adventure stories throughout the 1940s, 1950s and 1960s.

But most interesting is the use of satire, criticism and irony by the poets when they in effect take vengeance on the international first world powers by placing Brazil and its own leaders and artists on a pedestal in a defense of cultural nationalism, to be seen in the final part of Album VIII. The Brazilian point of view will take the form of the now familiar anti-hero, the Brazilian "quengo," "amarelo" or even "cangaceiro," in this defense of national pride, so evident in some of the stories.

As in Album VII, chronological time is the best way to consider how "cordel" has seen the world, so this chapter begins with the earliest extant international stories, those on World War I and how it affected the Northeast. Collection of original stories plus Xerox copies from major collections has provided Portrait with a good sampling of these one hundred years of international current events. As usual, limitations of space dictate that quotes of excerpts of important poems from each phase of the story be used along with summarizing and paraphrasing of the poets' voices.

The reader will recognize the names, personalities and style of many of the poets, since they are the same people who wrote chronicles of national life in the twentieth century. João Melchíades Ferreira da Silva who wrote of the War of Canudos, Leandro Gomes de Barros, the best poet of the first twenty years of "cordel," Francisco das Chagas Batista, chronicler of wars and banditry, João Martins de Atayde, the "entrepreneur" from Recife, their successors from the 1920s to the 1960s and the poets of recent years are the "voices" of the people who will report, inform, judge and opine, and teach and counsel in this Album.

1 World War I and the Dream Thereafter

World War I was the first major event outside Brazil reported in the "cordel" of the twentieth century. Even though Brazil had no direct participation in the War (it did send supplies and had plans to send officers), it came close enough so that a national military draft in the form of a lottery was established, the national economy was directly affected, and the particularly deadly Spanish Influenza of 1918, contemporary to the end of the War, was felt at home. It should be no surprise that the war itself with its massive destruction of humanity along with the loss of life to the international flu epidemic were seen by the poets as moral consequences of humanity's actions. An apocalyptic scenario was often used to describe the conflagration and its aftermath. And in addition, the description of individual heroes and villains was done using the same language as that of describing bandits and heroes in the early twentieth century in Brazil.

João Melchíades Ferreira da Silva, the author of The War of Canudos, wrote The First Great War and the Victory of the Allies ["A Primeira Grande Guerra e a Vitória dos Aliados"][2] from his home in João Pessoa, Paraíba in 1918. He believes the "Central Empires" are certainly losing to the Allies, but puts it in cordelian fashion:

> "The Emperor of Germany
> The greatest monster of the War
> Wanted to take captive
> All the world's powers
> He wanted to be like a God
> But the criminal always errs."

The greatest sins of "cordel"—pride and unlimited ambition—in effect, wanting to be like God, is the flaw of Kaiser Wilhelm just as it was for Lucifer in Album I. And the poet uses the same language to describe the villains in Germany as he would in a story of extreme perversity, of a heinous crime. Good and Evil battle and of course the Good and the Virtuous must conquer. This is another excellent example of how topic and form converge in "cordel."

Journalism is also present when the poet presents the "facts" in a summary of major events of the war: Austria invades Serbia, eliminates its king and advances toward Greece. Germany invades Russia, the Tsar falls and is executed by the Bolsheviks. Brussels and Belgium fall before the onslaught of the Kaiser. And just four months before the poet pens this account, Germany is "the terror of the world" with its "infernal machines of war."

General Von Hindenberg is described like other villains in "<u>cordel</u>;" he is "full of himself," just like the backland's bully who invades the local fair and roughs up the humble peasants.

But the tide has turned: the Allies are preparing to "take from its lair" the monster Kaiser in Berlin, the same Kaiser who wanted to spread his "assassin's ambition" to South America and especially to the German citizens of Rio Grande do Sul and Santa Catarina, states in southern Brazil! The poet presents the Kaiser wrapped in chains with the head of a tiger but with a human face. Wilhelm is "The Beast of the Apocalypse/ At war with the Allies."

France, England and now the United States have the Germans on the run and are marching toward Turkey to "cut off the head of the Sultan." The Kaiser has sued for peace and President Wilson has presented his fourteen points in order to secure an armistice, points the poet details one by one. In particular he is happy about the disarmament of Germany with its "war snakes," the early submarines developed by the Kaiser, a "new and treacherous" mode of making war. The poet makes no secret of his views:

> "Finally, Germany
> Wanted to be authoritarian
> It invented war
> And became the most bloodthirsty . . . ."

To make matters worse, the poet reports that the Germans attacked a Catholic Church on Good Friday, killing Christians during mass and at the moment of receiving Holy Communion! There can be no greater insult to God and Religion! Thus there is just reason for Germany's defeat, the fall of the Kaiser and the humiliation placed on its people with the Fourteen Points. Evil is punished and,

> "President Wilson
> He is the great chief
> Of the politics of the Allies
> International in every respect
> In defense of honor
> And the rights of the world."

There is word of a possible counter-attack late in the war, but <u>America</u> is a rising star which will destroy Germany and its war machine!

Almost as an afterthought, the poet details the thousands of Brazilian deaths as a result of the Spanish Influenza which came at the end of the war in 1918. Humanity, especially the German leaders, have been "so arrogant and proud" before an all-powerful God, that He sent this "Spanish General" to wreak havoc and punish the guilty. It is easy for the poet to launch into a general complaint of the moral state of the world—the evils of the new cinema, drinking at parties, loud, raucous music (and rock and Roll had not been invented) are more examples of man's evil. The poet counsels the leaders of nations to imitate the King of Nineveh in scripture, to repent of personal sins in the hope of diminishing the devastation of the flu and the war. His final words remind that,

> "If you live by the sword
> You will die by the sword
> As you do unto others
> So will they do unto you
> In the proverbs of Jesus Christ
> The people are guaranteed!"

Quite a different view of the war and its aftermath can be found in a myriad of poems by the great humorist and satirist of early "cordel," Leandro Gomes de Barros. Seemingly waffling between pacifism and the concept of the just war, the poet produced a series of cordelian jewels during the times. Like other contemporary cordelian narrations, there is a minimum of facts, really just enough to set the scene. From that point on the poet creates in great style via his commentary. He deals more with the social and economic consequences of the war and the way the poor masses reacted to them. In his verse joy is contrasted to great sadness and levity to the most serious of moments.

In The Afflictions of the war in Europe ["As Aflições da Guerra na Europa],[3] after he gives gruesome details which result from the war, Leandro Gomes de Barros describes its future hero:

> "Oh! Great North America
> Land of an enlightened people
> Intervene in this misery
> Consider a defeated world
> Where a man kills his brother
> Like a desperate dog."

America in 1915 is not yet the international power known for its capitalism and economic expansion; England still plays that role. America is the "sleeping giant" which promises great things to come.

In <u>Memories of the Past</u> ["Lembranças do Passado"]⁴ Leandro tells of the sweet, delicious times before the war and contrasts them to the atrocities now being committed, but he cannot help but show his humorous side. All the western nations are involved, even tiny Portugal (recalling the love-hate relationship Brazil has for its founder, conqueror, and colonizer):

"Portugal says here I am!
And I'll not give an inch!
If England shouts for help
I'll hear it and come running
Women will go, soldiers will go
Dogs, cats and everybody."

When Leandro Gomes de Barros turns to the effects of the war at home, his humor and satire reign supreme. Even though lamenting the economic hardships the war has caused, the poet says there is something potentially much more serious: the military draft via a national lottery and the very real possibility of facing death in Europe. In a series of poems about the draft, the poet says,

"An old outlander said
I'm not going no matter what
It's easier to just free myself
Of some fools I've got
I'll just send the daughters
And the old lady." . . .

Even as old as I am
About ready to croak
I can't even run anymore
When the "action" starts
But I'm still afraid
They'll toss me into this fray.

But a way to get out of the draft is to be newly married with family, so

"That's why there is so little choice
In marriages out in the country
A girl sees a boy
And it's a done deal
When the holy missions come
Dogs are marrying cats."⁵

The poet refers to the phenomenon of the annual mission when a priest often travels hundreds of miles to a local priest-less community once a year to do baptisms, confessions, holy communions and weddings for a church-starved public. One recalls the great giver of missions Friar Damian of Album II.

João Martins de Athayde in Recife reported attacks on small businesses of Germans or descendants of Germans in the capital city of Pernambuco state during the war and waxed philosophical about the warlike nature of that people. Yet, between his lines there is an admiration for the German's prowess in war, his strength and his courage in battle. But the poet also is offended by the Germans' burning of churches, the murder of priests—acts of savagery! He blames Germany for the first recorded air attack in history, bombs dropped from biplanes over Paris. In The End of the War and the Victory of the Allies ["O Fim da Guerra e a Vitória dos Aliados"][6] Athayde remains true to the cordelian vision, saying the world is now free of the "barbarity" and the "abyss" created by Germany and its leader the Kaiser that "Author of misery" and "Expansionist Monster." That "Infernal Emperor of Prussia" was punished by God and defeated by the "Angel of Peace" who crushed this "new Satan."

But Atayde ends saying the country bumpkins can show their faces in town again without fear of being drafted, and in fact are celebrating in the streets, drunk on sugar cane rum [cachaça]. He himself immediately bought a bottle of fine wine to celebrate the good news and "If you do not like my story/ just blame Rocha Leão wine." Thus the poets ended their chronicle of the first great war of the century, reporting a minimum of facts but linking the atrocities to an accustomed moral vision.

With the aftermath of World War I, the 1920s seemed to present a time of peace and a return to prosperity, a world imbued with faith and idealism in man. It is at this time in "cordel" when the United States as the newest "great" nation, fresh from real and moral victory against the evil Kaiser, begins to be seen as a new star rising, the epitome of the modern dream of democracy, freedom and especially the land of promise. "Give me your tired, your meek, your poor" promises the lady in the harbor of New York, and the poor begin to believe it. Thus an aura is slowly established, but the subsequent bright image will be tarnished by later events.

When crime is linked to the ideals of liberty, justice and freedom for all which the United States represented to the old world of Europe and the young democracies of Latin America, it brings a certain irony to this portrait of a people and nation. Such was the famous case in 1921 when the Italian immigrants Sacco and Vanzetti were condemned to die in the electric chair for a crime they denied doing. Sacco e Vanzetti in the Eyes of thee

World ["Sacco e Vanzetti nos Olhos do Mundo"][7] told the story of two Italian immigrants who came to America with the vision shining in their eyes. It narrated the unfortunate series of circumstances where Sacco and Vanzetti were imprisoned and condemned to death for murder. But more importantly, it told of how such a thing could happen in the U.S.A.:

> "Leaving one's native country
> Traveling to a foreign land
> Dreaming of freedom
> Dying in prison
> This life is strange
> How much lost hope
> Like castles in the sand."

Equally shocking but in a totally different way was the "hideous, perverse, monstrous crime" of the kidnapping and death of the son of Charles Lindbergh, the great American hero of the early century and perhaps its most tragic figure. In The Mysterious Kidnapping of the Lindbergh Child ["O Rapto Misterioso do Filho de Lindbergh"][8] and The Death of Hauptmann in the Electric Chair ["A Morte de Hauptmann na Cadéia Elétrica"][9] the bards of "cordel" found all the drama they could handle in telling a twentieth century adventure no less powerful than the death of Roland and the struggles and victories of a hundred fairy tale lovers.

Not only the story of an international hero, for Lindbergh was the pilot who captivated the world's imagination the most until man would make the journey to the moon in 1969, but great for its qualities of suspense and perversion, the poem also fulfilled the romantic dreams of its humble readers. After making the first non-stop, solo flight across the Atlantic to Paris, Charles Lindbergh was declared a national hero. Handsome, courageous, strong, and a man of great deeds—he fulfilled the heroic vision of "cordel!" His wife, described as having "the aura of a princess," had other fairy tale traits: she was beautiful, but delicate, with "blue eyes reflecting purity," and the "royal" lineage of a daughter of a United States ambassador, Dwight Morrow, ambassador to Mexico. The arrival of their first child is like a romance: Charles Junior is a "flower from heaven" and the parents' love for him is idyllic.

But one day the parents discover him gone, kidnapped by unknowns. Days and weeks pass, public appeals are made to the unknown captors, and false alarms and false hopes bring a roller coaster of emotion not only to the family but now to the entire nation. Delivery of ransom money to a supposed agent of the kidnappers in no less than a cemetery and the discovery of the tiny body ten days later bring emotions to a national frenzy. But in a very Brazilian ending, the author reports that a witness, a believer and medium in Kardec Spiritualism, announces the body is not that of the Lindbergh child. Consequently, the poet will write a second story when more details are available!

But "black fate" has ruled and the tragedy reaches its denouement when another immigrant, a German carpenter by the name of Bruno Hauptmann, is arrested, tried and executed for the crime. The Lindberghs flee the subsequent post-trial publicity and escape to Europe in 1936. The poet's description of the whole affair is highly theatrical and is written in the old cordelian style of quatrains; it emphasizes the mother's desperate pleas to the captors to at least provide medicine to the child "who suffers from malaria" and needs frequent medicine. But after the child's tiny body is discovered, the criminal apprehended and tried, the poet cannot restrain himself:

"Oh! Bandit of bandits!
Monster of monsters, abortion!
Butcher from another world
Who would sell a dead angel?

"Scoundrel of the Devil
Who chose a cemetery
To sell a life
Already consigned to a morgue!

"Hangman, turn on the electric current
Fill and fry his heart
Bruno was the biggest hunk of beef
That the electric chair has ever burned.

"Undertaker of the Devil
Nail the boards in his coffin
Made of the macabre scaffolding
Of the German carpenter."

This was cordelian high drama—the tragic death of an innocent victim, son of a true "prince and princess" of the United States of America! Justice was done with the deserved death of the doer of evil deeds, of a crime so perverse, so hideous, so vile, and so repellent! It is a great story of Portrait, one more example that the dream was fragile, that a star had fallen.

Beginning in the 1920s "Cordel" used photo-clichés of Hollywood Movie Stars to illustrate its covers, with the stars most times having little to do with the content of the story-poems. The use of the movie stars really was following another innovation, the use of European romantic post cards to illustrate cordelian covers. Stars appeared: Ingrid Bergman as Joan of Arc or Victor Mature in Samson and Delilah. But there was also the unexpected with unlikely photos having little or nothing to do with the story in the chapbook. A smiling Gene Autry at the side of his trusty steed Champion appeared on the cover of The Valiant

Sebastian, a tale of backlands heroism. There was a young Mickey Rooney on the cover of Chichuca the Professor of Thieves, a cordelian story with a clever picaresque rogue as hero. Better yet are William Holden and his leading lady on the cover of The Proud King at Supper Time, a story of romance in medieval Europe. John Wayne and Maureen O'Hara graced the cover of The Fidelity of Edgar and the Love of Adelina, one of hundreds of cordelian love stories.

Whatever the rationale or lack of the same, there is no doubt cordelian poets and public enjoyed seeing the Hollywood stars. The phenomenon was brought to "cordel" because photos of film stars were cheap to obtain from local newspapers which had used them to advertise the previous week's attraction. In addition, the humble cordelian public was exposed to the large movie posters in front of modest cinemas to the side of the São José marketplace in Recife where they gathered to hear the poets recite "cordel" and offer it for sale.

So both the evils of arrogant leaders of nations bound to increase their wealth and power and the goodness of real life heroes like Lindbergh and Hollywood "good guys" brought a vision of Europe and the United States to the humble backlands of the Northeast. However, the image would be magnified both for better and worse with the portrayal of monumental real life adversaries of the next Great War. Adolph Hitler, Benito Mussolini, Hirohito, Franklin Roosevelt, Winston Churchill and Joseph Stalin would be the protagonists of the greatest drama of the age: World War II with its epic struggle and forty-eight million deaths in a battle which changed the course of world history and indirectly brought Brazil into the international mainstream.

2 World War II[10]

Twenty-one years after the conclusion of hostilities in Europe in 1918 an even greater cataclysm would erupt. The horrors of World War II would be known in the Northeast via the media of the age, but "cordel" accompanied the events in verse in its stories with language common to the humble masses. "Cordel" at this time had reached its numerical apogee with the João Martins de Athayde operation in Recife. And it had been adapted and recreated for a large public in the Amazon Basin via the Guajarina Press in Belém, the capital of Pará state. Bahia on the southern fringe of the North East had a vibrant production during the war years stimulated by half a dozen active poets. And a handful of poets were now writing and publishing in Rio de Janeiro. So a totally new generation of poets would comment on and judge the evil powers of the Axis and its leaders. The resulting poetic accounts are truly an incredible record of the times and in one sense are the best of the news stories. Only the suicide of Getulio Vargas in 1954 and the tragic sickness and death of Tancredo Neves in 1985 would provide "cordel" with such drama and romantic discourse.

Due to the evolution of the means of communication, the scale of the war and the eventual participation of Brazil itself, there was a significant growth in interest by the Brazilian public in international affairs. There was news via film clips in the cinema, daily newspaper coverage and especially the use of short wave radio for first hand reports. Novelist Jorge Amado of Salvador da Bahia provides us one of the best descriptions of the moment with an atmosphere full of suspense and emotion. Amado wrote of the times both in fiction and non-fiction. In his thesis novel treating the preservation of Afro-Brazilian culture in Brazil and especially in Bahia, The Miracle Shop ["Tenda dos Milagres"],[11] Amado describes the final moments in the life of his hero Pedro Arcanjo who dies in 1943 in the middle of the war:

> He had gone to listen to the radio, to the foreign
> stations, the BBC from London, Central Radio from
> Moscow and the Voice of America; his friend Maluf
> had acquired a radio that got the entire world. The
> news that night was great, the "Aryans" getting the
> hell beat out of them. Everyone cursed the
> Germans, "the German Nazis," "the monstrous Germans,"
> but the old man only referred to them as "Aryan bandits,"
> assassins of Jews, Negroes and Arabs.

In his best work of non-fiction, the guide to the city of Salvador, <u>Bahia de Todos os Santos</u>, Amado wrote in the chapter "Characters—the Poet" specifically of Cuíca de Santo Amaro, the best known of the cordelian poets during the war:

> He explores a humorous vein in his anti-fascist poetry and laughs at those that wore the green shirts [the Integralists, a Fascist style political party in Brazil]. He laughs at Hitler's aversion to women, and at the cheap theater of Mussolini. In one of his booklets of verse he tells how Plínio Salgado [Brazilian Green Shirt leader] deceived everyone with his Integralist demagoguery. And he tells of the end of this fifth-columnist on a trip to Europe . . . . Another story narrates Hitler's marriage to Satan's daughter in hell. Hirohito and Mussolini are the best men . . . . In yet another story Satan decides to send Adolph Hitler to hell where the Nazi chief can pay for his crimes.

Brazil has a personal interest in this war culminating in the participation of the Brazilian Expeditionary Force [<u>Força Expedicionária Brasileira</u>] in combat in Italy in 1944 and 1945 under General Mark Clark. The same Brazilian officers who served in Italy would later form the corps of "protectors of the constitution" in the revolution of 1964. Back home, ethnic groups in Brazil, the Italians, Germans and Japanese, would be pulled like taffy from one extreme to another as a result of reports favoring now the Allies, now the Axis powers. And the battle between political factions in Brazil was no less important: the Communists were allied with Russia and Stalin, the Integralists favored the fascist states, and a centrist government which was pro-Ally tried to balance between the two extremes.

The German propaganda machine was active in South America, including Brazil, with pitches via the radio. But it was the German submarine activity in the South Atlantic which resulted in the sinking of Brazilian cargo ships and loss of life that finally convinced and converted the masses to the Allies.

Poets accustomed to writing dramatic fictional accounts of love, suffering and adventure found themselves applying the moral and religious rules and recreating the fictional arch types of hero and villain in this real life drama of good and evil. The discourse of the two different types of cordelian poems could be astonishingly similar. Mussolini and Hitler, especially Hitler, were placed in a love-hate relationship with the reader, and hate won the battle. The war was turned into a true epic, a battle of heroic proportions, and the public of this folk-popular poetry with heroic roots was thrilled daily with the saga.

No one knows the exact number of poems written and published about the War, but poets from Rio de Janeiro, São Paulo, all the Northeast and a very active press in Belém in the Amazon Basin contributed to the drama. The totality of these texts provides one of the most emotional and exciting parts of the entire international chronicle. <u>Portrait</u> provides its flavor.

The poets wrote of the preamble to the war, the Spanish Civil War. Manoel Tomaz de Assiz, an old veteran and a true backlands poet in Paraíba, wrote <u>The Atrocity in Spain, Horror of Horrorss</u> ["A Atrocidade na Espanha, Horror de Horrores"].[12] He gave emphasis, as might be expected, to the atrocities committed against the Catholic Church, its clergy and believers. He was sure the old prophecies had come true: the end of the world is near, and Paganism and Atheism in the form of Communism in Spain have brought indescribable misery, personal humiliation, suffering and death. Young girls were dragged into the streets and raped, nuns raped and forced to run naked through the streets, a priest burned alive, and churches, monasteries and convents sacked and burned. Italy and Germany are rushing to the defense of the rebels under Generalísimo Francisco Franco and Spain is embroiled in war. Russia on one side, Italy and Germany on the other, and the Condor Flights over Guernica would make Spain a disaster from 1936 to 1939.

Poets in both Rio de Janeiro and Belém do Pará would tell simultaneously of the Italian invasion of Ethiopia and the overwhelming slaughter of civilians due to the modern weapons of war of the invader. A great hero would emerge on the world scene, Emperor Haile Selassie, "The 225th Emperor of the Solomonic Dynasty, Elect of God, Lord of Lords, King of Kings, Conquering Lion of the Tribe of Judah."

Amador Santelmo was a pioneering popular poet in Rio de Janeiro who linked the evils of the Italian invasion to the plight of the black race shared by Ethiopia and Brazil. He describes the white Italian invaders and the suffering blacks under Haillie Selassie and defends the spunk and mettle of the latter:[13]

> "Mussolini well knows
> That Abyssinia is a hot country
> Not a soup
> That you gobble up quickly
> It's hot, Bahian style
> And scalds a lot of people."

Abyssinia is not without friends, France, England and Russia among them! The black race of Ethiopia has a role in history in its defense of Christianity from the Moslems, and there is a link to Portugal: Dom João II sent troops to Ethiopia to help drive the Moslems from the country. Criticizing the general ignorance of people about Ethiopia and its people, the poet adds with tongue in cheek that in that country,

"There are still savage tribes
Very warlike Abyssinians
That eat people, it's true
Principally foreigners,
Italian soldiers
Are true treats.

The people say and I believe it
Therefore you can too
That Italian barbecue
If well-seasoned in the fire
The smell alone makes you hungry
It smells like burned macaroni."

The poem becomes a defense of black heritage ["negritude"], including the same in Brazil, contrasting the former to the vile actions of the invading white Italians, an inferior white race which enslaved millions:

"The Italians have airplanes
The plague of the entire world
Poisonous gases
True killers
But we have the mosquito
Which bites like a shoemakers' awl.

"Greedy Italy
Has acted only with guile
And it's not just her
Look out for Germany as well
Hitler the crafty Nazi
Also itches to fight."

The poet predicts the years to come: blood will flow and Italy will drag Germany, England, France and even Japan into the fray. The League of Nations implores peace, the Pope prays, but "perverse hearts" rule the day.

And the worst comes. The poet Zé Vicente from Guajarina Press in Belém writes Germany Eating Fire ["Allemanha Comendo Fogo"][14] detailing the partition of Poland by Germany and Russia. Deladier and Chamberlain send telegrams while Hitler and Mussolini fall over laughing. The poet uses great humor and verve, employing stereotypical notions of the participating nations along with place names to characterize the protagonists in the war. Hitler disdains the Poles and will "make sausages of them," will drink German beer in Paris trampling the weak French, and will "put his toe in the North Sea and turn London upside down." All this will happen while the Russians are looking on from afar, not quite ready to enter the fray. Hitler like a cat "addicted to eating baby chicks" swallows up Austria and then Czechoslovakia. Then the <u>blitzkreig</u> comes and Poland is enveloped by the Nazis.

The poet chides the Brazilians who are entertained by it all:

"But we here in Brazil
Playing on our neutrality
We just go on selling manioc flour
And bananas in the streets
Our war is a war of words
Fought on the street corner

"Our war is being fought
By more than 100 generals
All of them operating
In the press rooms of the journals
Each at war's end
Trying to see who "shined" the best."

The poet sends warning that it would be an easy thing for Hitler to send one of his submarines right up to the docks of the famous "Check the weight" [<u>Ver-o-peso</u>] Market in Belém and "sink some of our canoes." But we are the land of carnival; why worry!

Another poet chronicles events closer to home like the amazing saga of the German war ship the <u>Graf Spee</u>[15] which was sunk by its commander rather than ceding to the British warships surrounding it outside Montevideo. The commander's heroism in the face of overwhelming odds appeals to the poet and his public. All happens while the German <u>Wehrmacht</u> spreads over northern Europe engulfing Finland, Holland, Belgium and France. The only hope is England which is soon embroiled in "A Battle of Two Giants" ["Allemanha Versus Inglaterra, a Batalha de Dois Gigantes"], a story which describes the battle like two boxers set to enter the ring. The German is dangerous, is like a cat with nine lives, fearless and seemingly invincible. The Englishman says little and is workman-like, just plugging along, but slowly gaining the advantage, and with a great leader:

"The minister of this people
Is truly valiant
Even seeing the rain
Of bombs upon his city
He takes measures
And doubles his preparations."

The battle in the skies over England and the Channel rages with both sides inflicting horrible damage and carnage; Germany has the original advantage, but England now bombs as far as Berlin. Italy, fresh from losses in Ethiopia and now North Africa, is "Just like a piranha caught in a net, Hanging by its mouth; It would like to fight, but can't."

Britain still rules the seas and is tightening a blockade of Europe with the aim of stopping the flow of supplies to the Axis powers. The days of the blitzkrieg are over and Hitler is caught in a slow, monotonous battle with Britain.

Suddenly a major new development shocks the world: Pearl Harbor takes place and the United States declares war against Japan. One of the poets writes Japan Is Going to Get It ["Japão Vai Se Estrepar"]¹⁶ on December 12, 1941. The poem is a tremendously racist diatribe against the Japanese invasion, emperor and people. Far different from the occasional praise the poets have for the strong, seemingly invincible Germans (and the jokes they make of the spaghetti-eating Italians), this enemy is not admired.

There had been much Japanese immigration to Brazil since the beginning of the twentieth century. In their odyssey to survive, the immigrants by and large avoided intermarriage with other Brazilians and expressed disdain for the "others," the "gaijim." Brazilian fear of the enigmatic Japanese appears in the chapbooks, whether from a lack of knowledge or even ignorance. The caricature of Japanese physical traits including the sound of their speech to Brazilians appears in the poems. The diet and the ambition of the Japanese are used against them. Portrait paraphrases the poet: They with their own language and sneaky ways are the epitome of the Fifth Column or spies in Brazil. The Japanese are a warlike people and Hirohito wants to be another Napoleon! Their alliance to Germany and Italy will bring down a rain of destruction upon them:

"Japanese is very ugly
With a frog's face
If you see one
Don't trust the SOB
His eyes look like
Watermelon seeds.

The Jap's tongue
Makes animals run away
When he is conversing
He makes a rat-like sound
He only knows how to make toys
Cheap imitations at that."

The poet goes on to explain that the Japanese are most often street vendors in Brazil, but be careful, because they keep their eyes and ears open. Spies all of them! Chang Kai Chek will eventually defeat them in China, and they won't get any help from "Mr. Hitler" who is now embroiled on the eastern front with Russia. And America is now in the war, viva America!

The Battle of Russia and Germany ["A Batalha entre Rússia e Allemanha"]¹⁷ comes next when Germany once again relies on the blitzkrieg and Hitler eventually sends four million

German soldiers to the Eastern Front! The poet comments on the fragile and strange alliance between the fascist Hitler and the communist Stalin which was useful only for awhile before being suddenly broken. Even odder is the new alliance of the capitalist West with Russia, strange bedfellows to be sure. The poet Zé Vicente describes the carnage in ironic terms: Germans are dying like "xuxu" (a common Brazilian vegetable) and so many Russians are dying that "it makes you sick." Civilians drop like "trampled ants" amidst the war's devastation, a true disaster.

The poet spends pages describing the Nazi propaganda machine of the Gestapo and how the German people themselves are unaware of what really is going on. He means the devastating losses to their Reich and even the lack of bread in Berlin or the destruction of the industrial zone of Germany by British and American bombs.

Europe Bathed in Blood ["Europa Banhada em Sangue"][18] continues the description at this time of the war, but once again with an apocalyptic tone: this is the war foretold by Isaac, by Daniel, by Jeremiah, and even by the Messiah in the Gospels. There is utter and total devastation, the population is decimated, and Europe has been made into "an ugly desert."

Meanwhile Brazil has entered the war. At first straddling the line of neutrality (recall the large German and Italian population in Southern Brazil,) but chided by the U.S. to combat German submarine attacks on merchant ships in the Atlantic, Getúlio's arm was twisted. Brazil broke relations with Germany, later declared war and had its own merchant ships attacked with loss of life, But an important result was that Brazil sent officers to serve under U.S. General Mark Clark in Italy in 1944. These same officers would later form the basis for leadership in the infamous "Redeeming" Revolution of 1964.

In 1945 the end of the war is near and finally comes. Poems like The Victory of the Allies ["A Vitória dos Aliados"][19] repeat an old refrain: Hitler declared himself to be a God and wanted to rule the world. The great sin of deceit [falsedade], among the greatest sins "cordel," is also his. The poet traces Brazil's entry into the war and the invasion of Europe by the Allies at Normandy: They all "entered the dance." The Russians and Americans race to Berlin where they find only barbed wire barricades, trenches and underground bunkers, and the Nazis fighting to the last in hand to hand combat. The time of the demise of Mussolini and Hitler has come, so the troops are returning home and "a true patriot/ will buy my book!"

One of the most inspirational of all poems of the war is by Delarme Monteiro da Silva in Athayde's shop in Recife, The End of the War and the Deaths of Hitler and Mussolini ["O Fim da Guerra e a Morte de Hítler e Mussolini"].[20] In classical cordelian language reminiscent of the great romances of love and adventure the poet says,

"The black shroud was torn
That enveloped the entire world
Saving millions of souls
From the bars of captivity
From Moscow, Paris, Washington
London and Rio de Janeiro.

He details the death of Mussolini who was hung and his body burned on the streets of Milan. And days later the news of Hitler comes:

"The body was found
Of this unspeakable monster
Shot through with bullets
Totally torn to pieces
Only his soul was not found
Beelzebub had already taken it."

The last photos of the World War II Album are the poems which looked back on the war, often in a humorous way. They became, in effect, the epilogue to the drama. They often left the realm of reality and fact and moved into the familiar cordelian world of fantasy. It was Cuíca de Santo Amaro from Bahia who helped close the album with poems like The Arrival of Mussolini in Hell, The Arrival of Hitler in Hell and The Arrival of Stalin in Hell. Such poems make fun of the leaders sending them to their everlasting in hell, thus using a cordelian device common to any villain the poets want to ridicule. Even though Hitler in particular brings his thirst for dominion with him to battle with Satan, in at least one poem he is mocked by the poet when he dances drunkenly with Satan's wife.

Arinos de Belém closed the album with Hitler's Last Will and Testament.[21] The poet narrates in first person:

"I Herr Adolph Hitler
Fuehrer of Germany
Was born in famous Austria
At first with no ambition
But I soon became a man
And did not even think of women . . . ."

The poet traces the Austrian housepainter in his meteoric rice to power as Chancellor of Germany, then as "der fuehrer" who commands the slaughter of the Jews, ironically according to the poet, to make Germans eventually pay for it. But it is the provisions of the will that summarize his feelings: he leaves the whole mess to the "stupid Germans who followed him," specifically,

"To Von Rommel the legs
Of a valiant runner
To run from Lybia
To the surrounding desert
And a goodbye from Mussolini
His "compadre" and protector.

"To Goering the wings
Of all the airplanes he wants
And a torn parachute
For him if he wants
To ask the English' blessing
That is, if he has time.

"To Goebbels I leave a bundle
Of newspapers full of lies
Speeches and more speeches
And a half million sheets
Of propaganda that he did
Full of Nazi ideology.

"To Von Papen if he wants
And may it be to his advantage
What in Turkey
I gave to that guy
Get out of my sight
Because I am already fed up.

"To Von Paulus the skulls
From the streets of Leningrad
Two vials of poison
And a revolver
After being fired as head
Of the defeated army.

"To Ribbentrop and he many choose
An old piece of iron, a cannon
An old bicycle
A plane's wing
A buzz bomb
It does not matter to me.

"I leave to the infamous head of the Gestapo
A hangman's noose, a whip
A flame, a punch
. . .
. . .
A portion of the carnage to fill his belly.

To all the Field Marshalls
I will leave in pieces
That so-called "Great Germany"
Which today is nothing
And to each one
A piece of the German Swastika."

There is more, but one gets the idea. The poem is illustrated by one of the most powerful of all the caricatures of the times: Hitler with his usual hair style and mustache, the armband with the swastika, high leather boots, but with his head in a hangman's noose, tongue swollen, eyes bugged out, and a blackbird of death hovering above his head. Thus in this poem which is totally ironic, "cordel" says goodbye to the greatest villain of the century.

It is clear that cordelian poets did not always have access to the facts, and when they did, they were capable of ignoring them or at least not emphasizing them to instead focus on the emotions and moral consequences of the greatest tragedy of the century. The horrors of war and particularly this war did not escape them.

3 International Conflicts in the Modern Era[22]

"Cordel" would continue to report and judge the events of the next half century, focussing on international conflict as usual as well as other newsworthy events such as a death of a statesman, a pope or other major event. Once again it is the United States of America which is portrayed most often, but not in the same light as pre-1945. To be sure, the U.S. is still seen mainly as the leader of the Western world, a truly democratic republic with ideals of freedom and justice for all. But as the world enters the age of the "Cold War," as early as 1948 with the Russian occupation of East Germany and part of Berlin and the need for the Berlin Airlift to supply the rest of that city, tension between East and West, Communist and Capitalist world grows. The U.S. will occasionally be depicted as the imperialistic, capitalist expansionist state and Russia and its Allies as a solution for the workers of the world. But "cordel" will still trust and believe by and large in America.

The advent of the Third World Movement and its philosophy with adherents all striving in their own way to join the First World will create new protagonists. And the importance of the oil producing countries, those primarily of the Middle East, and the Israeli-Arab disputes will become important in Portrait.

Two gaps in the chronicle are apparent: the Vietnam War and the War in Central America between socialist and capitalist contingents. Infrequent references to them exist, but few titles exist specifically about them, a phenomenon perhaps explained by the Brazilian Military Regime during that time and its alliance with the U.S. and need for the latter's economic and military support. Another explanation is perhaps simply that the dramas seemed distant and did not directly involve Brazil.

The Korean War was an issue seen in poems like Russia's Civil War Against the Nations ["A Guerra Civil da Rússia Contra as Nações"] [23]by João do Cristo Rei of Juazeiro do Norte. The poem mentioned Korea but really was a diatribe against Communism and its treatment of the Catholic Church in Russia. It was Rodolfo Coelho Cavalcante, the avowed anti-communist of the era in "cordel," who hit hardest in his poem War in Korea ["A Guerra na Coréia"].[24] The communists infiltrated into North Korea via Japan, and,

> "Korea thus became
> Totally enslaved
> By the Muscovite creed
> It was contaminated
> And that is when it began
> To be made a martyr.

The poet contrasts the U.S. troops under General Douglas Macarthur in the South to Russia "governing" the North. While the Americans are "civilizing" South Korea, Stalin is implanting slavery! The "Reds" invaded across the Naktong River in 1950; South Korean resistance produced the loss of General Kang-Kin of North Korea and the loss of Tejon and Aegam. It is still early in the war and no one can predict the outcome; both sides battle along the Pusan perimeter.

With nothing more to report, the poet launches into an attack on Stalin, accusing him of the same mentality and illusions of Hitler, both tyrants espousing a pure atheistic materialism. Whatever the name—Fascism, Communism, Marxism, Leninism—they represent a pure materialism that does not respect God, patriotism or the family! The hammer and sickle symbolize a lack of freedom, and

"Their slogan is two names:
Hunger and capitalism
When they distill the venom
Of all Stalinism
Which hates democracy
And is the greatest fanaticism."

This poem sets the tone for the Cold War struggle for years to come. Yet it is important to see that the poet closes praying to the Blessed Virgin Mary to save the world from Russia and a third world war. The messages of Fatima from Portugal resound in Brazil.

The Korean Conflict remained in checkmate with an armistice but no real resolution; both sides are yet today poised across a no man's land of barbed wire ready to resume the battle. The conflict between Russia, its allies and the West would boil over again in an unexpected place in 1956: Egypt. England and France challenged Egypt for the control of the Suez Canal which linked the Mediterranean to Eastern waters, and Russia, courting another piece in its puzzle of domination, backed Egypt. The War in Egypt and the Horrors of the World ["A Guerra no Egito e os Horrores do Mundo"][25] summarizes the moment.

Much closer to home the poets write The Revolution in Argentina ["Revolução na Argentina"][26] in 1955 registering the fall of Argentine strong man Juan Perón. Even though Argentina was a close neighbor, "cordel" never was strong in writing of Argentina or other Spanish-speaking neighbors, but Perón was too much to ignore. Portrait paraphrases: Arriving to power as an army colonel, Juan Perón created a strong base of support from the Argentine workers from 1943 to 1946 and created the "Justicialista" Party pledging support for the poor working class, the "shirtless" ["descamisados"]. Helped enormously in popularity by his beautiful and charming wife Evita, Juan and Evita became semi-gods by virtue of the party and social benefit agencies set up to aid the poor. But by trying to shift the balance of traditional power from the country and the ranchers to urban industry and labor, Perón rattled a few too many cages.

Evita's campaign to become vice-president (she had founded a woman's sector of the Justicialista Party) was seen as a threat to succeed Perón in power and was blocked by the military, but all Argentina would cry and lament her death from cancer in 1952. The poem is written in the years after her death when the military is preparing to oust Perón and send him into exile in Spain under Franco. Cuíca de Santo Amaro establishes a parallel between the dictator Perón of 1955 and Hitler and Mussolini ten years before. Perón is guilty of the classic "cordelian" sin of unbridled ambition.

Perón is battling the military but also the church, not only because the latter is a traditional ally of the landholders, but also because it refused to quickly canonize Evita upon Perón's demands. The poet tells of the dramatic scene of national mourning when for an entire month millions waited in long lines to see and touch the embalmed body of Evita, this while a despondent Juan Perón remained closed up at home in mourning in the Pink House, the national presidential palace. The poet says that when Perón was confronted by the papal requirement of a thirty-year waiting period for canonization, he blew his stack and gave an ultimatum to Rome: either canonize her or get out of Argentina! He drew up a new law for separation of church and state and began a campaign of persecuting the Argentine clergy.

The military are standing by, ready to act, but the poet believes there will be divine intervention against Perón for turning Argentina into an atheistic state.

Perón is ousted in 1955, but not forgotten; it is just the beginning of the myth.

Perhaps the most important and long lasting event for the hemisphere and one directly affecting Brazil in 1964 was the successful Revolution of Fidel Castro in Cuba in 1959. It brought two of the most anti-American poems in all "cordel:" The Story of the Invasion of Cuba or the Revolution Against the Regime of Fidel Castro ["História da Invasão de Cuba ou a Revolução Contra o Regime de Fidel Castro"][27] and the vitriolic Letter to Mr. Kennedy ["Carta a Míster Kennedy"],[28] both poems with a view from the left.

The first was written in 1961 after the failure of the Bay of Pigs invasion of Cuba by counter-revolutionaries backed by the United States. In it the author presents the view of the left in regard to Castro, Cuba and the United States. In spite of its propagandistic slant and either paid authorship or a pseudo-cordelian author, the poem did circulate in the markets and fairs thus providing a chance for the common man to read it. From the beginning it praises Fidel:

"Fidel as a strong
Nationalistic man
In Cuba freed the people
From the claws of the imperialists
After defeating the false
Batista dictatorship."

The Castro line is summarized: Batista was a dictator, the Cuban people were starving, Batista was controlled by North American interests, and there was no freedom. Anyone opposing the regime was arrested, tortured and their lands confiscated. The great Cuban industries of sugar and tobacco were controlled by foreign firms which took the profits out of the small island country. But even worse was the moral climate in the country: girls were forced into prostitution by the mafia, "American trusts" controlled gambling and night clubs and were taking all the profits. Even the famous Havana hotels, cinemas and restaurants were controlled by gangsters.

But Fidel brought a "classic" revolution of the "working masses" and peasants. Castro's justice was swift: "Serious punishments" (the firing squad) were meted out to the Batista followers who did not succeed in fleeing the country. The author details the revolutionary tribunals set up to judge Batista's army officers captured in the revolt. All prisoners "with all legal evidence" were subject "to the severe orders of Fidel Castro" and with "great vigor." Castro converted the army into a popular militia and sent traitors to the firing squad, but his greatest feats were the defeat of the "American trusts" and expulsing Batista from the island.

The last two pages of the poem deal with the failed invasion by contras led by Miro Cardona in 1961 in the provinces of Matanzas and Oriente. Castro used Russian fighter jets to rain down machine gun bullets on the invaders, and he won easily.

One needs to recall the atmosphere in Brazil in the early 1960s and especially developments in the Northeast where "cordel" was still strong as a popular medium of expression. One cannot underestimate the enthusiasm of many Brazilians for the "Cuban Model" as a solution for the poor masses and especially a successful challenge to the "Colossus of the North." Francisco Julião's Peasant Leagues and the cry for land reform based on the Cuban model, wide student support and even favorable comments from the Liberation Theology clergy were all factors from 1961 to 1964. The primary justification of the Brazilian military for the takeover in 1964 would be the perceived communist threat.

The Left propagandized using the cordelian format in the story Letter to Mr. Kennedy by one "Firmino Terra." The poem uses language and discourse uncommon to the traditional cordelian poet: stanzas of eight lines, the emphatic and rhetorical use of the familiar pronoun "you" [tu], and inflammatory ideological language not used in traditional "cordel.". But the poem was sold in the same markets as "regular" poems. It is addressed directly to President Kennedy, attacks the United States, defends Brazil's sovereignty, and praises Cuba as the only hope in the hemisphere against "North American imperialism." It lists Brazilian conservatives like Moreira Salles, Roberto Campos and especially Carlos Lacerda as "sharks" who want to sell Brazil to the U.S. The old oligarchy and the International Monetary Fund are presented as the villains and agents for the defeat of Brazil. The narrator predicts an armed conflict between present and future socialist countries in Latin America against the U.S. And he closes the poem in language indicative of the entire poem: "INDEPENDENCE? PROGRESS? ONLY AFTER THROWING YOU OUT!"

Events would multiply. In the very next year John F. Kennedy would directly challenge Khrushchev's nuclear missile bases in Cuba and demand their removal. The stalemate was solved after a tense give and take of messages and threats when Khrushchev backed down and the peace was maintained. But then on November 22, 1963, the unthinkable happened: Lee Harvey Oswald shot the President as he passed in a motorcade in Dallas, Texas, and the whole world saw it via a home movie taken from down the street.

Combining international political high drama, tragedy and a heinous crime, the event made for sensationalistic stories the world over and "cordel" was no exception. There had been nothing like it since the Lindbergh kidnapping, the assassination of João Pessoa in Brazil in 1930, and the suicide of Getúlio Vargas in 1954. Kennedy's death caught the attention of the cordelian bards and public as well as the poets of other nations. Lamentation was intense because this was the death of a respected international hero, but it became even greater because it was a crime of suspense and drama as well.

Literally dozens of poems were written, but Rodolfo Coelho Cavalcante's is perhaps the best.[29] It is at once an emotional tribute to Kennedy the man and the leader, a journalistic account of the murder, and a summary of the hopes that Kennedy represented to the poet and the people of Brazil and Latin America. No American president was ever so loved in the Americas and for so many reasons. The poet opens,

> "To all the Americans
> I send my condolences
> For the death of John Kennedy
> Victim of violence
> A heinous crime
> Perverse and without conscience."

The poet speaks of Kennedy's great civil rights record, calls him a successor to Abraham Lincoln, and recalls his firmness in dealing with Russia and Cuba. He praises the new Alliance for Progress, a real program in partnership with the countries of Latin American that offered true hope for social and economic betterment in the hemisphere. (Kennedy would always be identified with this program.) But Rodolfo's poetic description of the moment of death recalls other poems and other images by learned poets of the ages:

> "When John Kennedy died
> At 1:30 in the afternoon
> The entire world was enveloped in clouds
> In truth it seemed
> That nature itself was crying
> The wind itself stopped blowing
> Feeling the melancholy."

Rodolfo ends by asking a blessing on great America, home of democracy and on his own Brazil in its battle against Communism and tyranny. One needs to recall that the country is at the height of the Jango Goulart administration and his social politics of the Base Reforms, all to end in 1964 with the military revolution.

No less a moment would astound the world six short years later with another American feat—the first landing of men on the moon. A plethora of poems would follow the tense days of the flight, Armstrong's first "great step for mankind" and the happy return home. It was a victory of American know how and the free, capitalistic system which utilized it. The discourse in the poems is more like that of the old romance-adventure stories, and the astronauts are described in no less heroic language. The dangers and obstacles confronting them and their courage to conquer heretofore unexplored space once again remind the reader of old European romances. There were also curious moments: a strange rumor of disbelief was propagated at the time that the whole thing was a hoax contrived by the American media, so the poets had to convince their backlands readers of the opposite. They did it through great detail of the voyage, close attention to dates and times, even to the point of meticulously describing the astronauts' meals in space. Aside from the interesting question of how one could eat in zero gravity, such attention probably reflected an awareness of the chronic hunger experienced by many of "cordel's" public.

The challenges of the 1970s and 1980s followed. There was the Falklands Islands war reminiscent in "cordel" of the old Graf Spee story but this time with British warships with nuclear missiles steaming toward the Falklands. There was brief mention in <u>cordel</u>" of the Sandinistas and the Marxist-capitalist conflict in Nicaragua which spilled over into the rest of Central America.

But the main international scenario would shift to the Middle East when "<u>cordel</u>" would tell of the two oil embargos with devastating consequences for the Brazilian economy, the capture of U.S. diplomats and officials who were held for years in Tehran, Iran, the bungled attempts to free them, the Israeli-Palestinian conflict and continued wars between Israel and the Arab States. But perhaps it would all be epitomized by the war against Iraq in January, 1991.

J. Borges would write <u>The War in the East or the Inferno in Iraque</u> ["A Guerra no Oriente Médio ou o Inferno no Iraque"][30] from a tiny town in the interior of Pernambuco state saying the war is once again a sign of the times. The end of the world is near and the threat of world war had been predicted by no less than Father Cicero to happen in 1990! After invading Kuwait and threatening neighboring Saudi Arabia, Saddam Hussein paid no attention to a United Nations wrist slapping. It would end only when the brunt of the United States war machine fell upon him in a rain of cruise missiles and stealth bombs. The poet dwells on Hussein's stubbornness and his indifference to world opinion while hidden in underground bunkers no bombs could reach. After sacking the country of Kuwait and allowing the rape of its women by Iraqi soldiers, there was no doubt of the evil leader's ruthlessness. But the poet has confidence that God himself will do in Hussein, principally because of the latter's "ecological" war with its devastation of the oil fields in Kuwait before withdrawing and suing for peace. It is a sin against God himself, the creator of this beautiful earth and its resources! The sea is covered with petroleum, the sand with the blood of the war's victims, and Hussein destroys his own country and people by a refusal to listen to reason.

J. Borges closes expressing confidence that Hussein will be defeated, but adds a contemporary Brazilian note, common to "<u>cordel</u>," in a plea to his own president Fernando Collor de Mello to send his own troops to the Northeast to finish off the robbers and muggers, the "armed gunmen," along with the kidnappers and business sharks that exploit and kill our own people.[31]

4 Satire from the Third World to the First World

To close this album <u>Portrait</u> chooses a more recent text by a contemporary "protest" poet of the medium. Franklin Machado who worked in São Paulo is sharply satirical and not afraid to step on toes. Here is Machado's "revenge" on the First World.

This poem, poetic justice by a humble or perhaps not so humble Brazilian chronicler with a bit of vengeance thrown in, is Franklin Machado's <u>Lampião in the United Nations Defending the Third World</u> ["Lampião na ONU Defendendo o Terceiro Mundo"]. [32] In a sense it summarizes the cordelian chronicle since the beginning of the century for it directs its satire at first world nations and leaders that in the poet's mind have always kept Brazil and the poor nations down. It is the epitome of the cordelian structural pattern of challenge and response, a sort of modern oral poetic duel [<u>peleja</u>]. And the tone is totally Brazilian.

Lampião has come from the "other world" as a spirit taking possession of a speaker at the dais at the U.N. In first person singular narration, the poet protests the rich nations and defends the oppressed, each day more hungry to the point of needing to take a "hunger pill" (recall the recent birth control pill brought from the First World and opposed by many in the Third World as a capitalist plot to limit Third World population). The pills, of course, are made by the multinational firms

> ". . . Which treat our countries
> Like true back yards
> Imposing their dictators
> To be the foremen
> Of other social classes."

President Reagan stands up and says he supports Lampião and he will provide money, arms and food "to friends of the system." This incites Lampião's reaction:

> "Lampião addressed the subject
> Answering without fear:
> I don't fear an old "leading man"
> With starched hair
> Like a well dressed mummy
> Who shows no sign of life
> A senile, decrepit old man.

> "Who does not govern his own State
> But lets others give orders
> The damned capitalists
> They only want to exploit
> The mineral resources
> Of other nations
> Anywhere and everywhere."

And as for Reagan's friend and ally Margaret Thatcher:

"With Reagan she formed a team
Lady Margaret Thatcher
Turned into a beast
"Stuttering . . . .
"Mr. Lampion knows nothing
He does not think about what he says
He's like a dog, he just barks.

"After that outburst
And a finger pointed in his face
Lampião said, "I'll give you a beating
If you don't stop this business."
Of being a man in a skirt
Like a Scotsman in drag
In order to hide his "stick."

All the excitement woke up General Pinochet, he of recent fame, prisoner in London for murders against humanity and recently deceased in Chile, who protested:

"I'm not a killer
Assumed the dunce
Waking from a doze
And he got it in the nose
From a police dog
A really cool answer
For that off the wall remark."

Andropov the Russian minister bangs his shoe on the podium protesting Lampião (the poet Machado remembers when Lampião in a real life scene battled communist rebels near Juazeiro do Norte in his encounter with the Prestes Column in 1926).

The poet then makes fun of the macrobiotic dieting Japanese representative and Indira Gandhi's condescending and ethereal attitude toward Brazil.

At that moment Fidel Castro's Habana suddenly explodes "like a Molotov cocktail," and Lampião disappears in the midst of the confusion. Some say it was all caused by the KGB, others the CIA, but the poet concludes:

"That episode became
Known as "Lampiongate
With the testimony of mortals
The Heads of State
And here ends Machado
And Raimundo their story."

It is fitting and proper to end this international chronicle with this wonderful parody of names, speech and politics telling of the First World and its encounter with Lampião, Northeasterner, bandit and wise guy. It is a lesson in cordelian vengeance.

1   Many of the cordelian poems seen in this album come from the great Brazilian archives, public and private. We owe much to the cooperation of the Ruy Barbosa Foundation in Rio de Janeiro, the Institute of Brazilian Studies at the University of São Paulo, and especially to the private collection of a now deceased friend and mentor, Orígenes Lessa, of Rio de Janeiro, and to Maria Eduarda Lessa, his widow, who continued to allow us access to his archives after his death. We also mention the wonderful collection of Átila de Almeida in Campina Grande, PB. Another fine source for this album is Vicente Salles' prize winning book Repente e Cordel, Rio de Janeiro: FUNARTE-Instituto Nacional do Livro, 1985.

2   João Melchíades Ferreira da Silva, A Primeira Grande Guerra e a Vitória dos Aliados, Parahyba: Editora Popular, 1918. The complete title of the poem is: A Vitória dos Aliados, a Derrota de Allemanha e a Influenza Hespanhola.

3   Leandro Gomes de Barros, As Aflições da Guerra na Europa, Parahyba: Typografia da Popular Editora, julho, 1915.

4   Gomes de Barros, Lembranças do Passado, Recife, 1917.

5   Gomes de Barros, O Sorteio Obrigatório, Duas Noivas Trocadas, Recife: Typografia Mendes, n.d.

6   João Martins de Atayde, O Fim da Guerra, Vitória dos Alliados, Recife, 1918.

7   Atayde, Sacco e Vanzetti aos Olhos do Mundo, Recife, n.d.

8   Zé Vicente, O Rapto Misterioso do Filho do Lindbergh, Belém: Guarjarina, May 28, 1932.

9   Amado Santelmo, "A Morte de Hauptmann" in: A Tragédia Lindbergh, Rio de Janeiro, May, 1934.

10 Our summary of the details of history in this part of <u>Portrait</u> owes much to <u>A History of Brazil</u> by E. Bradford Burns (already cited), to <u>Half of Spain Died, a Reappraisal of the Spanish Civil War</u>, Herbert Matthews, New York: Charles Scribner's Sons, 1973; to David Mitchell, <u>The Spanish Civil War</u>, n.p., n.d.; to Askale Nagash, <u>Haille Selassie</u>, New York: Chelsea House Publishers, 1989; <u>World Book Encyclopedia</u>, vol. 21; to Martin Gilbert, <u>The Second World War, a Complete History</u>, New York: Henry Holt and Company, 1989, and to Joseph Luyten, "Os Japoneses na Literatura de "cordel"," <u>A Literatura de "cordel" em São Paulo: Saudosimo e Agressividade</u>, São Paulo: Edições Loyola, 1981.

11 Jorge Amado, <u>Tenda dos Milagres</u>, São Paulo: Livraria Martins Edta., 1969.

12 Manoel Tomaz de Assiz, <u>'Trocidade da Espanha, o Horror dos Horrores</u>, São Francisco Soledade, PB, n.d.

13 Amador Santelmo, <u>A Guerra Italo-Abyssínia, Dr. Jacarandá Minhas Memórias</u>, Rio de Janeiro, Coleção Orígenes Lessa, s.d.

14 Zé Vicente, <u>Allemanha Comendo Fogo</u>, Belém: Guajarina Edta., n.d.

15 Zé Vicente, <u>O Afundamento do Vapor Alemão 'Graf Spee'</u>, Belém: Guararina, 1939.

16 Zé Vicente, <u>Japão Vai se Estrepar</u>, Belém: Guajarina, December 12, 1941.

17 Zé Vicente, <u>A Batalha da Alemanha contra Rússia</u>, Belém: Guajarina, n.d.

18 Manoel Tomaz de Assiz, <u>Europa Banhada em Sangue</u>, n.p., n.d.

19 Manoel D'Almeida Filho, <u>A Vitória dos Aliados</u>, Aracajú, 1945. Coleção Orígenes Lessa.

20 Delarme Monteiro da Silva, Editor João Martins de Atayde, <u>O Fim da Guerra e a Morte de Mussolini</u>, Recife, 1945.

21 Arinos de Belém, <u>O Testamento de Hitler</u>, Belém: Guajarina Edta., 1945.

22 Besides the books already cited by Vicente Salles and E. Bradford Burns, please see Joseph Luyten, <u>A Notícia na Literatura de "cordel"</u>, doctoral dissertation, USP, 1981; <u>World Book</u>

Encyclopedia, Vol. C; and Raymond Cantel, "Les Poetes Populaires du 'Nordeste' Brésilien et les Mortes Célebres," and "De Sicile au Texas, ao Mexique et au Brésil, Quelques Complaints sur la Morte de John Fitzgerald Kennedy," Cahier do Monde Hispanique et Luso-Brésilien, França, Caravelle, 1965.

23 João Quinto Sobrinho, "João do Cristo Rei," Guerra Civil Mundial da Rússia contra as Nações, Juazeiro do Norte, n.d.

24 Rodolfo Coelho Cavalcante, A Guerra da Coréia, Salvador, September, 1950.

25 No author indicated, A Guerra no Egito e os Horrores do Mundo, n.p., n.d.

26 Cuíca de Santo Amaro, Revolução na Argentina, Salvador, n.d.

27 José Porfírio Costa, A História sobre a Invasão de Cuba ou a Revolução contra o Regime Fidel Castro, n.p., n.d.

28 "Firmino Terra," Carta a Mister Kennedy, n.p., n.d.

29 Rodolfo Coelho Cavalcante, A Trágica Morte de John Kennedy, 2nd. ed., Salvador, December, 1963.

30 J. Borges, A Guerra no Oriente ou o Inferno em Iraque, Bezerros, PE, 1991.

31 As in Album VII, one has to finish somewhere at some time, thus this "folheto" will be the last reported at this writing, that is, the first war in Iraq. There was a flood of story-poems over the next few years on subsequent international events. Everything got worse during the administration of George W. Bush: the war against the Taliban in Afghanistan, the terrible attack on the Twin Towers in New York by Alquaeda, the reaction to the same with the second war in Iraq by Bush Son with its devastating consequences for the entire world, a world threatened ever more by international terrorism. The titles reveal the antipathy of the public of "cordel" not only against the terrorist Bin Laden, but against the President of the United States himself! Bush was called "tyrant" and "dictator" and both he and Bin Laden end up in the moral hell of "cordel."

32 Franklin Machado, Lampião na ONU Defendendo o Terceiro Mundo, São Paulo, n.d.

Album IX

Life Is Not Getting Any Easier

Introduction

As the poets and public of "cordel" reached the millennium, it became very clear that there were not only new variations on an old theme, but quite often a change and evolution in attitude as well. "Cordel" in the large majority of poems produced and sold since the 1960s dwells more and more on the here and now, on current events and problems. The age of the old European or assimilated northeastern long, narrative poem [romance] of 32 pages with its stories of love, suffering, adventure and the hero conquering all are now largely a matter of collections in archives. The old romances are still occasionally reproduced by a single large publisher in São Paulo, but the short eight-page account of an event or commentary on the same has predominated in this the most recent and perhaps final stage of this portrait of a people and their country.

As the title of Album IX suggests, the essence even of the most recent chapbooks is life itself and a preoccupation with quality of life. Though individual topics may follow the old vision of good and evil, they are definitely "modern," end-of-century concerns. The recent chapbooks can often be reduced to a preoccupation with rights of humanity itself, and then of diverse segments of humanity: women, the unborn, abandoned children, husband and wife and the right to divorce, and the marginalized of gay Brazil who face an immense battle against AIDS. Such preoccupations concern not only the humble cordelian readers but all of modern society. A less philosophical but just as important area of concern is the concrete violation of these rights of life—violation seen in the day-to-day life at the end of the twentieth century. Bishop Dom Hêlder Câmara, a pioneering hero of the progressive church in the 1950s defined it well when he said Brazil suffers from violence of all kinds, and the greatest is the violence of poverty and hunger. It manifests itself in the city and the countryside, and today in the land itself, the future of Brazil.

The vision which provides the foundation for the story-poems of Album IX rests not only on traditional beliefs of right and wrong, but observation of what has happened and how life really was in the second half of the twentieth century. The cordelian response to the challenges of life, even if seemingly utopist or theoretical, does in fact exist and portrays this people and nation.

Life and the quality of life—that is the question for much of recent "cordel." A positive way to see the big picture is in Apolônio Alves dos Santos' poem Our Modern World ["Nosso Mundo Moderno"].[1] The poet, a native of the northeastern state of Paraíba but long time resident of greater Rio, begins by saying that the world has evolved and tradition has disappeared. He simply and incredibly poignantly says, "I am not what I used to be." Indeed, the recent poets and public of "cordel" are not what they used to be. As life changed, so did they. The poet lists for his readers all that has changed: the telephone, the transistor radio, astronauts on other planets, organ transplants and the increase of the life span, automobiles everywhere, the air shuttles to far off cities and back in one day, television and the ability to videotape television and see programs another day, almost instantaneous news from the entire world, and modern technology to solve crimes in our cities. The poet Apolônio loves the sound of today's specialists: oculists, dentists, anatomists, and scientists! And he is optimistic in telling of new government retirement agencies that offer guarantees for workers and new ways to combat illiteracy. He ends simply, asking the public to analyze what he has said, to see the evolution and without any hyperbole on his part!

An opposite view is that of Raimundo Santa Helena. He puts it all differently in a dark poem with a catchy title We the Urban Human Beings ["Nós, os Seres H'urbanos"].[2] In bad verse but very relevant detail, the poet summarizes life in contemporary urban Brazil, in this case Rio. He says life in the city today is that of malnutrition, a lack of hospitals, corruption and the mass population reduced to being marginalized Brazilians. He calls Rio "a concrete jungle" where "to live you have to kill." And "in this scary jungle" you find the "lost of the night," the homosexuals who come to Rio's famous lush south zone by the beach at Copacabana and Ipanema to sell themselves to survive.

It is a city where the poor trade what little they have for food, where some are reduced to picking up the popcorn others have dropped at busy Plaza XV near the ferry docks to Niteroi. The poet speaks of the long lines of the "sub-world" that wait for everything and that have grown in his seventeen years as poet in the city. The poor experience no calm in their lives; life becomes a neurosis.

The poet tells of being assaulted by a young boy with a knife on the streets of Rio, of being threatened with his life. He tells of two beggars fighting with knives over trash in the streets. He tells of the old historic Rio street of Mem de Sá where skinny whores work for their gigolos and of a famous bar in the area where even the police take advantage of the women. The poet's conclusion: "Our dreams have been poisoned."

Whether Apolônio's or Raimundo's vision is true or not is answered in the cordelian <u>Portrait</u> of the end of the twentieth century when the poets and their public will see it all as a question of rights and the violation of the same.

1 Life Itself and the Most Basic of Rights: the Right to Be Born

With the era of widespread television via satellite communication systems of the 1960s came a new Brazilian cultural institution; some say its most visible contribution to contemporary popular culture, the national "soap opera," [telenovela]. One of the earliest and most successful was called The Right to Be Born ["O Direito de Nascer"]. The topic of the show was universal—abortion. It was an important national phenomenon, unspoken by most but on everyone's minds. A plethora of story-poems in "cordel" took advantage of the moment and wrote of the issue, basing stories above all on the "telenovela" (one of the earliest instances of the "folk communication" phenomenon when "cordel" retold topics from radio and television with their now ubiquitous access to the humble classes).

Rodolfo Coelho Cavalcante, the arch-conservative from Salvador da Bahia, based his poem on the TV soap opera and used the same title, roundly condemning abortion and "today's women who avoid via their orgies the right to be born." The poem is more than an attack on abortion; it is a desperate cry of defiance to the changing times:[3]

> "Many upper class women today
> Don't want to even hear about staying at home
> They prefer to have their jobs
> And not wash clothes or sew
> They abandon the home
> For them the right to be born
> Is just a masquerade."

The woman who kills her child through abortion is subject not only to personal suffering but has violated a divine law! And with so many women desperate to have children but cannot! Maternity is a mission; it is the law of creation! Why does marriage exist? Why have husbands? (Little did the poet realize that a portion of Brazilian women were of course asking themselves the same questions and concluding that indeed marriage and a husband might not be necessary.)

The poet condemns not only women, but husbands who urge their wives to use the birth control pill for "economic" reasons. It is nothing but "pure anarchy" says the poet. And there are the male doctors who are nothing less than murderers who make a living doing abortions. Under any circumstances, it is the "modern" woman who wants to experience all pleasures who "profanes" the natural order and God himself by giving in to abortion. But God is just and God punishes; another diluvium will resolve the problem! Rodolfo spends the rest of his story condemning the characters in the "<u>telenovela</u>" and concludes his story saying that he always has a moral view in his poems. That is his mission. He may respect the government, but he answers first to the divine judge, God himself! And many of his public will agree with him.

This same "soap opera," one of the first huge successes of the genre in Brazil, was really a transplant from Cuba which originated first radio and then television soaps which were imported by the young networks in Brazil which would soon far surpass the Cuban production. But Cunha Neta "the backlands poet" from far off Piaui state summarized the same soap in the style of the thirty-two page cordelian romance with its great lessons on the value of life.

The topic caught fire and poets wrote titles like <u>The Right to Kill</u>,[4] <u>The Woman Who Conceives a Child but Later Kills It Without Reason</u>,[5] or <u>The Ways of the Woman Who Wants No Childrenn</u>.[6] In the first case the "Apostle Troubador" Minelvino Francisco Silva of southern Bahia condemns all murder, including that of women having abortions. The second story-poem responds to those who say abortion is a social problem; for the poet it is strictly a moral decision.

The poet's conclusion is that women are dying today in the maternity wards as a result of these pills! They leave orphans and widowers marrying again in search of happiness!

2 The Right to Be Different—the Modern Feminist

But what if you are a woman and want it your way? Perhaps the most volatile issue for a traditionally conservative, "old church" religious and moral public will be another social type which challenges the old paternalistic, male dominance of the poets and public of the cordelian northeast—the modern feminist. Portrait can report titles only by one author writing in one city only, but the fact that this author lived and wrote on the streets of São Paulo for twenty years and the fact he chose to write successive titles (not likely if they were not of interest to his public or commercially successful) warrants space as snapshots of the times.

Franklin Machado, born and raised in the northeastern state of Bahia, is a university graduate, a rarity among the poets of modern "cordel." Until recently he wrote and published his story-poems in greater São Paulo, the largest "northeastern" city in Brazil because of the massive migration in the twentieth century (greater São Paulo has twenty million inhabitants and an estimated one-third of them come from the Northeast). His forté is social commentary, satire and parody, most often in a very contemporary style and language. Dressed like a 1960s hippy with leather vest and hat, wearing round granny-glasses and beard, Maxado for years was the "vanguard" of "cordel" in São Paulo, selling his poems on the streets and in the markets of that city, especially Rua Augusta and the Plaza of the Republic in the city center where tourists and others came to the "hippy" fair.

Of his many titles on the subject, Machado's best poem and perhaps the most unique is his The Debate between Lampião and an American tourist ["Debate de Lampião com uma Turista Americana"][7] It tells of the outlandish, hilarious and very entertaining fictitious encounter between the macho bandit Lampião and Ms. Betty Friedan, America's famous pioneering feminist. The story is unique in "cordel" (except to Maxado) and is worth telling.

The title does not prepare the reader in any fashion for the real theme, but immediately attracts the attention of the typical male purchaser of "cordel" in the market—no one can resist both Lampião, the greatest northeastern hero and the love-hate relationship most Brazilians have for North Americans. Maxado's idea is to present "Beti Fridi" as an American tourist doing research in the Northeast. She is portrayed as a feminist "indoctrinating" all who come in contact with her "atheistic principle." The poet uses the device of the spiritualist medium in the person of Betty's tour guide who "receives" the spirit of the bandit Lampião and becomes "possessed" by him. A debate or discussion follows (using the format of the traditional poetic debate in "cordel") in an exchange of ideas which turns out to be all one-sided.

The macho bandit from the very beginning lets Betty know his view as to modern woman and feminism:

> "That business of feminism
> Is the art of the ugly woman
> Who can't find a real man
> To whip a little sense into her
> So she grabs another woman
> And then does whatever she wants
> With her foreign doctrine."

The bandit's diatribe continues for several pages, but then the reader sees Betty's response:

> "Mister, you are an ignoramus
> And you are a chauvinist pig as well
> You don't understand people
> Much less a feminist
> You're one of those 'ole machos
> Who is an enemy of a woman
> You just don't know how to make a conquest."

Hearing this, the bandit loses his cool, blows up, calls Betty some choice names, and "like the Cisco Kid when in danger," gives her a real whipping (with "kinky" connotations implied):

And he really lays on the leather.
The "gringa" then began to shout—
—O my darling, oh únderful!
(And the more she was beaten):
—Veri gude, véri matiche.
Sânquio, iou me did xeque-mate
(She did not know what she was saying).

—Now I have found my "man"
I'm going to quit running and shouting,
On the streets of the States
And taking off my brassiere
I accept you along with a thousand
Other women in Brrrezil
No longer am I going to protest.

Betty says she is going to return to the kitchen, prepare the meals and be a good housewife,

"I learned my lesson well
The woman's place is in the bed
In the kitchen and in the pantry
Knowing how to be a real woman
And not being like any common broad
Disgraced and still unmarried!

At this point Lampião smiles, says goodbye to all present and returns to the spirit world. He threatens to return again, should the need arise, and give a good beating to any women who have not seen the light. But the poet closes <u>admitting</u> that maybe things have changed a little since Lampião's days.

For the reader who knows "<u>cordel</u>" well, and by this time that includes the readers of this book, it is evident there is more than one way to interpret this story. The poet probably should not be taken very seriously. Satire, after all, is quite often no more than a device the poets have used for years to comment on the changing times. What is different in this story is the bilingual text, a rarity in "<u>cordel</u>," but certainly more plausible in greater São Paulo than a tiny town in the northeast. The public who would gather in São Paulo to hear Maxado recite his verse was largely a male public, people who probably attended American movies upon occasion, students, and perhaps even Americans and other English speaking tourists in the Plaza of the Republic on Sunday morning. It is unlikely that any traditional public of "<u>cordel</u>" would know as much English as the poet uses in the text, but the poet may have been directing it to university students or foreign tourists as well.

The poem seen today, almost thirty-five years after its appearance in 1981, and after the early waves of international feminism, really fulfills the cordelian function of informing <u>after the fact</u> and serving as a portrait of the age. Its words now seem antiquated and kitsch to us, stereotyped relics of the age, but they do reflect the period and the social situation: how a given segment of the Brazilian population would react to a social phenomenon coming from outside the country and influencing and changing Brazilians themselves. The poet's main purpose was to get a laugh from a mainly male, macho public, and he certainly did that through a declamation amidst asides and guffaws in the public plaza. He certainly insulted today's sensibility. The story-poem may be a portrayal of a scene of male domination and the changes to come, changes which would forever alter the face of Brazil.

3 Rights of a Man and His Wife

But what can be said of the well-being of the procreators themselves—man and woman, husband and wife? What of their rights of marriage and rights of divorce? Another of the major issues of the times which dates from the late 1970s is the legalization of divorce by civil law passed by the Brazilian congress in 1977. In a traditional Catholic country which prior to that time allowed only civil separation and no legal second marriages, this was a major change in the way of life of an entire nation. "Cordel" captured the debate prior to passage of the law, discussed the pros and cons, and perhaps surprisingly revealed changing attitudes from a supposedly conservative voice representing a large portion of Brazilian society.

The poets welcome the new law of 1977 but tend to hedge on the issue. They all believe that a happy marriage is what God had in mind, but all recognize that it is the human element and human error that cause bad marriages, unhappiness and perhaps even violence. So the law is a way out. One finds much of the northeastern, male psyche in the poets' words and attitudes. Azulão in Rio de Janeiro writes Only Divorce Solves the Problem ["Só o Divórcio Conserta"][8] in 1975 prior to the actual passage of the law but during the hot debates in congress. The poem summarizes the views of the great majority of his colleagues. His main point is found in strophe one:

"When the couple does not succeed
In living a certain [true] life
Let's give to each one
Freedom and an open door
If you deny this
You deny there is an error
That only divorce solves."

He applies logic to his belief: why prohibit a law which solves a great error? Believing marriage is eternal is closing your eyes to the world today. Obliging a couple to stay married when things go bad is only to continue a living hell for them.

Marriage is a crap shoot; you don't really know what your partner is like until you have lived with her/ him for awhile. And no one is perfect, man or woman. In a civilized country a divorce law is neither a crime nor a business; it is a necessity. In Brazil without it there are countless discombobulated families—husbands living with other women and their own wives "shacked up" [amigadas] with other men. This situation needs to be "moralized." No one wants to go back to living together in misery, but each searches for happiness with a new partner. And Brazil's legal separation [desquite] solves nothing because it does not allow for a legal second marriage after the separation. A country without divorce simply can have no discipline. Divorce moralizes, dignifies and gives a doctrinal base to life.

Divorce existed long before Christ and was part of divine law. God is present in the man who lives in peace and in a moral way. Otherwise you return to the legal separation mess—so many cases that they cannot even fit into the archives. And worst of all, there are children who do not even know who their legitimate parents are. There are more separations than marriages today; it's a mess.

But divorce must be regulated and allowed only after several attempts at reconciliation, perhaps only after five to six years of legal separation. It must be desired by both parties. Whoever marries and fails must not remain like a prisoner tied up in a frustrated marriage.

Remember, marriage is a union of personal interest and pleasure. It is not God who determines living together until death. If there is a mistake, it is a human mistake. I say to those that claim that God does not consent to a second marriage and that it is a sin, why is it not legally prohibited in Brazil to live together and not be married ["se viver amasiado"]? Those that know their Bible know that Jesus did indeed baptize but he never married anyone. Look at the examples of the Old Testament:

"The man that married the most
Was the great Solomon
But God gave him the wisdom
To govern the nation
And also to build his temple
And I'll cite another example
Of Delilah and Samson."

So my thesis is based on our ancestors and he who contradicts my poetic voice ["minha lira"] is saying that sacred scripture is a lie!

The majority of poets of recent "cordel" then are unanimous in welcoming the new law, and each is cognizant of tradition and Biblical teaching. Though Rome and the Church may forbid divorce per se, even the humble and unlettered accept the same reality and remedy as their middle and upper class counterparts in modern Brazil.

4 Rights of the Children

If abortion is condemned, if other means of birth control are ineffective for whatever reason, the result is another of the most serious social problems of Brazil—the unwanted and abandoned child and the resulting street children found throughout large cities in the entire country. Recent decades of exacerbated poverty and the moral and social disintegration of the nuclear family have drastically increased the problem. A tragic corollary is that phenomenon the Brazilians call the "death squads," para-military groups taking the law into their own hands and "eliminating" undesirables and the marginalized, including children from the streets. The cordelian poem The Justice of "White Hand" of the Death Squads[9] is a case in point when the poets praise this "patriotic" vigilante justice.

The Candelaria Massacre of several street children in 1993 in Rio de Janeiro was a horrible case in point. Well intentioned Brazilians responded with efforts to address the problems both from the capital Brasilia and private sources. "Cordel" has addressed and opined as to the problem, reporting the bad with the good, especially since the issue evolved in the 1970s into a national campaign to at least try to do something about it.

5 Rights of the Marginalized—Gay Brazil and AIDS

In the stories condemning abortion one could have talked of another way to avoid having babies—the condom—but this topic would impact much more directly the "man's world." It is a different story and reveals yet another important reality in Brazil. The condom or "preservativo" as they call it in Brazil obviously would safely avoid conception as well. But in "cordel" it is almost exclusively discussed in a totally different vein: as protection against the plague of the century—AIDS. That many Brazilian men would not consider it their responsibility or role to use a condom for anti-procreation purposes (one of the poets says up front "it is not our custom") is one reason for recent rights advocates condemning the "selfish Brazilian male." But when it comes to self-preservation in the AIDS crisis, then the condom—"Venus's little shirt" ["Camisinha de Venus"]—becomes an issue intimately related to the "scourge of the century."

The snapshots themselves reveal the range of reaction and sentiment as AIDS hits like a pile driver in the Brazil of the 1980s. Contagious AIDS Killing Humanity, AIDS the Fear of Humanity, AIDS, the Sickness of the Century, or The people Don't Want to Do It Anymore for Fear of AIDS explain the disease and how it ravages the world. "Venus's Little Shirts" for Everyone, AIDS, Fimosis, Vasectomy and Gay Power, and Sexual diseases instruct of means to avoid it. And AIDS Has Arrived Killing Queers of Every Variety mounts a scurrilous attack on homosexuals as perpetrators of the disease in Brazil.

Azulão puts in his two cents worth in Rio de Janeiro with "Little Shirts" [condoms] for Everyone ["Camisinhas para Todos"][10] combining seriousness in teaching about the disease with his usual sardonic humor, treating it as just another of Brazil's predicaments. He informs that you don't have to stop kissing; it is transferred via blood, so be careful of transfusions, visits to the dentist and using a needle someone has already used. Since it's also transferred via the genitals, don't have sex with pederasts or concubines! He chides husbands with "a wife at home as pretty as the moon" who still are not satisfied and have sex with street women—use a condom! And if you have sex with a "queer" and then a neighbor lady and she in turn with her husband, use a condom!

He even chides virgins to put a condom on their finger before doing what they all do alone! And young guys, the palm of your hand can transmit AIDS too!

The poet explains that Sacred Scripture warned us all that when man loses his faith in God and disobeys the divine master, war, nudity, madness and diseases with no cure will come to punish us all. Satan planted his "evil seed" in the world and invented all manner of sexual disease. Advice from priests and the pope himself does no good because no one listens. We will all be destroyed just like the people of Sodom. Now we see women with their "rear end hanging out" on TV and on the streets! There's no more shame! Naked women and queers rule!

The real cause of all this abuse is television:

> "Our kids can't
> Watch television
> Because on all the channels
> There's just screwing around
> Naked couples, crazy scenes
> Sucking on tongues and mouths
> Teaching perdition!"

AN ASIDE: By the way, in the cordelian story The Evil that the "Telenovela" Brings[11] the poet Alberto Porfírio rails against those addicted to the television nightly soap opera. Things are so bad that priests have had to change the time of mass so people will not have to choose between mass and the soap opera. And social life has been ruined. You do not just knock on the door and visit in the parlor like the old days. The TV is on and no one pays attention to you, so you might as well give in, make a drink at the bar and see the show. END OF ASIDE

Azulão assures us that God above is watching, and AIDS is an example of the immorality of the world. Scientists may labor, but there is no cure. And the medicine that does exist to help slow it down is so costly that only the rich, the "millionaire capitalists," can afford the medicine, and the poor are "screwed as usual." So the old adage still is true, "The rich live because they can/ the poor survive only out of stubbornness." That's the opinion of the poet.

What is clear first of all is that "cordel" did not shy away from addressing such an important issue of life. Indeed, as the century evolved so did the issues the "voice of the masses" addressed in his "newspaper of the poor." In the absolute majority of the poems, the attitude is first of all to inform, then to teach. While most poets will make an occasional joke or use a witticism to describe social customs and mores in Brazil that expose the population to AIDS, they often unintentionally reveal sexual practice and social acceptance of less than traditional Catholic moral standards.

6 The Next Step: the Case of Roberta Close

Perhaps no cordelian story-poem of the recent past struck such a modern note as Expedito F. Silva's poem <u>Roberta Close the Phenomenon of the Twentieth Century</u> ["Roberta Close, o Fenômeno do século XX"].[12] The poets, as <u>Portrait</u> has seen, were only too aware of the AIDS epidemic assailing the country and the sudden spotlight thrown onto the homosexual segment of Brazilian society. Whether sympathetic to the plight of active homosexuals or radically opposed to them as an aberration of society, the male, often macho poet of "<u>cordel</u>" in 1984 had to deal with a related but slightly different phenomenon—the tongue in cheek election of Brazil's most famous transvestite and later transsexual Roberta Close as Brazil's "most beautiful woman."

Long famous for its transvestites and especially their role in the famous carnival ball held annually in Rio de Janeiro, Brazil also had to choose its response to the phenomenal popularity and visibility of Roberta. This writer wrote a tongue-in-cheek paper on the matter when it happened called "What Do You Do If You Are Catholic, Conservative and Write "Cordel?" The answer is found in this poem.

Expedito, a veteran on the Rio de Janeiro cordelian scene, begins with the classical appeal to the muses to inspire this poem done "upon request" about the charms of Roberta. She has become a headliner on television and the dailies, "Causing envy for some/ and happiness for others." Singing or not, modeling or not, Roberta is applauded by the masses! The world is in transition, so Roberta does not have to be a stage or screen star to prove herself because she was born beautiful, by the law of creation.

The poet says he does not understand those that accuse her. After all, in the march of progress they forget that being a "phenomenon" can be a formula for success. Roberta is a headliner, the most beautiful in history. She may be a transvestite, but the poet Expedito knows that she has well deserved glory. The press raved about her because it thought she deserved it. "I've never seen such a phenomenon/ Without a reason/ and never a person like her!"

He raves on: she was born beautiful, born an artist. <u>Portrait</u> paraphrases: she has a face beautiful even without makeup, an attractive smile (which I [the poet] saw on TV). That is when I decided to write this poem. If there is a prettier woman out there, show me! Roberta now can be on radio or television anywhere, anytime; there is no limit. She is elegant, has charm, health and maturity to handle any challenge! Some say she is a curiosity. The other models say not even Satan himself can withstand her temptations.

She became a national hit when Chacrinha invited her to his TV program to be on the judges' panel (along with the regular beauties). She topped them all and pleased the public. No one talks of anything else. And not just the common folks who watch TV. The artists themselves seem to be obsessed with her on all the programs.

As Elke Maravilha (a well known star) says, whether it's a "he" or a "her," what matters is fame, and she's got it!

> Exuberant Roberta
> Has a sculptured body
> Man or woman—whatever
> He's coveted by the public
> An image of today that
> Leaves the world in wonder."

She is "the delicious plate of the day." The poet says he wrote the poem in Bahia and was applauded for it. He adds that some are going to say he is "unfaithful" to "cordel" to write a book like this, that it's a waste of paper. "I only did it because I thought Roberta would make a good "cordel."

One has to remember Album III which dealt with the moral example and phenomenon to realize the why and wherefore of this story. Roberta Close, above all, is news! And she is in addition a "phenomenon" of the times. The poet surely sold out the printing quickly exactly because of that. And if the reaction of his public was like that of the masses of Brazilians who witnessed the Roberta phenomenon of those years, it shows at the least, a Brazilian tolerance for an incredibly beautiful transvestite (to become transsexual) and a willingness in the modern days for a poet from this arch-conservative poetic tradition to not only report the times but to courageously admit that man or woman—this beauty turned him (and his public) on!

All the segments of society seen thus far in their right to basic life were and are challenged by forces which can end that life, and violence, violence of all types, is the common denominator. It is this violence which preoccupied the poets as they chronicled the Brazil at the end of the twentieth century.

7 The Real Violence—Murder in the streets

As any visitor to Brazil who reads the dailies or watches TV news knows, and as those who actually live in the cities, on the farms and on the ranches of Brazil know better, the problem of violence is huge and far from alleviated. Its darker side is reflected in "cordel" by early poems of the 1960s of vigilante justice like Carlos Lacerda and the Beggars in Guanabara Who Were Thrown into the Rio da Guarda as well as later poems like Minelvino Francisco Silva's Story of the Death Squadrons in the 1980s. Such violence has been a major topic in urban "cordel" for the past four decades. Most recently, statistics on the number of weapons in Brazil's cities, the number of crimes and the recent national referendum on gun possession, draw attention to the problem.

Urban poems like God, Man and Violence, Violence in Rio, Drugs Are Just That, Drugs, The Death of the Racketeer Marquinho and I Don't Know Whether to Cry or Laugh Over the Violence in Rio all tell the story. The poems are repetitive in the story they tell, but each offers a small vignette of the entire sordid situation.

Gonçalo Ferreira da Silva, one of Rio's best contemporary poets who never minces words when speaking of national politics or the social scene, in I Don't Know Whether to Cry or Laugh Over the Violence in Rio[13] takes a more cynical tack. He says the general population is desperate for a solution. Rio's Roman Catholic leader, Cardinal-Archbishop Dom Eugênio Sales offers a Christian solution: return love for violence; turn the other cheek. He believes the violence is a result of the abandoned children. The poet says the good priest would change his tune if he were subject to a mugging like everyone else. Children abandoned out of poverty are not the reason—we the northeasterners who migrated to Rio came in the worst poverty, and it never crossed our minds to rob or kill. No, the solution lies elsewhere and most certainly not in opinion polls run by national TV which come to nothing.

The authorities who try to dissolve the death squads are themselves involved with the "bandits." One solution only exists for the "cruel marginalized" who criminalize Rio: an "accident" by the police who round them up when they try to "escape." Citizens who try to be honest and turn in crimes or criminals become suspect themselves when they give witness to what they have seen and are often killed by the bandits. The poet returns to his original theme: the religious may say that justice will be done in heaven and criminals will have to pay for their sins after dying, but "for us materialists," there is a better solution: pay here and now for the crimes committed. The church's drivel is no more than "lies to piss us off" ["papo furado/ para nos encher o saco"]. Enough already! says the poet.

The poet Gonçalo says there are those who will say he is full of "baloney" and is a real "clown;" his answer is a hypothetical conversation with Jesus Christ himself. Jesus would say, "I already sent Ghandi and that did no good. I went myself, died on the cross for you, and when I last took a look, the world was more violent than ever." Jesus' conclusion to the poet: "You had it right. The criminals have to die in a "duel" with the police."

8 Violence in the Countryside

The alternative to the violence of the city, both physical and environmental, is the old dream of escape, of somehow finding a piece of land in the country to eke out a living. There now is less of a chance of accomplishing this in the old traditional Northeast because of centuries old landholding patterns and policies and the even greater emphasis on cash crops such as sugarcane which was converted in the 1980s and 1990s into combustible alcohol to fuel the massive amounts of new autos and trucks manufactured in Brazil. The Mecca of rich agricultural lands in the Center and South of Brazil also offers less opportunity even for seasonal labor because of Brazil's conversion of its agriculture into a modern, mechanized system of large crops to be sold for dollars in the external economy. This policy has produced a lessening of emphasis on growing basic food crops for internal public consumption (see "cordel's" The Soybean Planters Are Doing in Brazil), so the country became desperate. The seasonal pickers' [bóias frias] options have become even less viable.

The military solution from the 1960s to the mid—1980s and the solutions since have been to resurrect the old concept of land reform espoused by the great Getúlio Vargas in the 1930s and João Goulart in the 1960s. It represents the dream to open new lands in the Far West and North, the last frontiers, the last chance. What seemed like a simple solution to the military regimes from the 1960s to the 1980s of giving title to peasants who would work vacant land for a stipulated number of years, establishing a residence and improving the property, turned out to be a nightmare. Supposedly vacant land turned out to have owners, and hired gunmen of landholders were sent to expulse the squatters [moradores ou posseiros].

Complicating the issue was the support by the progressive wing of the Catholic Church in Brazil espousing the Liberation Theology "preference for the poor" strategy, a topic seen in "cordel" by Franklin Machado writing from São Paulo in The New Catholic Church and the Christian Socialism of Friar Leonardo Boff.[14] The poet says that if the times are changing, so must the Church, even if it requires a socialist bent. He traces church history in Brazil noting the alliance of the old church with the rich landholders, even though some of the former defended the rights of the Indians, slaves and poor. But now, in the 1960s there is a different kind of priest, disciples of Gustavo Gutiérrez who first formulated Liberation theology.

The example of such clergy is Father Leonardo Boff who disdains the old rich church and wants the church as an arm for social justice for the poor. Basing his thinking on the gospels themselves with Christ's teachings about the poor and the difficulty of a rich man entering heaven, Boff has had to defend his ideas before the pontiff in Rome. The poet tells of the new martyrs, a priest killed in Chile and Archbishop Romero in El Salvador. Basing his story on Boff's book, Machado tells how the new wave clergy defend the poor and the right to make revolution under tyranny (a right traced all the way back to the writing of St. Thomas Aquinas and the concept of just war taught by the Scholastics in Salamanca in Spain.) He tells of Camilo Torres the "revolutionary priest" martyr in modern Colombia and Father Ernesto Cardenal, a Sandinista leader in Nicaragua.

He goes on to say that Brazil had its own radical religious leaders—Antônio Conselheiro, Father Cícero and Francisco Julião, "A lawyer for Christian Marxism/ Sacrificed for the people" as a result of the Peasant Leagues in Pernmabuco in the early 1960s. The new leaders are progressive, want wealth divided and distributed, and are not Communists, but neither do they espouse the "capitalist bosses." They are not Socialists, for that is the result of an atheistic materialism, but they do prefer "Theology of Liberation." They use the term "socialization" basing their ideas on the papal encyclical Rerum Novarum which Pope Leo XIII pronounced to combat Marxism. And Maxado ends speaking of John Paul II himself, a product of a Marxist nation, who fears the new direction of Liberation Theology priests and calls them to task. The poet ends saying that the new church knows it must do more than preach the gospels and has to actively help the people to force land distribution.

> "If not
> It will turn into folklore
> Or a museum piece with its history
> With empty sermons
> Losing its glory
> Of resistance, of its martyrs
> Who reached for victory."

As a result of such thinking and leaders in the 1980s and 1990s the church actively supported migrants and squatters' rights to land and offered both moral and legal support. Violence ensued and clergy were beaten and killed.

9 Violence to Planet Earth

Environmental questions are tied both to the cities and the land, but have a slightly different twist in each. They began to become an issue in modern Brazil as early as the arrival of the atomic bomb on the world scene and then with the question of nuclear power symbolized by the plant at Angra dos Reis existing on a fault line in southeast Brazil. Perceived in traditional "cordel" as being a product of atheistic "mad" scientists contrary to the natural order of things (God's creation of the universe) and man's desire to become like or more powerful than God, the bomb and nuclear power became feared not only for their destructive power but their proven poisonous effect on nature. Poems like Rafael Carvalho's Atomic Bomb are cases in point and date from the turbulent nationalism and anti-U.S. sentiments of the early 1960s.

It was not much of a leap to more recent times and concern over environmental questions with the massive government sponsored mining in the Amazon Basin where the land was strip mined on the one hand (Carajás) or dug shovel by shovel in the Brazilian version of Hollywood biblical scenes where masses of slaves built pyramids—the hole-in-the-ground gold mine of Serra Pelada where the poets reported the mad rush for the elusive nuggets in titles like Serra Pelada. The use of large quantities of mercury to separate the precious metal from the ore, especially in the vast rivers of the North, fed fuel to the fire.

Once the concern for the land became a movement with international celebrities like Sting playing an important role in publicizing the new rape of the land, the poets reported developments in stories like Eco 92 (the large environmental congress in Rio de Janeiro) and poems like Devastate Brazil? or Amazônia forgotten.

But equally important was what was happening right in front of the Brazilians' eyes close to home—poisonous air and environmental disaster in the industrial center of the country. The situation came to a head in 1984 with an oil pipeline exploding and burning nearby slums in Cubatão, the infamous industrial center thirty-five miles from São Paulo center. It was reported by Raimundo Santa Helena in Rio de Janeiro in Tragedy in Cubatão[15] where the muckraking cordelian journalist laid the blame for the disaster directly in the hands of the national oil company Petrobrás when he said the company was warned ahead of time. The ensuing fire killed nearly one hundred residents of Vila Socó and thousands lost their homes. The poet warns the same thing can happen as well in other industrial zones of Brazil.

Raimundo Silva in Rio de Janeiro as early as 1981 takes an historical approach: it all began with the Trans-Amazon highway and the military's decision to open up the forests to poor northeasterners, the squatters [posseiros] already seen in a previous story. As a result, over 100,000 families migrated to southern Pará state. But with the Geisel administration in 1970 the utopist land plan changed: the multinationals were invited in to exploit Amazonia, the best example being the Jari Project of international capitalist Daniel Ludwig. Then the military regime shook hands with the Japanese and Itaipu Dam was built devastating millions of square miles of former forested land in south central Brazil. The landholders now expulse the same squatters [posseiros] who had been given government promises of prosperity in the late 1960s. The culmination is the American photography project via satellite which will reveal formerly hidden riches to be exploited by the multinationals. The poet urges Brazilians to wake up—the only answer is democracy and freedom from the current hegemony of military dictatorship which has sold out to the U.S

The culmination of all these poems is the poignant The Death of Chico Mendes Left Nature Sad[16] by Manoel Santa Maria in December, 1988, in Rio de Janeiro. Mendes' story takes place in the Amazon and is the most famous case combining concern for the people and the land. The area was originally populated by poor northeasterners and local crossbreeds [caboclos] in the rubber plantation region. What was originally a battle for workers' rights and the locals to hold onto land they had used for generations evolved into a cause célebre to protect the forest and the Amazon. A local labor leader, Chico Mendes, was converted into a national and international icon in his cause which was only strengthened by his murder and martyrdom.

In this poem the author has it correct when he pays tribute to Chico Mendes, "Our martyr of the forest/ Our astute labor union leader/ Our fearless ecologist," for Chico was all that. First battling for the rights of descendants of the original rubber zone workers in Xapuri in the jungle, Chico expanded his efforts in a general plea to save the forest itself. His murder by a hired thug in the employ of a local landholder [fazendeiro] brings a plea from the poet for an end to the killing and the destruction of the area. The press calls Mendes "The Gandhi of the Rubber plantations." According to the poet, even the United Nations felt the impact of Chico Mendes' death, and this poem is to "Jab the wound/ Of the landholders and their evil gunmen/ Who think they can run our lives."

The poet is quick to notice that it was the international press with its clamor, principally the New York Times, which caused the rusty (except when greased), slow-moving wheels of Brazilian justice to notice the death and take action. A Brazilian government desiring the monetary backing of foreign capital "To invest in the nauseating/ Pseudo-development and financial scandal" springs into action! This is the Brazil at the end of the twentieth century which is drowning in the "cauldron" of political parasites; the Brazil doing only what is in error. Such corruption and bad administration could be corrected by the new constitution

(1988), but instead the corrupt are protected by it. The poet cites cases where the Macuxi Indians were pursued and robbed of their lands, of rich ranchers who literally destroyed the forest with clear cutting, burning and then allowing cattle to feast on and trample what was left until the treeless soil was baked by the Amazon sun.

The national organization to control "development" in the Amazon, the IBDF, is lax and exerts no real control. It all has become a "false colonization," the "cruel destruction" of Brazil's natural reserves. The technocrats, the multinationals, and one political party, the UDR (National Democratic Rural Union, the party of the landholders) are at fault. The UDR has defended the large landholders who order the killing of "peaceful small farmers, priests and union leaders." It is in fact the UDR which was responsible for drafting a part of the new constitution of Brazil which in effect "killed Agrarian Reform." The consequences are here and now:

> "The Indians cry for help
> The Atlantic rain forest is in tears
> The Amazon agonizes in its death throes
> And a foul smelling breeze
> Terrifies and suffocates us all."

The result is climatic disequilibrium (the cordelian "world upside down" motif has come true) not only in the Amazon but in other parts of Brazil and a good part of the world. Drought in the south, who ever heard of it! And floods in the Northeast! And there is a biological holocaust in the Amazon itself. But all is not in vain; the death of Chico Mendes and his blood will "irrigate the earth" and other Chicos will come, just as mountain chain follows mountain chain. It will be a war to the finish in 1988.

So thought the poet. In 1992 ECO 92 was held in Rio de Janeiro, an international congress to address the devastation in the Amazon and the effect of the attack on the environment of the entire world. But the new cordelian poets, street-wise veterans of the devastation since the 1960s, thought otherwise. Seeing Brazil as a perennial victim of exploitation since colonial times, the poet in Eco 92 blames his fellow citizens for being complacent, for getting used to giving in. At the end of the twentieth century the dollar is devastating the poor Brazilian "cruzeiro" and the national economy. The International Monetary Fund has Brazil by the throat with its huge international debt and interest rates which can be paid only by a cash exportation economy which has ruined the stability of a formerly self-sufficient nation. ECO 92 is only the latest and the culmination: an international "fair" to inform other nations of Brazil's remaining riches so they can come and exploit them. It is a plot not to protect the beauty of the Amazon, but to once more steal its riches.

Not only does the Brazilian government not stop the fires in the rain forest, but does nothing to punish those who start them. How can any Brazilian not condemn what is happening? Notice that Peru, Ecuador, Venezuela or Colombia are not in question, for those peoples have backbone; they shout and make revolution. And we the Brazilians are only used to being trampled. Let's defend Brazil and keep the Amazon from being divided by them!

These, then, are the stories of end-of-century cordelian journalism. It is not a pretty picture, but is this all there is? Gonçalo Ferreira da Silva's feigned poetic conversation with Jesus Christ and the latter's solidarity with the poet in solving the problem of criminal violence in Brazil was no accident. When man fails, when all else fails, the cordelian poet and public return to basics: God as Messiah and solution to the unsolved problems and unresolved issues of life. Nowhere is this better seen then in the poems about death and the end. In "cordel" death is not the end, and man's most important reality is that very human heaven when the gods talk to man. Album X provides such conversations and restores the reader's faith in the northeasterners, the Brazilians and Brazil.

1   Apolônio Alves dos Santos, Nosso Mundo Moderno, Benfica, RJ, n.d.

2   Raimundo Santa Helena, Nós, os Seres H'urbanos, Rio de Janeiro, n.d.

3   Rodolfo Coelho Cavalcante, O Direito de Nascer, Salvador, n.d.

4   Minelvino Francisco Silva, O Direito de Matar, Itabuna, n.d.

5   Severino Cesário da Silva, Mulher que Concebe o Filho e Depois Mata Sem Razão, n.p., n.d.

6   Rodolfo Coelho Cavalcante, 3rd. ed. A Maneira da Mulher que Não Quer Filhos, Salvador, 1973.

[7] Machado, <u>Debate de Lampião com uma Turista Americana</u>, São Paulo, n.d.

[8] José João dos Santos, "Azulão," <u>Só o Divórcio Conserta</u>, Engenheiro Pedreira, 1975.

[9] No author indicated, <u>O Justiceiro Mão Branca do Esquadrão da Morte</u>, n.p., n.d.

[10] José João dos Santos, "Azulão," <u>Camisinhas para Todos</u>, Engenheiro Pedreira, n.d.

[11] Alberto Porfírio, <u>O Mal que Causa a Novela</u>, Fortaleza, n.d.

[12] Expedito F. Silva, <u>Roberta Close, o Fenômeno do Século XX</u>, Rio de Janeiro, 1984.

[13] Gonçalo Ferreira da Silva, <u>Não Sei se Choro ou se Rio da Violência no Rio</u>, Rio de Janeiro, n.d.

[14] Franklin Machado, <u>A Nova Igreja Católica e o Socialismo Cristão do Frei Leonardo Boff</u>, São Paulo, n.d.

[15] Raimundo Santa Helena, <u>Tragédia em Cubatão</u>, Rio de Janeiro, n.d.

[16] Manoel Santa Maria, <u>A Morte de Chico Mendes Deixou Triste a Natureza</u>, Rio de Janeiro, December, 1988.

Album X

This Is Not the End

Introduction

Recalling the albums of <u>Portrait</u>, one sees that <u>cordel</u>'s vision of Brazil and the Brazilians—of its poets, its public and their reality—is essentially religious, moral and heroic. In Albums I ("God Above and Below: In This We Believe"), II ("The Manifestations"), and III ("The Wages of Sin: What Not To Do") the reader was introduced to the religious and moral foundation of <u>Portrait</u>. The real life models for living out the vision were found in Albums IV ("A Model To Live By: the Heroes of 'Cordel'"), VI ("But We Have Our Distractions"). However, life's heroes are not necessarily the traditional models of the powerful or famous; just as often they are the personages of daily life as <u>Portrait</u> revealed in Albums V ("Life Is a Struggle and Life Is a Saga") and IX ("Life Is Not Getting Any Easier").

In this religious-moral-heroic vision of life, all eventually leads to death and its reward or punishment: eternal life in heaven or perhaps the perils of hell. But before death, one hopes and dreams in cordelian fashion of the best of life here and now. Leandro Gomes de Barros, pioneering master of old <u>cordel</u>, wrote <u>A Trip to Heaven</u> ["Uma Viagem ao Céo"] which in turn became a model for one of the most unique and really beautiful poems of the entire cordelian portrait: <u>Trip to St. Saruê</u> ["Viagem a São Saruê"]. This poem by Manoel Camilo dos Santos of Paraíba State is the epitome of the poets and public of <u>Portrait</u>'s dream of heaven on earth. This story-poem, above all others, forms a bridge between the humble poet and public of <u>cordel</u> and their fellow citizens, the middle and upper class primarily urban Brazilians who know a similar utopist vision in the Modernist poet Manuel Bandeira's "I'm going to Passárgada," ["Eu vou á Passárgada"] a poem-icon of Brazilian high culture. One gives credence to the other and both show the aspirations and dreams of Brazilians.

But since life is not perfect at this the beginning of the new milennium (just ask the poor Brazilians facing the realities seen in Album IX), one is left with life as it was, is, and shall ever be. Hence, much of Portrait is a remembering of what life was. One cannot help but recall the words of Brazil's great modern day novelist João Guimarães Rosa in his twentieth century epic masterpiece The Devil to Pay in the Back Lands ["Grande Sertão:Veredas"] when his bandit heroes, modern "knights of the backlands" of Minas Gerais and Bahia States, ponder why they live like they do and conclude that the main reason is simply "to be remembered." Thus cordel remembers in the hundreds of poems intitled "Life of . . ." and "Death of . . ." dealing with heroes running the gamut from Jesus Christ to a national soccer playing hero. Such stories form the second in the final snapshots of this final album of Portrait. In the remembering of these protagonists, people and what they stand for converge.

But, after remembering life and after death, one is rewarded or punished, so cordel presents a plethora of story-poems which deal with man's ultimate fate, heaven or hell. Portrait's heaven is not nebulous or mysterious, not composed of gauzy clouds or robed angels playing on harps. It is a continuation of man's conversation and interaction with God, Jesus, Mary and the saints or of man's final confrontation with Satan in hell itself. Cordel possesses dozens of poems about heroes who reach the pearly gates but communicate with earthy brethren who are not yet so fortunate. There are "letters from heaven," "advice from heaven" and more importantly "the arrival in heaven" stories. Heaven and earth become one with the virtues of the former and the foibles of the latter in plain sight. Such encounters encourage the living to keep the faith, to stay on the right path. But for those who waffle or ignore the vision, there are the stories of the vilest of mankind, "the arrival in hell."

A final, unique poem in cordel tells of life in its largest dimensions, the end and the hereafter. In this writer's opinion, no poem in Portrait better summarizes a vision, recalling the past and expressing hope in the future than Rodolfo Coelho Cavalcante's All on Earth Must End ["Tudo na Terra Tem Fim"]. This is an opinion shared by the writer who perhaps owes most to cordel, Ariano Suassuna, and colleagues in Recife, Pernambuco, who awarded the poem in manuscript the prize of monetary support for its publication. Once again, this poem bridges the gap between the poets, their public and the other Brazilians. It harks back to the book of books, the Bible of both the Old and New Testaments. When one reads All on Earth Must End, one thinks of the poet(s) of Ecclesiastes, the New Testament Gospels of Jesus, and a famous late medieval model for Spanish and Portuguese poets (whose folk-popular poetic "cousins" were the precursors of cordel and its kindred), the poetic vision of the great Spanish poet Jorge Manrique in "Verses upon the Death of his Father" ["Coplas por la Muerte de su Padre"]. "Vanity of vanities" and the reward of another life converge in this humble cordelian poet's verses and remain the great truth. Such is the importance of these last examples of Brazil and the Brazilians that Portrait chooses to quote directly, paraphrasing some texts in their entirety.

1 Utopia on Earth: <u>Trip to St. Saruê</u>[1]

This poem is of an extremely rare style in <u>cordel</u>: it combines the usual vehicle of the poets, narrative poetry (telling a story), with lyricism, and the fusion produces a true "jewel" of <u>Portrait</u>. Its author, Manoel Camilo dos Santos, who was active in cordelian production in the city of Campina Grande, Paraíba, in the 1940s, 50s and 60s, took great pride in his "gift of poetry" and his capacity of using the Portuguese language in the humble booklets of verse of <u>cordel</u>. He had his own printing shop called "The Star of Poetry," a name which seemed a bit euphemistic when we interviewed the poet in 1966 in the poorest part of town, in his ink stained work clothes at his humble house with a printing shop in the back. He was known for his bombastic and at times eloquent defense of authors' rights (printed on the back covers of his booklets of verse) when he raved of thievery by "unscrupulous and indecent poets" and threatened legal action against infractors from his "stable" of lawyers.

<u>Trip to St. Saruê</u> is really an escapist poem, "a living portrait of flight, by means of a dream, of a people who suffer" (in the words of the writer Orígenes Lessa who in a speech at the Brazilian Academy of Letters compared the poem to the great Modernist poet Manuel Bandeira's "I'm going to Passárgada"). The strange thing is that Manoel Camilo considered the poem "Just a poem I really composed quite easily; it was really nothing." According to the poet, the title came from an old folk adage in the Northeast: "Only in St. Saruê where the beans sprout with no rain." For him, St. Saruê is "the improbable, the day of St. Never, a silly little thing the people find funny" (quotes once again from Lessa).[2] Be that as it may, the greats of the Brazilian Academy, including the highly reknowned poet Carlos Drummond de Andrade, found the poem to be a small gem, a small masterpiece.

It is a poem that purposely or not expresses the dreams of the Northeasterner in language and terms significant and dear to him. It is a flight from harsh reality to an utopist dream world where happiness is finally found for the northeasterner and on his own terms. The poet ironically gave it little value, thinking much more of his <u>romances</u> (the lengthy narrative poems of Album IV: "Our Heroes"). But it says so much and in such a beautiful way that we choose to quote extensively from it in this the final chapter of <u>Portrait</u>.

"Doctor Master Thinker
Said to me one day:
You Camilo, go visit
The country of St. Saruê
Since it's the best place
There is to see in this world.

Ever Since I was young
I had always heard tell
Of This So-called St. Saruê
I destined myself to travel
And by order of Thought
I went to see the place.

"I started the trip
At four o'clock in the morning
I took the car of the breeze
I passed by the dawn
Near to the waves breaking at the shore
I dumbfoundedly stared at the dawn.

As the day passed the breeze stopped, calm came over all, and the poet felt the "tiredness" of the day. Sunset came amidst secrets and mysteries. Night then took command and the poet transfered to the car of cold snow in which he saw the mysteries of the night awaiting the day.

"Upon the surging of the new dawn
I felt the car stop
I looked and I saw a beach
Sublime and enchanting
The rebelling sea bathing
The dunes along the shore.

"A bar of pure gold
Serving as a placard I saw
With letters of diamonds
And drawing closer I read
It said: St. Saruê
Is this place here.

"The people in St. Saruê
All experience happiness
They get along well, dress decently
There is no contrariness
No one needs to work
You have as much money as you want.

"There I saw rivers of milk
Hills of roast beef

"I saw a city
Like none I had ever seen
All covered with gold
And trimmed in cyrstal
No one poor lives there
Everything in general is rich.

"When I saw the people
I was absolutely overwhelmed
A happy and strong people
A civilized people
Good, approachable and charitable
I was embraced by them all.

"There the bricks of the houses
Are of crystal and marble
The doors pure silver plate
With locks of ruby
The roof tiles are of gold leaf
And the floor of satin.

The Stones in St. Saruê
Are made of cheese and rock candy

Lakes of bees' honey
Ponds of buttermilk
Reservoirs of Port wine
Mountains of stewed meat.

"Beans come up in the field
Mature and already cooked
Rice comes up in the river bottom
Hulled and ready
Turkeys are born ready to eat
And are well fed without eating.

"Fish there are so tame
And so used to people
They leave the sea and come to your house
They are big, fat and well fed
You just pick them up and eat them
They are already cooked.

Orchards with only money trees
That gets your attention!
The branches with big bills
Wow, they drag on the ground
And silver and gold trees
Are as common as cotton.

"There when a child is born
It is no trouble to raise it
It is already speaking and knows how
To read, write and count
The child leaps, runs, sings and does
Everything he is asked.

"There they have a river
Called the fountain of youth

The cisterns have coffee
Freshly made and hot
And everything else
Exists in great abundance.

"Hens lay every day
Instead of eggs, capons
Wheat instead of grains
Produces loaves of breae
Butter over there falls from heaven
Piling up on the ground.

"Everything there is good and easy
You need buy nothing
There is no hunger or sickness
People live to enjoy
They have everything; nothing lacks
And there is no need to work . . . .

"Trees of 1000 denomination
They are all over the place
And you can pick all you want
The more you pick, the more they sprout
And aside from the branches
Even the leaves are all bills . . . .

"There you do not see anymy homely women
They are all young and beautiful
Well educated and brought up
Well dressed and amiable
It is like a garden of fairies
Replete with close and cinnamon.

It is a magnificent place
Where I spent many days

Where a hundred year old man
Bathes whenever he wants
When he leaves the bath
He seems to be twenty years old.

"There exists every type of beauty
Everything that is good and right
It appears to be a holy and blessed place
Or a garden of divine nature
It imitates very well through its grandeur
The ancient Promised Land
To which Moses and Aaron
Led the people of Israel
Where they say milk and honey ran free
And manna from heaven fell to earth.

Well satisfied and enjoying
Pleasure, health and happiness
I occupied myself the entire time
Reciting my poetry.

"Everything there is festive and in harmony
Love, peace, good will and felicity,
Rest, calm and friendship
On the night before my departure . . .
I gave a speech I verse there
They awarded me upon the judge's command
A ring of diamonds and rubies
And all manner of beauty
On which the following is said:
"He who visits this country is happy."

I am going to finish by advising
Any little friend whomever
Who may wish to travel there
I can show him the way
But I will only show it to him
Who buys a poem from me."

This vision then is what the poets and public of <u>cordel</u> could dream of in a less than perfect life. (One in North America remembers the classic "Rock Candy Mountain" of folk fame.) All the needs of a people are imagined and fulfilled. The final touch of course is the prize of the good and the just <u>poet</u>: to be heard, appreciated and even rewarded. One recalls the cordelian poet Azulão's plea for poetic and economic justice for the poor spokesman of the masses, the poet of <u>cordel</u> in <u>The Injustices of the Artist</u> in Album VI. Manoel Camilo has dreamed and answered, not just for the poet but for all the poor Brazilians. One imagines the poor, humble public in the market listening to the poet recite the lines of verse and the fulfilling of each person's needs, physical and emotional. When one sees the very real poverty and difficult living conditions yet today for many of the Brazilians, including the public of <u>cordel</u>, the intense beauty of St. Saruê, the goodness and generosity of its people, the immense excess of its basic foods and drink, the never lacking quality of shoes, of clothes, the ease of daily existence with no need to work, even in the raising of children, and the beauty of the ladies in a true land of milk and honey, then one realizes life on earth as <u>Portrait</u> would have it.

But, alas, it is only a dream. And the end comes. In <u>cordel</u> death is first a remembering; through the hundreds of "Life of . . . ," "Death of . . . ," and "The ABCs of . . ." story-poems Brazil and the Brazilians remember as well.

2 Remembering Brazilians—the Life and Death of . . . [3]

Portrait derives much of its value as a document of Brazil and the Brazilians in the Twentieth Century from the hundreds of story-poems precipitated by the death of an important national or international figure and the homage paid by the cordelian poets to such figures. In the pages of Portrait seen thus far the Brazilians remembered their greatest hero in the "Life, Passion and Death of Jesus Christ." By no coincidence the life and death of Brazil's most beloved political figure Getúlio Vargas was also remembered using the same title!

In such poems, titles, topics, protagonists and story lines converge, but death is the greatest and most important occasion for the poets to reminisce and to register for all time in Portrait the gamut of great Brazilians. The essence of the stories is biography. The poems use various titles such as "The life of . . . ," "The death of . . . ," "The ABC of . . . ," or "Homage to . . ." to tell their stories.

They tell of famous religious leaders like Father Cícero or Friar Damian, the bandits of Northeast Brazil, local and regional political figures, but especially national political heroes (international political leaders, popes and famous personages are included as well). Famous poets, novelists, TV soap opera composers and actors, musicians, singers, intellectuals and writers are also eulogized. In the cordelian homage, deceased greats of the world appear as well, from the Greek philosophers, to Galileu, to heroes of Brazilian independence, abolition of slavery, and major national events prior to the advent of cordel. The sum total of these story-poems is a folk-popular biography of Brazilian and world personages. It is the way the public of cordel learns of a world beyond the small towns of the backlands and cities of the Northeast.

Some stories come about by catalysts like disasters and tragedies such as a fatal automobile accident causing the death of the great national builder of Brasília, President Juscelino Kubitschek, or the assassination of Dr. João Pessoa which precipitated the Revolution of 1930, or yet the airplane crash killing the first military general of the Revoluation of 1964, President Castelo Branco. Heinous crimes on the international scene produced a major story in cordel in the 1960s with the assassination of John F. Kennedy. And of course it was the suicide of President Getúlio Vargas that produced debatably the most memorable of all such moments in national history, the death of Getúlio Vargas.

The "king" of the life-death-homage poems was Bahia's Rodolfo Coelho Cavalcante. Perhaps no poet wrote more homage in all such forms than this national leader of cordel for four decades. The poet made a living late in his career writing almost exclusively in the format of such homages at the death of a famous personage. Erudite writers, especially those linked in some way to the northeastern reality, like Luís da Câmara Cascudo, Brazil's most famous folklorist, and especially, famous poets like Castro Alves "the Poet-Apostle of the Slaves" are eulogized in Rodolfo Coelho Cavalcante's cordel. Benefactors of humanity, including scientists and inventors like Santos Dumont "the Father of Aviation," are chronicled at the time of death. Popular singers, TV stars, and even opera composers are heralded. Leaders of Brazil's black culture, from the rebel Zumbi of slavery days, to modern candomblé priestesses and capoeira masters are recalled. Even Greek philosphers fill the pages of Cavalcante's cordelian tributes.

Perhaps the epitome in the cordelian portrait of the "death" stories, one among the hundreds of such titles and dozens of excellent biographies, eulogies and homages, one that expressed deeply the sentiments of the Brazil and Brazilians who comprise the public of cordel, is The Death of the King of Northeastern Music ["A Morte do Rei do Baião"]: the death of Luiz Gonzaga of northeastern music fame.[4] A native of the backlands town of Exu, Pernambuco, scene of political feuds by backlands political demagogues, region of the youth and legend of Lampião, Gonzaga became known as the best and most popular composer of traditional northeastern music with the song called the baião, in analogous terms, the "samba" of the Northeast. Accompanying himself on Brazil's version of the accordion or soundbox [a sanfona] in a trio completed by a triangle and drum played for rhythm, Gonzaga became the epitome of such music in Brazil. The music became known as forró and caught on to become a national fad and mania in the 1970s and 1980s, even becoming "chique" in dance halls, restaurants and nightclubs in major cities of Brazil's center and southeast.

It was not just the sound or the rhythm of the baião, but its lyrics that captivated Gonzaga's northeastern public spread throughout Brazil by the migrations seen in Album V "Life Is a Struggle." His lyrics in the medium of northeastern pop music dealt with most of the topics of everyday cordel, the life and loves of the nordestino. But three major links were the most important: (1) he always dressed for the stage in a stylized version of the apparel of the northeastern bandits and cowboys: the wide brimmed leather hat adorned with "stars of Solomon" attributed to Lampião and his cohorts, (2) he expressed a life-long devotion to Father Cícero in Juazeiro do Norte, and (3) most of all, he wrote and sang the song that became the "Northeastern national Athem." "White Wing" ["Asa Branca"] poetically, musically, and with poignant emotion told the story of the droughts, the sad goodbyes, the departure, the odyssey of travel of the northeastern migrant [Pau de Arara] to Rio or São Paulo, and the never ending dream of returning home after the rains (see Album V). (This

256 Mark J. Curran

author can scarcely keep a dry eye yet today when hearing a Luiz Gonzaga performance of the song.)

Of the many poems written at Gonzaga's death Portrait chooses Gonçalo Ferreira da Silva's <u>The King of the "Baião" Died</u> ["Morreu o Rei do Baião"]. After factually stating the death of the composer of such classics as "White Wing" and "Juazeiro" at 5:20 a.m. on the second of August of 1989, the poet says:

"With Luiz Gonzaga the North
Gained another dimension
He showed the Northeast to the world
Through his "baião"
And he ended "northeasternizing"
Our great Nation."

Of "White Wing" ["Asa Branca"] the poet says,

"White Wing" is a song
Of such refined sentiment
Linked in such a way
To the Brazilian heart
That it has now become eternal
As a true anthem.

How many times the North East
Has already suffered the horror
Of pitiless droughts
Now it cries from the pain
Of the sad and definitive
Departure of its singer." . . .

The poet notes that in a recent Soviet Union documentary of Brazil the producers chose "White Wing" as the background music to represent all Brazil. But of even more importance for Gonzaga, <u>cordel</u> and all the Northeast (and personally by this author who has had a career long passion in divulging such culture),

"After Luiz Gonzaga
The dark prejudice
That others had for the Northeast
Was more than rightfully set straight
And was substituted in turn
By a sincere and pure respect."

The body prior to burial in Gonzaga's home town of Exu was transported by air to no less than the city and the tomb and church of Father Cícero Romão in Juazeiro do Norte, Ceará, where the multitudes paid homage to another in the seemingly never ending stream of northeastern cultural icons (Father Cícero, Friar Damian, Lampião) and now the King of the 'Baião' himself.

But death is not the end; there is a heaven and hell.

3 The Arrival in Hell or Heaven

All that matters in <u>cordel</u> does converge. <u>Portrait</u> previously alluded to the evil bandit Lampião's arrival in hell, a humorous poem by José Pacheco, a classic in the poetry. Other poets picked up on the fantasy, and when the devil could not put up with the bandit any longer, they packed him off to purgatory and then to heaven. When other classic villains came along, the pattern was already established, so Hitler, Mussolini and even Stalin ended up in cordelian hell. In a scenario closer to home, the economic minister of the hated military regime (called a dictatorship by most Brazilians) of twenty-one years from 1964 to 1985, Delfim Neto, the so-called creator of the "Economic Miracle" which made a few Brazilians fantastically rich and most a lot poorer, was immediately consigned to hell as well.

Having already seen "The Arrival of Lampião in Hell," associated with bandity in the North East, <u>Portrait</u> chooses as an example of the best of the "hell" poems the story penned coincidentally by the folk-popular "Hell's Mouth" of Salvador da Bahia, Cuíca de Santo Amaro, <u>The Arrival of Hitler in Hell</u>.[5] Written at the end of World War II when emotions still ran high due to the unspeakable tragedy and loss of life caused by Hitler, the poem measures out cordelian justice but entertains at the same time. The poet's fanatical fans expected no less.

Hitler is greeted at the gates of hell by Satan himself with a branding iron in hand; the Nazi leader is a bit taken aback by the place but likes its looks, regretting he had not arrived six years sooner and avoided WW II. But he wonders if his old friend Mussolini had already arrived:

> "Hitler, seeing Mussolini
> Said to the poor slob
> You were the cause
> Of our being defeated
> Even though I backed you
> You ran like a scared deer.

> "You Italians
> You were toally undependable
> Everywhere in the world
> Considered the dregs of the Axis
> Mussolini listened to him
> With his hand resting on his chin . . . .

Mussolini's response is that if Hitler wants to thank someone, he should thank the Portuguese, for they were the only nation to declare a national day of mourning with the fall of Berlin: "Go thank them/ And don't complain about me."

Cuíca then leaves his political commentary and commences to tell a hilarious story of the rest of Hitler's experience in hell (for as the poet once said, "Just give me a fact or two and I'll take care of the rest."). Satan gets Hitler drunk on sugar cane rum [cachaça] and the Nazi leader dances to a "baião" in hell dressed just in his undershorts. He becomes enamored of Satan's mother who appears to encourage him, saying her son is gettinhg old and hell needs a new boss. After a big kiss from her, Hitler is convinced and says he will ask for her hand in marriage from Satan himself. She has married eighty times and the only one left is Ferrabraz (the Moorish villain of Charlemagne and his Twelve Knights stories); all the others could not take it and have kicked the bucket. Mussolini falls over laughing, saying "This was the last straw/ You marrying the Devil's mother!" This riles up Hitler:

"Hitler then said angrily
What else do you expect?
I lived there in Germany
Running away from women
I died like I was born
You figure it out."

So the poet combined an anti-Nazi stance with cordelian vengeance and poetic justice. But Cuíca the poet could not help making his public laugh as well bringing the Brazilian mother-in-law jokes and Hitler's dubious tendencies into play. So the infamous Hitler joined the company of Lucifer himself and other great villains of history like the bloodthirsty Lampião in immortality in the cordelian hell.[6]

But those were the bad guys. Much more common and in tune with the cordelian moral vision was the arrival of the deserving great hero in heaven. Once again, all converges. Portrait spoke in Album I of the great religious classic The Play of the Arrogant Soul when the unrepentant soul arrived in heaven and was set for eternal damnation by a just Jesus when Mary his mother (and just as importantly, a woman) intervened in her role as lawyer for the defence and convinced Jesus to spare the soul. The great northeastern playwright Ariano Suassuna picked up on the same topic but adapted many other themes and personages dear to cordel when he created the final judgement scene of corrupt clergy, bandits, small-time capitalists and the classic cordelian conman John Crickett with a similar end (all this in his The Rogues' Trial).

Perhaps because of the Brazilian sense of humor or because of the intrinsec nature of politics itself (promises, promises, and promises) national political figures became the most common of cordelian protagonists to be singed in the fiery flames or arrived to have a Brazilian cafezinho with St. Peter, Mary and Jesus in heaven. In just a quick perusual of the poems, one sees that João Pessoa, the assassinated candidate for vice-president on Getúlio Vargas' ticket in 1930 arrived in heaven sucessfully. Juscelino Kubitschek, leader of modern industrialization in the steel and automobile industries and founder of Brasília in 1955 was just as fortunate. Even the first military general and dictator of the 1964 Revolution, coincidentally a native son of Ceará state (a fellow nordestino from cordel country) was consigned to the pearly gates. The most recent bigwig was "St. Tancredo Neves," "Martyr of the New Republic," the politician from Minas Gerais who succeeded in bringing to an end the twenty-one year military dictatorship with his "Direct Elections" campaign of 1983 and 1984 and successful election to the presidency in 1985. Falling ill just days before his inauguration in 1985, he suffered seven surgeries before succumbing to death before national lamentation with millions of Braziians praying to no avail in the streets.

Probably no national figure in heaven was more important and more controversial than the "Father of the Poor," the icon of Brazilian politics President Getúlio Vargas. His story in one sense ties together the issues of Album X: many believe that he attempted to create a utopist, benevolent society with his support of a minimum wage for workers and the establishment of what in effect is the Brazilian "social security" and national retirement plans. But like Manoel Camilo's poem Trip to St. Saruê, the dream came to a shocking end with Getúlio's death by suicide in 1954.

Getúlio became the "most remembered" of all national figures in Portrait, and his arrival in heaven by virtue of poetic rationalization made him the greatest of the secular heroes of all cordel. The great president's death was, if not the most, then one of the most important events in the entire history of cordel. The reason is simple: the man and the emotional loss felt at his death affected the poets, public of cordel, and in fact all Brazilians more than any other prior political event in the twentieth century.

The poets had to write quickly, running with their manuscripts in hand to the printing shops, waiting in some cases for the story to be printed, and rushing to sell the story like hotcakes on the streets. Almost any cordelian poet who deemed himself a poet in the mid-1950s wrote of the event. Orígines Lessa in his book on Vargas quotes the poet Azulão in Rio as having sold 200,000 copies and Antônio Teodoro dos Santos another 280,000 in

São Paulo. By virtue of dozens of poets and many dozens of titles, the poem easily reached one million in sales from 1954 to the present (it is still sold in the markets almost fifty years after Getúlio's death).

Such agitation and interest were not caused just by the death, but by its most unusual circumstances. In a traditionally Catholic nation (and with a traditional Catholic public buying cordel) the most beloved national leader of all time had just committed suicide. It presented a great problem for the poets: what to say of Getúlio's fate as a result of the suicide? The way out was found in the circumstances of the death: Getúlio left a "letter-testament" to the Brazilian people before shooting himself to death with his own revolver. By virtue of his motives (he said he did it because of unrelenting, mysterious pressures from diverse national and international forces), he permitted Brazil and the Brazilians to see him as a sacrificial lamb who killed himself for the good of all to avoid national civil war.

The poets had two choices: the first was to say Getúlio died defending the presidency with honor, not giving in to death and dishonor at the hands of his enemies. The second was that Getúlio died to avoid further bloodshed of Brazilians who would be embroiled in a national civil war which might have taken place had he not died. In other words, Getúlio died to save his people and was now a victim of a complicated (and yet to be explained) series of intrigues by his enemies.

In the cordelian archive Getúlio is more often than not identified with Jesus Christ: he is the "messiah" who "saved" his people through the workers' legislation and retirement laws and was killed by the forces of evil on earth. But the story could not end there: Getúlio had to have a final judgement. So the poets dusted off an old cordelian tradition—the hero who arrives at the gates of heaven and faces judgement—but in the form of a human trial with prosecuting attorney, attorney for the defence and judge.

Orígenes Lessa cites no less than six different cordelian accounts of Getúlio's arrival in heaven. There were many important precedents (already seen in Portrait): the arrival in heaven of saints, including St. Peter and St. Simian, and the problems of deciding who would control the pearly gates, the devil's many attempts to knock on the doors of heaven to have a man-to-man chat with Jesus over the state of the world, and of course the Play of the Arrogant soul, an early classic.

Rodolfo Coelho Cavalcante, in one of his own "classics," uses a cast which includes, modestly speaking, most of the great figures of Western Civilization to tell of Getúlio's arrival in heaven. He creates a tribunal in which Jesus Christ is the judge and Mary the lawyer for the defence. Case closed. Jesus is convinced of Getúlio's good intentions, "Even through he sinned gravely," and pardons him "for the good of the people." This is probably the best example of that great Brazilian custom, the "easy fix" [jeito], in all <u>cordel</u> and <u>Portrait</u>. Jesus even allows Getúlio to return to earth to take another crack at saving Brazil Thirty years later in another cordelian poem Jesus and St. Peter advise President Tancredo Neves to forget the whole thing; Brazil is not it!

4 <u>All On Earth Must End</u>[7]

As <u>Portrait</u> said at the beginning, Brazil is a land of great religiosity and characterized by its religious syncretism. Such a mixture of beliefs is applicable to the poets as well, and there is no better example than Rodolfo Coelho Cavalcante—born Catholic, converted to Protestantism and living the life of a preacher in his teens, and finally converted to Kardec Spiritualist as an adult. This poem by Rodolfo Coelho Cavalcante has a vaguely Kardec Spiritualist orientation that death is not the end but a fiction leading to yet another life. Its vision can be reduced to a simple question of semantics and compatible poetic imagery for most of the cordelian public who were traditional Catholics as well. The poets' vision is also is a happy coincidence when one recalls famous erudite poets who have called both life and death a dream. Rodolfo Coelho Cavalcante tells of an after-life he calls a "life-continued," his way of describing a spiritualist notion poetically compatible with the eternal life so often promised in <u>cordel</u>'s old church Catholicism. But whatever the semantics, the notions that life in all its possibilities ends and that another life awaits for those who have followed Jesus's axiom of "Love one another," made an impression at the Pernambuco State Department of Culture. Its director Ariano Suassuna, a famous fan of <u>cordel</u> and an author mentioned frequently in <u>Portrait</u>, deemed Roldolfo Coelho Cavalcante's poem <u>All on Earth Must End</u> as prizeworthy and arranged for its publication.

Sharing Suassuna's enthusiasm, <u>Portrait</u> includes a large part of the poem either by direct citation or paraphrasing. The poem treats life, death and the life to come with eloquence rare in <u>cordel</u>. The religious tone of much of the poem is really that of the bard of <u>Ecclesiastes</u>. The message the poet takes to the reader is that all the great personages of history have met the same end as the humble, that the sins of the people of this world with their materialism are all "vanity," and the only truth is that of Christ's message—"Love one another."

The humble reader of the Northeast interior, even without understanding every historic or cultural allusion in the poem, senses its grandeur and the eloquence of the poet. Few authors, perhaps even no other poet in <u>cordel</u>, could have written such a poem in such a way as did Rodolfo Coelho Cavalcante because of his autodidactism and interest in history, philosophy and religion. His familiarity with the Bible (he once said he nearly had it memorized, not textually, but episodically), and impressionistic knowledge of history fill the poem. So everything on earth ends, the body lies in the grave, the material world ends, only God, love and eternity exist. Never before or later have the personages of history (and <u>Portrait</u>) come together as in this poem:

"King Nebuchadnezzar
Was great in Babilonia
Solomon father of science
And Moses the legislator,
David, Isaac, Abraham
All are beneath the ground
Giving accounts to the Lord.

"Herod, Pontius Pilate,
Along with Annas and Caiaphas,
They crucified Jesus—
These exist no more
Julius Caesar up to Tiberius
Also Nero the criminal
They died long ago.

"Alexander, commonly called "The Great"
He also disappeared
Napoleon Bonaparte
Died at Santa Helena.
The Kaiser and Hitler of Germany
Each with his mania
Of domination perished!

Who still speaks of Mussolini
Who dominated Italy?
Stalin, Marx, Lenin
Each one "evaporated" . . .
Daniel, Abimelech,
Victor Hugo, Allan Kardec,
None remains on the earth! . . .

"And what of Roosevelt, Kennedy,
DeGaulle, Churchill—men
Who became famous
Defenders of nations? . . .
Today they are entombed
Although glorified
By all generations!"

Getúlio Vargas, dictator, ex-dictator, democrat and "Father of the Poor" in Brazil is on page three, before the pharaohs, the Chinese thinkers and Tiradentes (Brazil's martyr of Independence). August Comte receives equal space to Martin Luther and Calvin, "the Lights of Protestantism." Then come the great religious prophets of the world—Krishna, Buddha, Mohammed and Jesus—only "Jesus of Nazareth/ Did not end up in the abyss."

The vanity of courage but on the wrong side of the law is on page four when the poet remembers Lampião, Maria Bonita and the bandits of his own homeland, all "exterminated" as a lesson to mankind! Then the poet Rodolfo leaps forward to evil Naziism, Fascism, Anarchism and "even Communism/ the terror of the entire world"—"The first were dilacerated/ The last repudiated/ By the Brazilian people."

And the power of money? The billions spent to send astronauts to the moon? The earth continues to be reflected in its light, apparently its only purpose.

"Where are Truman, Abraham
Lincoln and their values?
They all die in this world:
Democrats, Dictators,
Field Marshalls and Scientists,
Nobles, plebeans and artists
And the wisest thinkers.

And what of great Charlemagne
Oliveiros and Roland
And the other knights of France,
And what about Samson?
The weak die like the strong
No one escapes death
With the cleaver in his hand.

"Pride does no good,
Egoism, vanity,
Money, opulence,
Abuse of authority.
The good dies, the evil one dies,
Everything on earth has its end
Only the law of the Divine remains!" . . .

Nature, woman and her beauty, man and his money, even tyranny—"Only poetry does not die/ Given by the true God."

"Everything is transformed
Lavoisier already said it.
Yet death is a dream
Difficult to understand . . .
A prolongued dream,
Hidden in our past
To later be revived!

"Everything on earth has its end
As I have proved,
For it is the spirit which continues
Which will be transformed
Into a different being
Born from a seed
From a fruit of the past!

"There are many philosophies
You can pick and choose . . .
One says that people die
And then are born again,
Another affirms that at death

Some say there is a hell
Others deny it completely
One says purgatory exists
For its purification.
Each one has his theory

The body dies and evaporates
And no one sees the soul.

"There is no going back
In the Law of Evolution,
No one escapes death,
But death is a fiction
Death, yes, is the Departure
For the True Life
There is no other explanation!

With its own philosophy
All of it is pure fiction! . . .

"Love one another"
All grandeur ends
Not even Rockefeller himself
Took his money with him . . .
Why do hate and vengeance
"Put out" the flame of hope
Causing war in the world?

"Everything on Earth ends
That is the true reality,
But after the end begins
The Life-Continuation,
If one goes away, the other stays
And that is how is explained
The Law of God, in Truth!"

No one could say it so eloquently; no one could say it with the curious summary of history. The ages old technique of ubi sunt or "where are they" of the great poet of Ecclesiastes is used successfully in this folk-popular medium by the cordelian poet Rodolfo Coelho Cavalcante. But aside from the rhetoric of the poem, its message comes through for the humble readers of cordel: believe and act well and the reward will come. The poet once stated that fifty per cent of his huge cordelian production carried such messages of moral example. In a larger sense, the folk-popular tradition of cordel has always emphasized just that, the moral message.

This then, is the message of a poet, but also of a Brazilian who was born Catholic, preached as a converted Protestant and found his own "ultimate truth" in Kardec Spiritualism. In a way the poem summarizes the poets and public of cordel, Brazil and the Brazilians. In many ways the poet has affirmed the basic reality and lessons of cordel and Portrait. The poet has reaffirmed Album I "God Above and Below: in This We Believe" and Album III "The Wages of Sin: What Not to Do" in the lesson of pride and other sins of vanity (the major sin of cordel) as well as sensualism and sex. He has recalled many of the heroes—from Charlemagne to Lampião to the great Getúlio and Churchill and

Roosevelt—and the villains as well—the protagonists of Albums IV "A Model to Live By: the Heroes of "Cordel," Album VII "In Politics We Hope but Do Not Trurst," and Album VIII "There Is a Big World Out There." Death is the great leveler, thus struggles of the downtrodden (Album V "Life Is a Struggle and Life is a Saga" and Album XIX "Life Is Not Getting Any Easier") and the dominion of rich over poor (a given in all of cordel) also end.

Rodolfo fulfills his role as poet, albeit a bit differently from the rest of his colleagues in "cordel," but whether different from them, one recalls he did publish 1,700 story-poems. He recalls Manoel Camilo's recitations and discourse in Trip to St. Saruê when he says "Poetry does not die/ A gift from God himself," for the poets of cordel believe it a gift [um dom] and one is born with it. Like the great Spanish poet Jorge Manrique in his Coplas por la Muerte de Su Padre, this life is but a passing moment, and death, "a fiction," is but the departure for the other, the true life, the pure reality, the one promised by God himself when he gave the greatest of the commandments, "Love one another."

So Portrait inexorably arrives to the real end (or beginning). Utopia on earth, however dreamed and desired, does not exist. No earthly messiah yet, in spite of promises or deeds, has succeeded in bringing material salvation to "the land of the future." So the poor Brazilians, the humble Brazilians, return to their roots and look for the spiritial messiah of Album I, the real messiah, Jesus Christ, who brought them the most important and basic of all messages: "Love one another."

So ends Portrait, but as the poet said, it really is just the beginning.

---

[1] Manoel Camilo dos Santos, Viagem a São Saruê, Campina Grande: Estrella da Poesia, 1965.

[2] Orígenes Lessa, A Voz dos Poetas, Rio de Janeiro: Fundação Casa de Rui Barbosa, 1984, p. 59.

[3] The poets since early drafts of this book continue the tradition of "The Life and Death of . . . ." New representative titles are "Goodbye Princess Diana" (November, 1994), "The Tragic Death of the Mamomas Assassinas (March,1996), "The Greatest Medium in the World Dies in the Hands of the People" (July, 2002), and new stories on the tragic death of Daniella Perez: "Violence Against Women; the Assassination of Daniella Perez."

4   Gonçalo Ferreira da Silva, <u>Morreu o Rei do Baião</u>, Rio de Janeiro, n.d.

5   Cuíca de Santo Amaro, <u>A Chegada de Hitler no Inferno</u>, Salvador, 1945.

6   And more recent villains of recent times are not far behind: <u>Bush Is Going to Reign in Hell</u>, <u>Bin Laden's Visit to Hell</u> and <u>The first Reunion of the World Leaders in Hell</u>.

7   Rodolfo Coelho Cavalcante, <u>Tudo na Terra Tem Fim</u>, Recife: Departamento de Extensão Cultural, UFEPE, n.d.

Bibliography of Secondary Works on "Cordel"

Álbum dos Presidentes, a História Vista pelo JB. Edição do Centenário da República. Rio de Janeiro, 15 de novembro, 1989.

Almeida, Atila de. <u>Dicionário Bio-bibliográfico de Poetas Populares</u>. 2a.ed. Campina Grande: UFEPB, Campus II, 1990.

Amado, Jorge. <u>Bahia de Todos os Santos</u>. 24a. ed. São Paulo: Martins, 1972.

Amado, Jorge. <u>Seara Vermelha</u>. São Paulo: Martins, 1946.

Amado, Jorge. <u>Teresa Batista Cansada de Guerra</u>. São Paulo: Martins, 1972.

Andrade, Manuel correia de. <u>A Terra e o Homem no Nordeste</u>. São Paulo:EditoraBrasiliense, 1974.

Andrade, Mário de. "O Marco de Lampião" IN: <u>O Baile das Quatro Artes</u>. São Paulo: Livraria Martins, 1932.

Barroso, Gustavo. <u>Almas de Lama e de Aço: Lampião e Outros Cangaceiros</u>. São Paulo: Melhoramentos, 1930.

Barroso, Gustavo. <u>Ao Som da Viola</u>. Rio de Janeiro: Departamento de Imprensa Nacional, 1949.

Batista, Francisco das Chagas. <u>Cantadores e Poetas Populares</u>. João Pessoa: Editora F. C. Batista Irmão, 1929.

Batista, Sebastião Nunes. "O Seu a Seu Dono" IN: <u>Encontro com o Folclore</u>. Abril de 1965.

Benjamin, Robero Câmara. "Folhetos Populares Intermediários no Processo da Comunicação" IN: <u>Revista Comunicação e Artes</u>. (São Paulo), 1, 1970.

Burns, E. Bradford. <u>A History of Brazil</u>. 2nd. ed. New York: Columbia University Press, 1980.

Calasans, José. "A Guerra de Canudos" IN: <u>Revista Brasileira de Folclore</u>. 6 (14).

Calasans, José. <u>O Ciclo Folclórico de Bom Jesus Conselheiro</u>. Salvador: Tipografia Beneditina Ldta., 1950.

Calmon, Pedro. <u>História do Brasil na Poesia do Povo</u>. Rio de Janeiro: Editora a Noite— Instituto Nacional do Livro, n.d.

Carvalho, Rodrigues de. Serrote Preto: Lampião e Seus Sequazes. Rio de Janeiro: Sociedade Editora e Gráfica, Ltda., 1961.

Cascudo, Luís da Câmara. "Da Poesia Popular Narrativa no Brasil" IN: 25 Estudios del Folklore (Homenaje a Vicente T. Mendoza y Virginia Rodríguez Rivera). México: Universidad Autónoma de México—Instituto de Investigaciones Estéticas, 1971.

Cascudo, Luís da Câmara. Dicionário do Folclore Brasileiro. V. 1. Rio de Janeiro: Instituto Nacional do Livro—Ministério da Educação, 1962.

Cascudo, Luís da Câmara. Vaqueiros e Cantadores. Rio de Janeiro: Edições de Ouro, 1968.

Chandler, Billy Jaynes. The Bandit King Lampião of Brazil. College Station: Texas A&M Press, 1978.

Curran, Mark J. Cuíca de Santo Amaro: Poeta-Repórter da Bahia. Salvador da Bahia: Fundação Casa de Jorge Amado, 1990.

Curran, Mark J. "Grande Sertão: Veredas e a 'Literatura de Cordel'." In: Brasil/Brazil (Brown University/ PUC of Rio Grande do Sul, 1995, pp. 3-50.)

Curran, Mark J. História do Brasil em Cordel. São Paulo: EDUSP, 1998.

Curran, Mark J. Jorge Amado e a Literatura de Cordel. Salvador da Bahia: Fundação Casa de Rui Barbosa-Fundação Cultura do Estado da Bahia, 1980.

Curran, Mark J. A Literatura de Cordel. Recife: UFEPE, 1973.

Curran, Mark J. "Literatura de Cordel" Today: the Poets and the Publishers" IN: Journal of Latin American Lore. 6:1 (1980).

Curran, Mark J. "A Página Editorial da Literatura de Cordel" IN: Revista Brasileira de Folclore 12:32 (1972).

Curran, Mark J. A Presença de Rodolfo Coelho Cavalcante na Moderna Literatura de Cordel. Rio de Janeiro: Edta. Nova Fronteira-Fundação Casa de Rui Barbosa, 1987.

Curran, Mark J. "A Sátira e a Crítica Social na Literatura de Cordel" IN:Literatura Popular em Verso. Estudos. T. 1. Rio de Janeiro: Casa de Rui Barbosa, 1973.

Daus, Ronald. O Ciclo Epico dos Cangaceiros na Poesia Popular do Nordeste. Rio de Janeiro: Fundação Casa de Rui Barbosa, 1982.

Facó, Ruy. Cangaceiros e Fanáticos. 4a. ed. Rio de Janeiro: Civilização Brasileira, 1976.

Ferreira, Paulo Roberto. "Literatura de Cordel: a Tragédia, a Sátira Social e a Política no Verso dos Repentistas" IN: Jornal do País. Suplemento Especial. Jan. 3—9, 1985.

Guimarães Rosa, João. Grande Sertão: Veredas. 6a. ed. Rio de Janeiro: Editora José Olympio, 1968.

Insight, August 17, 1987.

Kelly, Brian and London, Mark. Amazon. New York: Harcourt, Brace, Jovanovich, 1983.

Lessa, Orígenes. "Literatura de Feira" IN: Revista Esso (Rio de Janeiro), 27 (n.d.): 13-16.

Lessa, Orígenes. "Literatura Popular em Versos" IN: Anhembi (São Paulo), 21(1955):60-87. Rio de Janeiro, Ano XXVII, n.3.

Lessa, Orígenes. Getúlio Vargas na Literatura de Cordel. Rio de Janeiro: Editora Documentário, 1973.

Lima, Estácio de. O Mundo Estranho dos Cangaceiros.

Lins do Rego, José. Fogo Morto. 6a. ed. Rio de Janeiro: Livraria José Olympio, 1965.

Luna, Luís. Lampião e Seus Cabras.

Luyten, Joseph. A Literatura de Cordel em São Paulo: Saudosismo e Agressividade. São Paulo: Edta. Estação Liberdade, 1992.

Luyten, Joseph. A Notícia na Literatura de Cordel. São Paulo: Editora Estação Liberdade, 1992.

Maranhão Liedo. O Folheto Popular, Sua Capa e Seus Ilustradores. Recife: Fundação Joaquim Nabuco—Editora Massangana, 1981.

Matos, Edilene. Notícia Bibliográfica do Poeta Popular Cuíca de Santo Amaro. Salvador: Universidade Federal da Bahia, 1985.

Matos, Edilene. O Imaginário na Literatura de Cordel. Salvador da Bahia: Universidade Federal da Bahia, 1986.

Maxado, Franklin. Cordel, Xilogravura e Ilustrações. Rio de Janeiro: Editora Códecri, 1982.

Moreira, Thiers Martins de, ed. Literatura Popular em Verso. Antologia. T. 1. Rio de Janeiro: Ministério de Educação—Casa de Rui Barbosa, 1964.

Mota, Leonardo. Cantadores. 3a. ed. Fortaleza: Imprensa Universitária do Ceará, 1961.

Mota, Leonardo. Violeiros do Norte. 3a. ed. Fortaleza: Imprensa Universitária do Ceará, 1962.

Pombo, Rocha. História do Brasil. 14a. ed. São Paulo: Edições Melhoramentos, 1967.

Proença, Manuel Cavalcanti, ed. Literatura Popular em Verso. Catálogo. V. 1. Rio de Janeiro: Ministério e Educação e Cultura—Casa de Rui Barbosa, 1962.

Proença, Manuel Cavalcanti. Roteiro de Macunaíma. Rio de Janeiro: Editora Civilização Brasileira, 1969.

Salles, Vicente. Repente e Cordel. Rio de Janeiro: FUNARTE—Instituto Nacional do Livro, 1985.

Santos, Olga de Jesus. "O Povo Conta a História" IN: O Cordel, Testemunha da História do Brasil. Rio de Janeiro: Fundação Casa de Rui Barbosa, 1987.

Simmons, Merle. The Mexican "Corrido" as a Source for the Interpretive Study of Modern Mexico. Bloomington: Indiana University Press, 1957.

Skidmore, Thomas. <u>Politics in Brazil 1930—1964. An Experiment in Democracy</u>. New York: Oxford University Press, 1967.

Skidmore, Thomas. <u>The Politics of Military Rule in Brazil 1965-1985</u>. New York:Oxford University Press, 1988.

Slater, Candace. <u>Stories on a String: the Brazilian "Literatura de Cordel"</u>. Berkeley: University of California Press, 1982.

Suassuna, Ariano. "Coletânea da Poesia Popular Nordestina" IN: <u>Revista do DECA</u> (Recife) (5) 1962.

Suassuna, Ariano. <u>Auto da Compadecida</u>. 6a.ed. Rio de Janeiro: AGIR Editora, 1970.

Terra, Ruth. <u>Memórias de Luta: a Literatura dos Folhetos do Nordeste 1893-1930</u>. São Paulo: Global Edta.—Secretaria do Estado da Cultura, 1983.

Gallery of Poets and Artists

José Bento da Silva declaiming verse at the Mercado São José, Recife, 1966

Manoel Camilo dos Santos in front of his printing shop, Campina Grande, 1966

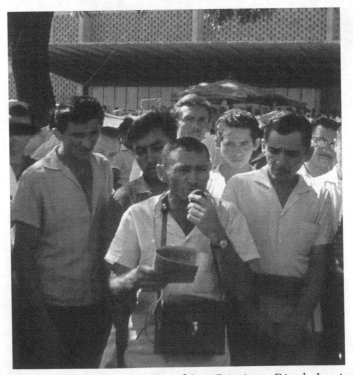

Azulão singing the story-poem, Fair of São Cristóvão, Rio de Janeiro, 1967

Poet-singers at the Fair of São Cristóvão, Rio de Janeiro, 1967

Rodolfo Coelho Cavalcante and correspondence. Bahia, 1985.

The artist Sinésio Alves working. Bahia, 1985

The poet Apolônio Alves dos Santos in his market stall.
Fair of São Cristóvão, Rio de Janeiro, 1978

The poet and woodcut artist Abraão Batista at his market stall, 100 Years of "Cordel," São Paulo, 2001

The poet and woodcut artist J. Borges at his market stall, 100 Years of "Coerdel," São Paulo, 2001

The poet and woodcut artist José Costa Leite at his market stall, João Pessoa, 2005

About the Author

Mark Curran is a retired professor from Arizona State University where he worked from 1968 to 2011. He taught Spanish and Brazilian Portuguese languages and their respective cultures. His research specialty was Brazil's folk-popular literature, "a literatura de cordel," and he has published many research articles and eleven books on the subject in Brazil, the United States and Spain. Subsequent books reflect civilization classes taught at ASU; they are from the series "Stories I Told My Students."

Published Books

A Literatura de Cordel. Brasil. 1973.

Jorge Amado e a Literatura de Cordel. Brasil. 1981

A Presença de Rodolfo Coelho Cavalcante na Moderna Literatura de Cordel. Brasil. 1987

La Literatura de Cordel—Antología Bilingüe—Español y Portugués. España. 1990

Cuíca de Santo Amaro Poeta-Repórter da Bahia. Brasil. 1991.

História do Brasil em Cordel. Brasil. 1998

Cuíca de Santo Amaro—Controvérsia no Cordel. Brasil. 2000

Brazil's Folk-Popular Poetry—"a Literatura de Cordel"—a Bilingual Anthology in English and Portuguese. USA. 2010

The Farm—Growing Up in Abilene, Kansas, in the 1940s and the 1950s. USA. 2010

Retrato do Brasil em Cordel. Brasil. 2011

Coming of Age with the Jesuits. USA. 2012

Peripécias de um Pesquisador "Gringo" no Brasil nos Anos 1960, ou, À Cata de Cordel. USA. 2012

Adventures of a 'Gringo' Researcher in Brazil in the 1960s. USA. 2012

A Trip to Colombia—Highlights of Its Spanish Colonial Heritage. USA. 2013

Travel, Research and Teaching in Guatemala and Mexico—In Quest of the Pre-Columbian Heritage, Volume I—Guatemala, Volume II—Mexico. USA. 2013

A Portrait of Brazil in the Twentieth Century—The Universe of the "Literatura de Cordel." USA. 2013

Professor Curran lives in Mesa, Arizona, and spends part of the year in Colorado. He is married to Keah Runshang Curran and they have a daughter Kathleen who lives in Albuquerque, New Mexico. Her documentary film <u>Greening the Revolution</u> was shown most recently at the Sonoma Film Festival. Katie was named "Best Female Director" at the Film Festival in Oaxaca, Mexico.

The author's e-mail address: <u>profmark@asu.edu</u>

His website: http://www.currancordelconnection.com